An Intimate Economy

An Intimate Economy

Enslaved Women, Work, and America's Domestic Slave Trade

Alexandra J. Finley

The University of North Carolina Press CHAPEL HILL

© 2020 The University of North Carolina Press
All rights reserved
Set in Merope Basic by Westchester Publishing Services
Manufactured in the United States of America

The University of North Carolina Press has been a member
of the Green Press Initiative since 2003.

Library of Congress Cataloging-in-Publication Data
Names: Finley, Alexandra J., author.
Title: An intimate economy : enslaved women, work, and America's
    domestic slave trade / Alexandra J. Finley.
Description: Chapel Hill : The University of North Carolina Press, 2020. |
    Includes bibliographical references and index.
Identifiers: LCCN 2019052078 | ISBN 9781469655116 (cloth) |
    ISBN 9781469661353 (pbk.) | ISBN 9781469655123 (ebook)
Subjects: LCSH: Slave trade—United States—History. |
    Slavery—Economic aspects—United States. | Women slaves—
    Employment—United States—History. | Women—Employment—
    United States—History. | Slavery—United States—History.
Classification: LCC E442 .F56 2020 | DDC 306.3/620973—dc23
LC record available at https://lccn.loc.gov/2019052078

Cover illustrations: *Background*, detail of Silas Omohundro Market
and General Account Book (courtesy of Library of Virginia); *label tag*,
© iStock.com/artisteer; *portrait*, detail of *A Quadroon* (courtesy of the
Historic New Orleans Collection, The L. Kemper and Leila Moore
Williams Founders Collection, 1965.90.281.8).

For my grandma, Mary Ann Kee,
who started me on this journey

Contents

Illustrations

Acknowledgments

In a project that stresses the importance of domestic and socially reproductive labor, it is only appropriate that I thank the friends, family, and acquaintances who opened their literal and metaphorical homes to me while I researched and wrote.

In terms of academic "homes," I couldn't have found a better place to "grow up" than William & Mary, and I thank all of the colleagues and mentors who helped "raise" me and guide me into the scholar I am today. I cannot thank Scott Nelson and Cindy Hahamovitch enough for their encouragement, brilliant insights, and spirit of generosity as mentors and friends. Karin Wulf has been a constant source of guidance and support throughout my career and I count myself lucky to know her. Jim and Carolyn Whittenburg inspired my love of history and William & Mary many years ago, and thus began my life as a historian. Sarah E. Thomas has provided amazing support for this project, and her encouragement, editing, and friendship have made the book what it is today. Laura Ansley has been with this work from the beginning and I thank her for her feedback throughout the project's life and, most importantly, for her friendship. Thank you to Hannah Bailey, Laurel Daen, Cara Elliott, and Casey Schmitt for being exemplary peers and friends. To Fred Corney, Andrew Fisher, Paul Mapp, Leisa Meyer, Hannah Rosen, Brett Rushforth, Carol Sheriff, and everyone I knew in Williamsburg, I say thank you.

Several institutions supported this project, giving me temporary intellectual homes in which to research and write. I received a Parker-Dooley Visiting Scholar Grant from the Southern Historical Collection at the University of North Carolina at Chapel Hill and a Betty Sams Christian Fellowship from the Virginia Historical Society. I owe a special thanks to John McClure at the Virginia Historical Society. The wonderful staff at the Library of Virginia have made researching a delight and gave me the opportunity to partake in the "To Be Sold" exhibit and conference in 2015. Particular thanks are due to Barbara Batson, Gregg Kimball, and Brent Tarter. My other archival home, the City Archives/Louisiana Division at the New Orleans Public Library, provided an endless treasure trove of materials, and I thank Greg Osborn and all the archivists there for helping me locate seemingly endless case files. Much of my early writing was done during a fellowship year at the McNeil Center for Early American Studies at the University of Pennsylvania. Thank you to Dan Richter and my entire cohort for your stimulating conversation and sociability during an otherwise solitary process. Many thanks are due to all of my amazing colleagues at my current academic home, the University of Pittsburgh, who have been incredibly welcoming and supportive of me and my research.

I have been lucky enough to research, attend conferences, and teach alongside many amazing historians. This project owes a great deal to Joshua Rothman and Calvin Schermerhorn, both of whom provided thoughtful feedback on the manuscript at several stages of writing. Their suggestions have strengthened my analysis and pushed the work forward. Robert Colby, Maria Montalvo, Seth Rockman, and Calvin Schermerhorn have all generously exchanged both materials and ideas with me, and my work would not be the same without their assistance. The intellectual support of Daina Ramey Berry, Laura Edwards, Henry Louis Gates Jr., Ellen Hartigan-O'Connor, and Stephanie Jones-Rogers has made this book what it is and I thank them for their input. A conversation with Justin Randolph about the adventures of archival research in court houses inspired the epilogue of this book. I am grateful to have received encouragement and insight from Mandy Cooper, Max Degenais, Rachel Engle, Jill Found, Sarah Gronningsater, Erin Holmes, Andrew F. Lang, Peter Messer, Julia Osman, Judith Ridner, Morgan Robinson, Courtney Thompson, and others who I'm sure I will remember as soon as this goes into print.

Thank you to Mary Caviness, Charles Grench, Jessica Newman, Dylan White, and everyone at UNC Press. Particular thanks go to Chuck Grench, who has believed in this project from the beginning. I appreciate the ways in which he has shaped this book, and I have valued our many conversations. I thank him for all his encouragement and his willingness to listen.

The Omohundro descendants with whom I've corresponded have been welcoming, open, and generous. Rene Tyree has been particularly helpful, and I thank her for her kindness and for sending me copies of the images of the Omohundros used in this book.

To my family, whose many forms of labor allowed me to do everything I do today, how can I say thank you? Besides housing, clothing, and feeding me from my birth to age eighteen, my parents, Joe and Deb Finley, also taught me courage, compassion, and the strength in being kind. For the many meals cooked, floors swept, illnesses nursed, and dreams inspired, I say thank you. My grandpa, Roger Minerd, has supported and eagerly awaited this work for what must seem like forever. I thank him for believing in me and inspiring me to speak my mind.

My grandma, to whom this book is dedicated, didn't live to see its publication, or even to see me become a historian. I hope she knows that her memory keeps me searching for human stories and putting words on the page. Mary Ann Kee's belief in my writing set me on the path that I'm on today, however circuitous the route. Her selflessness, her creative spirit, and her open heart inspire me to be a better person.

The socially reproductive labor of raising a child extends beyond the immediate family, and I want to acknowledge all of those family friends, extended family members, and public-school teachers who have mentored me over the years. Thank you for your support, your belief in me, and your role in shaping me into who I am today.

For the past several years, I've shared my domestic space primarily with two others. Capucine, my canine companion, has seen me through this work from the literal beginning. Thank you for warming my lap as I wrote, reminding me to periodically get up and walk, and always bringing a smile to my face. James has been my first and best editor and friend. I thank him for many things, but near the top of the list has to be his commitment to an equal distribution of household labor. Maybe now we can travel somewhere that isn't a research trip.

An Intimate Economy

Introduction

August 1855. The city of Richmond, Virginia, is waking; the once-empty streets are now populated with people going about the day in the summer heat. Two brothers, recently emigrated from Germany, make their way to work at Tredegar Iron Works. Medical students hurry to make it to class on time at the Medical College of Virginia's College Building, constructed to look like an ancient temple in an era of popular interest in Egypt. An enslaved woman weaves her way through the crowd, carrying a basket of vegetables to sell at the 17th Street Market in Shockoe Bottom. A free black sailor hurries past her, rushing to say one last goodbye before his ship moves down river.

On a side street off of 17th, Silas Omohundro exits his home and work-place, ready to attend to the day's business. As he walks toward Broad Street, he passes the residences, offices, and jails of many of his friends and associates. It is still early, and the agents of his fellow traders are just affixing red flags above the doors of the auction rooms around Wall Street. Perhaps Omohundro scans the scraps of paper pinned to the blood-colored fabric, comparing the descriptions of people for sale with the advertisements in that morning's paper. He hopes to make several sales himself at the ten o'clock auctions, but first he must attend to his financial business. His first stop is the auction rooms of Dickinson, Hill, & Co., one of the largest slave-trading firms in Richmond.

Omohundro tips his hat to Charles and Nathaniel Hill, partners in the firm, before addressing Dickinson. He and Dickinson have known one another for about ten years. Both are considered veterans of the trade, though Dickinson is more successful and well known, with several homes, race-horses, and a farm outside of the city. The two men exchange pleasantries. Omohundro offers his condolences for the recent death of Dickinson's young white son; maybe he also asks after Dickinson's children with the woman he enslaves. Turning to business, Omohundro removes $415 in banknotes from South Carolina from the pocket of his overcoat. Dickinson, in turn, holds $415 in banknotes from Virginia.

The money Dickinson holds belongs to an affiliated firm, that of Robinson & Smith. Robinson and Smith are frequenters of Dickinson's auction room. The two men were soon heading south to purchase more enslaved people, and they knew it was easier to have South Carolina bills on hand. While traders like Robinson and Smith were used to dealing in the notes of other states' banks, the less well-traveled folk of rural South Carolina—say, a small-town tavern keeper from whom they hoped to buy a drink—might be wary of taking the less-familiar notes of a Virginia bank. Because Robinson and Smith had an open account with R. H. Dickinson, they asked the senior trader if he would exchange the proceeds of one of their sales, in Virginia banknotes, for some from South Carolina.

Dickinson, familiar with most of the traders in town, knew that Omohundro had South Carolina money on hand. Rather than exchange the South Carolina currency at the bank for a fee (much like exchanging foreign currency today), Dickinson asked Omohundro to visit his office so he could simply switch $415 worth of banknotes from South Carolina for the same in banknotes from Virginia. Omohundro benefits from the exchange, as well; he trades infrequently with South Carolinians and the notes were not of much use to him. Having exchanged the bills, Dickinson turns to his clerk and nephew, R. L. Dickinson, and hands him the South Carolina money. R. L. Dickinson makes a quick note of the exchange in his uncle's account book.

Omohundro moves on, knowing the first auctions will soon begin. He walks past Franklin Street toward the Farmer's Bank of Virginia. The second-oldest bank in the state, it is located on Main Street, and Omohundro has been a longtime customer. Many of his associates also frequent the Farmer's Bank; his neighbor Robert Lumpkin received a handsome loan that allowed him to purchase a jail complex not far from Omohundro. Today, however, Omohundro needs only to make a deposit of cash. On other days he cashes checks, discounts bills and acceptances, or exchanges out-of-state bank bills for those of the Farmer's Bank. Depositing banknotes from Virginia, as he is today, is a fairly simple procedure, and it allows him to easily write checks to pay for more enslaved people, to give to his brother R. F. Omohundro for purchasing money, or to send to his older children in Cincinnati.

Upon reaching the Farmer's Bank, Omohundro greets the deposit clerk and hands him $300 to be placed on his account. He withholds the remainder of the exchange to make small purchases around the city. After making a note of the deposit in his bankbook, Omohundro leaves the Farmer's Bank and heads back to attend the day's auctions. Just before reaching home, he passes the rented building of Hector Davis, an old-timer in the market like himself, who is standing outside his auction room, debating the terms of a sale with a prospective buyer. Just behind him, an enslaved woman in her mid-twenties, Virginia Isham, walks into Davis's rooms, a basket of newly sewn white shirts in her hands. Omohundro does not have to trouble himself with hiring Isham to sew; he has another woman who prepares clothing for the slaves in his jail.

Omohundro sees her, Corinna Hinton, as he walks onto his property and makes his way to the jail behind the boardinghouse. She is headed to the kitchen, where other enslaved women have started to prepare food, carrying the fruits of her latest trip to the market in her hands. Just outside, his three children with Corinna, Silas Jr., Alice, and Colon play under the watchful eye of Patsy Clark, an elderly enslaved woman who assists Corinna in her household duties. Omohundro beckons to Corinna, needing to give her a bit of the cash in his pocket before it slips his mind. He hands her a $5 banknote, telling her to make sure the pantry is stocked before the next boarder arrives that night.[1]

AS THE BANKNOTE PASSES from Silas's hand to Corinna's, the sexual, domestic, and financial economies of the slave trade come together in one small but significant cash transaction. The monetary exchange between the two exemplifies the importance of domestic and socially reproductive labor to the financial success of the antebellum slave trade. Money accrued from the sale of enslaved men and women, facilitated by state banks, went to pay for more enslaved people and the food, clothing, and medicine they required. Women, enslaved and free, provided much of the domestic and socially reproductive labor needed to produce these resources, from sewing clothes to making meals. When enslaved women's sexuality was commodified as a key component of sale, or when slave traders forced enslaved women to become their concubines and household managers, the slave trade's sexual economy was equally important. While this scene is partially imagined, the circulation of cash among enslaver, slave trader, banker, and domestic laborer or household manager was a central component of the antebellum slave trade. The first three actors in this market—enslaver, slave trader, and financier—are well described in the historiography of the slave trade. The crucial role of women, enslaved and free, has escaped notice. Tracing the movement of cash from slave sale to bank deposit to the household is one way of highlighting the role of women's labor in the slave trade, a role obscured by a tendency to see *homo economicus* as just that—a man.

Hidden in plain sight, it was women who performed the day-to-day labor necessary to the functioning of the slave trade, and thus the spread of slavery to the lower South, the expansion of cotton production, and the profits accompanying both of these markets. Important historical work has been done on the slave trade and its connections to global financial markets, the cotton trade, and plantation slavery. In delineating the connections between British manufacturers, bankers and factors in Britain and the United States, and southern slaveholders, however, historians have missed one final but critical link in these Atlantic credit chains: the work of women. In the slave market, the "product" of women's labor—clean, healthy, and well-dressed bodies—were put up for sale in horrifying ways. In their crude, dehumanizing monetization of laborers, the buyers and sellers of enslaved people cast a harsh light on the value of work traditionally performed by women.[2]

Women gave birth to and raised the enslaved people from whose sale traders profited. Women fed the men, women, and children in the slave jails and yards. Women housed slave traders on their way to markets and while they did business there. Women sewed the sale outfits that the enslaved people on the auction block wore. Traders marketed women for their physical beauty and ability to reproduce. The slave market encompassed many classes of women: free white women, free black women, and enslaved women; the wives of slave traders, their enslaved concubines, their daughters and their sisters; women who ran boardinghouses; seamstresses; midwives. The place of women in the slave market was multifaceted and extensive. Different classes of women experienced the slave trade in very different ways. Some profited from the sale of other women. Some women were sold themselves or saw their children sold. Some women earned a living in the subsidiary markets that accompanied the sale of hundreds of thousands of human beings.

Recognizing women's work in the slave market is one way to acknowledge the role of women's labor in economic markets more generally. Ignoring the fact that the slave trade relied on women's domestic and reproductive labor further naturalizes women's work and elides the gendered and racialized ideologies attached to certain forms of labor. Economic systems require basic biological needs to be met, and these needs are most often fulfilled by women, though in largely unrecognized and uncompensated form.[3]

This book historicizes and critically analyzes work traditionally defined as feminine and its place in economic development through an examination of women's labor in the antebellum slave market. The four case studies that follow consider the ways in which the sexual and racial division of household labor facilitated the expansion of a burgeoning capitalist economy. Considering the function and value of such labor allows us to understand how ideologies of gender and race structure and benefit the marketplace, even as the marketplace can unsettle those very ideologies.

Domestic Labor

The word "economy" derives from the Greek *oikonomia*, meaning household management. While the economy's roots in the household have been all but lost in the term's modern definition, the history of the domestic slave trade allows us to see the ties between the financial economy and the domestic management signified by its original meaning. Just as in other markets, the traditionally feminine household economy intersected with the male-oriented financial economy of the slave market.

In the analysis that follows, I use the phrases *domestic economy*, *household labor*, and *domestic labor* to signify the work of running a household. This includes but is not limited to cleaning and maintaining the home, keeping the home supplied with necessities such as food and water, washing clothing and other linens, preparing meals, the bodily care of household residents, and helping to make ends meet through various cost-saving measures and prudent shopping, all of which took training and skill. Domestic labor can also refer to keeping up appearances: in an era when reputation was paramount to one's creditworthiness, it was crucial that a wife or household manager project the image of a home that met with a man's class and business aspirations. Domestic labor also often included *emotional labor*, which "requires one to induce or suppress feeling in order to sustain the outward countenance that produces the proper state of mind in others." Within the idealized antebellum household, this meant creating a sense of warmth, safety, and devotion for other residents, and appearing to happily do so out of love and devotion, even if it required suppressing one's inner feelings.[4]

In the antebellum United States, female authors such as Catherine Beecher recognized and stressed the value of a woman's labor in the home without challenging the appropriateness of such work for the female sex. In her many books and pamphlets outlining a woman's responsibilities, Beecher argued for "the relative importance and difficulty of the duties a woman is called to perform," challenging skeptical male readers to "become the member of a large household . . . let him fully comprehend all her cares, difficulties, and perplexities; and it is probable he would coincide in the opinion, that no statesman, at the head of a nation's affairs, had more frequent calls for wisdom, firmness, tact, discrimination, prudence, and versatility of talent, than such a woman." For Beecher and those like her, domestic labor, though it deserved acknowledgment and appreciation, was suited particularly to women. Women may have been capable of expanding their housekeeping capacities outside of the family home, but there was no question of their role as domestic manager.[5]

Even authors who challenged women's subordinate position in society rarely or only halfheartedly critiqued their responsibility for household duties. Instead, most emphasized the value and difficulty of household management to a public that, according to Jeanne Boydston, began "not simply to conceive of women as economic dependents, but to deny that they contributed to the household economy at all." While women continued to perform domestic labor, some form of which had been their responsibility for centuries, they did so in a society that was increasingly unlikely to acknowledge its importance. With the spread of classical economic thought, capitalist markets, and their emphasis on marketable products in the early republic, social commentators and family members recognized the value of household work less and less — except for when women attempted to leave housework behind for wages.[6]

While the nineteenth-century sexual division of labor deemed domestic labor the work of women, divisions of race and class meant that domestic labor was not the same for every woman. Domestic labor was never natural or constant; women learned from their families, peers, novels, and advice manuals what types of work they should perform, and what they learned varied by race, class, and region. The meaning attached to particular forms of domestic labor could change over time as it became associated in the popular imagination with particular classes of women. As more elements of clothing production, for example, moved from the home to the factory, and as sewing machines and drafting systems transformed home production, the perceived value of needlework shifted. Once a necessary and respectable task familiar to most women, by the second quarter of the nineteenth century, middle- and upper-class women associated plain sewing with working-class women and poverty.[7]

The domestic ideology of the era, while held up as a standard for all women, was a reality only for those with racial and economic privilege. The types of domestic labor that a woman did or, importantly, did *not* perform reaffirmed her status. This was particularly true in the slaveholding South, where white womanhood depended on distance from physically demanding domestic labor, which white southerners deemed more appropriate for enslaved black women. While never the reality for yeoman's wives, wealthier white women's successful direction of enslaved domestics confirmed her privilege, her whiteness, and her respectability. The language of domesticity in the South, as Thavolia Glymph has shown, "camouflaged difficult labor relations and conflict within the plantation household" as enslaved women resisted laboring for their enslaver's domestic ideals.[8]

Part of domestic laborers' daily experience has historically been the threat of sexual violence. In colonial America, for instance, many masters' "explicit mastery over a servant in his household also extended to sexual mastery." This vulnerability continued in the nineteenth century for household servants in all regions. In the popular imagination, domesticity was the place of wives, daughters, or female kin. When other women worked in the household, their motives were often seen as suspect. Enslaved women were particularly at risk of sexual abuse as they were without legal recourse against their enslavers. Equally significantly, racial ideology already portrayed women of African descent as sexually promiscuous and open to sexual advances. It is no wonder, then, that so many of the women who slave traders sold for sex were marketed as seamstresses, maids, and nurses.[9]

Socially Reproductive Labor

Drawing on feminist analysis, I consider procreation a social as well as a biological fact. While biological reproduction is obviously a crucial factor in social reproduction, procreation also requires significant day-to-day labor in the raising and care of children. Even adults, to be functional members of society, require certain basic needs to be met, including feeding, clothing, and nursing. I use the term *socially reproductive labor* to signify two distinct but interconnected forms of work. First, the physical act of giving birth to the next generation is a form of labor, as well as a way of considering the intergenerational transfer of privilege and inequality. Enslaved women literally reproduced the enslaved workforce when giving birth to enslaved children. As historians such as Jennifer Morgan have pointed out, enslavers throughout the Atlantic World were keenly aware of the value of enslaved women's reproductive capacity. The ability to reproduce was a key component of how slave traders marketed enslaved women. White women, too, reproduced a social class that, if not always slaveholding, was born free with certain legal privileges.[10]

Beyond biologically giving birth, women maintained life on a daily basis through the socially reproductive labor of feeding, clothing, cleaning, and otherwise caring for people of all ages. In this sense, socially reproductive labor often overlaps and intersects with domestic labor, as the household is the key site of the production of laborers. Domestic labor is always socially reproductive labor, but socially reproductive labor is not always domestic labor. Women employed in northern textile factories or women who worked as independent dressmakers, for instance, were not domestic laborers but they were performing socially reproductive labor by crafting clothing for people to wear. When women educated and socialized young children at home, they engaged in socially reproductive labor without providing domestic labor.

In the case of the slave trade, women's work daily reproduced both the laborers of the slave trade (such as the slave traders themselves and the enslaved people they forced to work in slave jails) and the human capital from which the slave traders profited. Women's reproductive labor was not the only way to maintain traders and enslaved people—at times slave traders had enslaved men "prepare" slaves before a sale, for example—but women's labor was the most common and economically efficient means of doing so.[11]

Though not legible in statements of profits and loss, or easily traceable in account books, socially reproductive labor created profit no less than other modes of production did. The exact value of that labor has long been a matter of debate for feminists, economists, and other activists and intellectuals. Most classical political economists, whose work influences the field of economics to this day, considered the household to be outside of the market and thus not a realm for serious economic inquiry. Many women, and some men, writing throughout the nineteenth and twentieth centuries countered this exclusion, making note of the crucial role of traditionally feminine work in raising and caring for laborers. Authors from disparate viewpoints—from antebellum American proponents of domesticity to European radicals—wrote in response to the male-centered literature of the classical economists. Many developed an analysis of domestic labor within broader economic markets. While the specifics of this analysis differed, the underlying argument was the same: while undervalued, women's work in the home was a central component of economic progress.

Marxist-influenced thinkers often drew on, as well as critiqued, Marxist analysis of production and value in relation to women, particularly Friedrich Engels's *The Origin of the Family, Private Property, and the State*, published in 1884. Engels argued in this work that "the determining factor in history is . . . the production and reproduction of immediate life. This, again, is of a two-fold character: on the one side, the production of the means of existence, of food, clothing and shelter and the tools necessary for that production; on the other side, the production of human beings themselves, the propagation of the species."[12]

While neither Marx nor Engels went much further in critically examining household labor, quickly abandoning a materialist inquiry of women and relying on familiar assumptions about female nature, Marxist feminists further developed their analysis. Mary Inman, an early twentieth-century Marxist writer, gained the ire of many of her contemporaries when she used Engels's ideas in *The Origin of the Family* to craft an extended critique of the orthodox view of household work being incidental to capitalist production. Inman's *In Woman's Defense* argued that "the principal error the feminists made was their failure to take into account the most important fact of woman's subjugation," or the economic role of women. For Inman, family labor was "the cheapest method of production." Later feminist Marxists followed Inman's lead and suggested that the sexual division of labor had deeper foundations than modes of production.[13]

Marxist feminists as well as non-Marxists continued to argue for the economic significance of women's household labor throughout the twentieth century. Authors such as Mariarosa Dalla Costa, Selma James, Gayle Rubin, and Marilyn Waring argued that domestic labor counted. Yet again, however, formal economists continued to overlook the place of economic woman. Even in the twenty-first century, gender is not frequently considered a useful category of analysis in economic thought. The discipline of economics has been one of the last to feel the influence of feminist analysis. Nonetheless, an outpouring of feminist-influenced literature led to the development of the International Association for Feminist Economics in 1991 and the subsequent publication of the association's journal, *Feminist Economics*, beginning in 1995. Feminist economists have challenged the discipline's focus on economic man, encouraged economists to consider the history of knowledge production, and challenged economists' acceptance of a divide between a (self-interested) public marketplace and a (altruistic) private family life.[14]

Sexual Economy

Slave traders' commodification of enslaved women's fertility and sexuality are key components of what Adrienne Davis refers to as the *sexual economy* of slavery. I employ Davis's terminology to describe the ways in which enslaved women's sexuality directly enriched slave traders and enslavers in general when they marketed enslaved women for their sexual attractiveness, ability to reproduce, and imagined sexual availability. While the sexual economy encompassed the entire slave system, and involved sexual violence against men as well as women, I focus specifically on women in the slave market, where slave traders openly marketed and exploited enslaved women's sexuality, as well as how enslaved women responded to and resisted such commodification.

Attention to the sexual economy in the slave market highlights the intangible, unquantifiable benefits that slaveholding brought to enslavers. As Emily Alyssa Owens argues, it "was not only sex acts that captured the attention and the capital of white men in antebellum New Orleans," when purchasing women for sex, but the affective objects attached to it, including the illusion of consent. Enslaved women sold for sex were not purchased to labor toward a tangible end product, such as cotton bolls, but they labored nonetheless, producing emotion, pleasure, and a sense of mastery in the person who enslaved them.[15]

In her tour of the United States, Swedish reformer Frederika Bremer noted the separate jails of the slave market that imprisoned "the so-called 'fancy girls' for fancy purchasers. They were handsome fair mulattoes, some of them almost white girls."[16] In this "fancy trade," the sexual economy of slavery is particularly apparent. Though "every sale of an enslaved woman was a sale of sexual labor," this work looks in detail at the "fancy trade" because in the sale of "fancy girls" the value of sexual labor is most explicit. Sexual labor occurred in many contexts in the sexual economy, including the sale of "fancy girls," interracial concubinage, and prostitution. Calling each of these a form of sexual labor highlights the value of sexual acts for enslavers outside of reproduction and "troubles narratives of choice while preserving the extent to which the women in this study acted like other enslaved and free laborers of color" in their daily navigations of the slave system. Sexual labor was not a choice or a route toward potential agency; it was often forced labor, and even when the women in question had some say in their labor, they acted within considerable legal, economic, and social disadvantages.[17]

The domestic, reproductive, and sexual labors of the slave trade are most visible when considering the enslaved concubines of slave traders, who had often been sold as "fancy girls." Many, if not most, slave traders sexually abused the women they enslaved. The slave market rested on sexual violence and exploitation. Enslaved people's accounts of slave traders frequently referenced the sexual violence they committed or the enslaved women they forced to live in concubinage. Moses Roper, for example, reported that traders "often sleep with the best looking female slaves among them, and they will often have many children in the year, which are said to be slaveholder's children, by which means, through his villainy, he will make an immense profit of this intercourse, by selling the babe with his mother." The papers of slave traders, too, are replete with crude sexual references to enslaved women.[18]

In many cases, slave traders, as Roper suggested, sold the women they raped. In other cases the traders kept certain enslaved women with them for a number of years, or even for a lifetime, relying on these women for domestic, sexual, and socially reproductive labor. As in other studies of interracial sex, understanding the dynamics, and the degree of coercion, is difficult because the enslaved women in question rarely left accounts in her own words to testify to her experiences. Without such evidence, the power differential between slave trader or enslaver and enslaved woman must remain paramount in analysis and interpretation.

In the absence of the legal ability to consent and with no laws criminalizing the rape of enslaved women, Emily Owens argues that the sexual lives of women of color "were marked by extreme vulnerability and that their consent was fetishized in the sex trade." I follow Owens's reasoning in an attempt to move beyond the debate over the presence of love and consent and to instead consider the complex, impossible specificities of enslaved concubines' lives. According to the logic of nineteenth-century contract law, enslaved concubines could not consent to a sexual relationship; yet white slaveholders fetishized their willingness. Faced with severe violence or other punishments, enslaved concubines faced a "choice" that was no choice at all. The men who enslaved them could thus create the *appearance* of choice for enslaved concubines. Historians must be careful not to interpret enslaved women's survival strategies and lack of options as consent. Trapped in impossible situations, enslaved concubines in the slave trade prioritized survival while still resisting in subtle but meaningful ways.[19]

I refer to the women in these case studies as enslaved concubines for a number of reasons. Historically, "concubine" has often been used to designate a sexual relationship between master and slave in which coercion is present. As historian Brenda Stevenson notes of concubinage, "Just as some form of slavery has manifested itself in virtually every major civilization in recorded history, including those of ancient Rome, Greece, Israel, China, Persia, India, various European and pre-Columbian American societies, as well as throughout Africa, so too did some form of sexual relations exist between owners and those owned in these societies." Concubinage is also how many residents of antebellum New Orleans referred to long-standing sexual relationships between white men and both free and enslaved women, including in two of the cases I consider in chapters 3 and 4. I have added the word "enslaved" before "concubine" to emphasize that, for the women I write about, the woman was considered of a lower social status, was ineligible for legal marriage, and had no legal right to refuse the man's sexual advances. Thus, the term *enslaved concubine* in this work designates an enslaved woman with sexual ties to a white man who had the social and legal privileges of slave ownership and race behind him.[20]

In the case studies in this work, contemporaries described all the enslaved concubines under consideration as "mulatta," "mulatto," "quadroon," or "yellow." The mulatta or mulatto concubine is both a historical and a mythical figure—both a real woman and a highly eroticized stereotype of black women's alleged sexual excesses with white men. The mulatta concubine, like the tragic mulatto and the quadroon, functioned as a cultural symbol of illicit sexuality and the privileging of whiteness. She can be found across the Atlantic World, and while the specifics of her life vary by place and time, the mulatta concubine is consistently described, as Lisa Ze Winters writes, as "light-skinned, female, and always beautiful, nearly always understood to be a New World subject . . . her body is evidence of the racialized and sexualized trauma, the violence of white male desire, the geographic displacement, and perhaps, most importantly, the fractured and interdependent reproductions of kinship and capital so central to economies of American slavery."[21]

While acknowledging the symbolic role of the mulatta concubine, the following case studies move beyond the trope of the tragic mulatto, the quadroon, and the octoroon to consider what experiences lie behind the myth. I am less interested in the literary figure or cultural trope and more in the historical actor who lived, resisted, labored, and formed emotional attachments outside of those to a white man/slaveholder. Women such as the enslaved concubine and the "fancy girl" are too often romanticized, with the available details of their lives and the very real work they performed veiled under the stuff of novels and folklore. Too often, their story is told not on its own terms but as an appendage to their enslaver's biography, as an anecdote to a grander and allegedly more significant historical narrative. Too often, the story of the "fancy girl" is subsumed within a narrative of white male power and privilege, her life viewed from the perspective of masculinity and mastery.

At least some antebellum men were aware of the significant labor concubines performed. As a young Louisianan reported to Frederick Law Olmsted in the 1850s, keeping a concubine was "much cheaper than living in hotels and boarding houses" for men financially unprepared for marriage. The man told Olmsted "it was cheaper for him to *placer* than to live in any other way which could be expected of him in New Orleans." Unlike a legal wife, the man claimed, "his placée did not, except occasionally, require a servant; she did the marketing, and performed all the duties of housekeeping herself; she took care of his clothes, and in every way was economical and saving in her habits." If he felt this way about living with a free woman of color, how much "cheaper" would it have been to have an enslaved concubine?[22]

THE LIVES OF enslaved concubines shed light on the very nature of slave systems. The sexual exploitation of enslaved women as concubines must be considered not as incidental to slavery but as constitutive of it. Within the antebellum United States, the enslaved concubine and especially the "fancy girl" were products of a slave trade imbued with a highly capitalistic mindset. While the history of enslaved concubines is old, what is distinct about their experiences in the internal slave trade is the degree to which enslaved women's sexuality was commodified and the complex financial relationships that facilitated the sale of enslaved women for sexual purposes. If part of capitalism's essence is the commodification of human feeling, then what could be more capitalistic than engaging in a bidding war over a "fancy girl"?

The development of capitalism in the United States has historically been linked to the Northeast, but recent analyses of the southern economy in the nineteenth century have troubled the traditional association of the South with precapitalist agricultural systems. The idea of the market revolution, once rooted in the North, has spread southward with studies of accounting practices, marketing strategies, and financing. Slave traders, for instance, were some of the first in the South to adopt new methods of accounting, allowing them to better measure profit and loss. They used standardization and marketing in attempts to turn human beings into commodities, and they extended credit to customers in hopes of making more sales. Traders and slaveholders alike borrowed money to purchase enslaved people and then used those same enslaved people as collateral for loans. Sven Beckert and Seth Rockman have labeled this particular element of capitalist development "slavery's capitalism." By showing how "slavery became central to and perhaps even constitutive of a particular moment in the history of capitalism," the idea of slavery's capitalism allows scholars to move beyond a strict divide between slavery and capitalism as two antagonistic economic systems and see how "slavery helped constitute capitalist modernity in the workplace, the counting house, the countryside, and the factory."[23]

Another way of tracing the development of slavery's capitalism, particularly in the urban South, is through a careful examination of women's labor. Studies of domestic and socially reproductive labor and the development of capitalism have almost exclusively focused on the Northeast and Midwest. Historians have studied the boardinghouse as both a symptom and a cause of expanding capitalist economies in the northern United States. On a smaller scale, and more concentrated in major urban centers, boardinghouses played an important role in the southern economy as well. Boardinghouses and other rented lodgings provided space and domestic comforts for a growing number of wageworkers, cotton factors, bank clerks, and others of the professional classes. Many slave traders relied on enslaved or free women to run boardinghouses that catered to their clients and agents.[24]

In the southern context, slavery imbued socially reproductive labor with a specific character. Slaveholders could simultaneously turn women's labor into a commodity through the commodification of an enslaved laborer's person as well as through exchanging wages for the domestic labor of a free black or white woman. In addition to paid white servants, boardinghouse keepers, renters of rooms, and hotels relied on enslaved labor to supplement their workforce. Slave traders marketed enslaved women as seamstresses, nurses, chambermaids, and cooks. Enslavers purchased outfits for themselves and the people they enslaved that were made of slave-grown cotton and constructed by a variety of hands: black and white, free and enslaved, northern and southern. Heads of household, slaveholders, and businessmen in the antebellum urban South "thrived," as Seth Rockman writes of early Republic Baltimore, "on [their] ability to exploit the labor of workers unable fully to claim the prerogatives of market freedom." The socially reproductive labor that slave traders required was cheap and readily available because of legal restrictions on and social attitudes about women's labor, particularly if the women in question were of African descent.[25]

Slave traders used some of the "technologies of capitalism," such as the quantification and abstractions of account books, to classify people as types. These attempts to standardize humanity—to turn individuals into "fancy girls," "A1 field hands" and "prime women"—were central to the violence of slavery. Too often, the archive reproduces these types and erases individual identities, turning enslaved men, women, and children into undifferentiated groups of laborers. In an effort to combat archival erasures of identity, I make my argument through four microhistories. I begin each chapter with a type or label that slave traders ascribed to enslaved women and then complicate and unsettle this type through a close examination of individual enslaved women's lives.

Each chapter also begins with examples of market transactions from women's lives: items purchased, labor sold, inheritances received. By highlighting these seemingly mundane monetary transactions, I consider what financial accounts can tell us beyond profit and loss, as well as what unanswerable questions they raise. In other words, these microhistories consider what questions about enslaved women's histories are still answerable, buried and unrecognized in ledgers and financial statements, and what parts of that history are unknowable.[26]

The histories that follow focus primarily on the period from 1840 to 1861, the period between the Panic of 1837 and the Civil War. The antebellum slave trade changed dramatically after the financial collapse of 1837, as traders struggled to collect due bills, promissory notes, and other financial promises. Some of the dominant trading firms of the era, particularly Franklin & Armfield, exited the slave trade; many of the earlier era's smaller, itinerant traders left the business of slavery as well. As the national economy struggled to recover, a number of trading "combinations" formed in the South's urban centers. These slave-trading partnerships, usually with business connections in multiple slave markets, came to dominate the slave trade of the latter 1840s and 1850s. By the 1850s, as Calvin Schermerhorn writes, "expanded transportation led to a slave market that behaved like a stock exchange." Previously correlated to the price of cotton, the price of enslaved people soared, even coming close to doubling in 1850s New Orleans.[27]

While chronologically focused on the later decades of the antebellum slave trade, the case studies center geographically on two of the trade's major markets—Richmond, Virginia, and New Orleans. These were far from the only slave markets in the South, but they were two of the largest and two of the most famous. In their letters, slave traders eagerly reported news of the "Richmond market" or queried about the "going prices" in New Orleans. Richmond was primarily, though certainly not exclusively, a place from which enslaved people departed. Traders who had purchased individuals from the Maryland, North Carolina, and Virginia countryside traveled to the large slave jails of Richmond and sought the city's many auctioneers. The large trading combinations often purchased enslaved people to sell to associates in New Orleans, the largest slave market of the South. New Orleans's slave trade made an estimated $8 million annually, which was more than both Richmond and Charleston, another major market, combined.[28]

Prominent, professional slave traders maintained connections in and traveled to and from Richmond and New Orleans, as well as other smaller markets. They often employed agents to make sales and purchases for them, but they made at least annual visits to colleagues in other cities and maintained active communication via letters, circulars, and, later, telegrams. That the large slave markets were both regional centers and urban spaces had significant implications, both positive and negative, for enslaved concubines. None of the women in the following case studies were isolated on rural plantations; their connections to broader urban communities, their access to urban economies, and the concomitant presence of wage laborers all shaped their daily experiences. A focus on Richmond and New Orleans allows us to see how the urban South differed from the agricultural South, and how enslaved and free women's lives and labors were distinct in the urban household from the plantation household.[29]

The first chapter, "Fancy," explores the "fancy trade" and the various economic roles women played within it. It focuses on the life of Corinna Hinton Omohundro, an enslaved woman, likely labeled a "fancy girl" herself, who then assisted in clothing other women sold as "fancies" by Silas Omohundro, a slave trader and the father of her children. Hinton gave birth to her first child with Omohundro when she was fourteen or fifteen. Over the next ten years, Hinton bore Omohundro six children and eventually positioned herself as Omohundro's wife to gain legal recognition as his widow. She assisted in clothing the enslaved people in Omohundro's jail and ran his adjacent boardinghouse, which catered to visiting slave traders. Although she received some wages for her domestic labor, much of her work cooking and cleaning she did for free. Running the boardinghouse, however, gave her an opportunity to market her domestic skills to visiting traders, and she earned money of her own sewing and washing, allowing her to occasionally loan small sums of money to her boarders. Hinton's labor—enslaved, compensated with wages, marketed to her customers—shows the many forms that women's socially reproductive labor took under slavery's capitalism.

Chapter 2 looks at enslaved women whom slave traders called "seamstresses." This chapter highlights the importance of needlework to slave traders who used clothing as a marketing tool. Before sale, slave traders generally gave enslaved people two suits of clothes, one of which was their "sale outfit" to be worn at auction. Slave traders acquired "sale outfits" in a variety of ways, but almost all of them included some form of women's labor. Some slave traders made the enslaved women they jailed sew or alter clothes as they awaited sale, while others paid free black or white women to sew for them. I focus here on the variety of women whom one Richmond slave trader, Hector Davis, depended on. I also consider how slave traders often employed the term "seamstress" as a euphemism for a woman to be sold for sex.

In chapter 3, "Concubine," the geographical focus moves to New Orleans to investigate the life of Sarah Ann Conner, a woman who became infamous as the enslaved concubine of Theophilus Freeman, the slave trader who sold the free man Solomon Northup in Louisiana. Conner forged a troubled path from enslavement to emancipation, purchasing her freedom with the proceeds of domestic and sexual labor. When she was the enslaved concubine of Theophilus Freeman, Conner used her personal savings to convince Freeman to buy her freedom. Through incompetence or trickery, Freeman's emancipation of Conner was incomplete, and the parish court attempted to sell her to pay Freeman's debts. As she struggled to solidify her freedom, the power of slavery's sexual economy continued to pull her in. As Freeman's enslaved concubine, she was a target of his creditors and the means through which they tried to recover their debts. Conner's story calls into question historiography that places accommodation and resistance in a dichotomous relationship, especially for enslaved women.

Chapter 4, "Housekeeper," considers the experiences of one of Sarah Conner's acquaintances, Lucy Ann Cheatham. Cheatham's story brings into focus the blurry line between enslaved domestic and enslaved concubine. Cheatham's life spanned the two major markets of the slave trade, Richmond and New Orleans. John Hagan, a major slave trader with national financial connections, purchased Cheatham in Richmond and took her as his enslaved concubine to New Orleans, where she lived for the remainder of her life. Cheatham managed his household and, after his death, made a living renting out domestic space. She maintained friendships with many women, enslaved and free, who also attempted to use domestic work to free themselves from the sexual economy of slavery. The relationships she formed with other enslaved women, and particularly other enslaved concubines, shed an important light on women's modes of resistance to slavery and the importance of female friendship for survival.

Considering the actions of women within the slave market requires examining and reevaluating many assumptions about the economy, slavery, and sexuality. This work not only illustrates that women's domestic labor was neither obvious nor natural; it also connects women to the study of more traditional economic questions. That women sewed and cooked for slave traders, or that enslaved women were sold in terms of sexual availability, was not a given but a product of specific discourses about the biological roots of gender and race. And the fact that women performed this work either for free as wives and/or slaves, or for cash amounts that varied according not to the labor performed, but instead the legal and racial status of the laborer, served the interests of slave traders and enslavers more broadly. The experiences of women in the slave market should be considered in light of Gerda

Lerner's argument that "economic oppression and exploitation are based as much on the commodification of female sexuality and the appropriation by men of women's labor power and her reproductive power as on the direct economic acquisition of resources and persons." Even when women were not or could not be direct market actors themselves, they performed the labor that sustained *homo economicus* in his self-interested pursuit of profit.[30]

CHAPTER ONE

Fancy

Silas Omohundro Market and General Account Book
Library of Virginia

8 January 1858
1 pair Earrings for Girl Jane & stockings 2.50

9 June 1860
Cash to Corinna for Market 50.00

23 December 1862
Dimont [sic] Ring Give to Corinna 100.00

Sometime after she was born in 1835, Silas Omohundro purchased Corinna Hinton, and potentially her mother, as well. After he started recording purchases in his market and general account book in January of 1855, Omohundro regularly noted purchases he made for Hinton and items he had her purchase on his behalf. In July 1855 he gave her cash to buy clothes for his children. In November he went to Binford, Mayo, & Blair to select three dresses for Hinton. In 1856 he paid for her to have her "likeness" taken. Over the course of the next six months, Omohundro bought Hinton four more dresses. In 1857 he paid Doctor Hudson to make Hinton a set of false teeth. He had her watch repaired later that year. In 1859 and 1860, Omohundro paid for more dresses, corsets, shoes, a mourning veil, silverware, and fabric. The list goes on—silk stockings, buckskin slippers, garters, bonnets, tea sets, jewelry—with entry after entry of material goods that a slave trader purchased for a woman he enslaved.[1]

Then there are entries for work Hinton performed, as well as work others did for her. Early in the account book, Omohundro paid Hinton "for negro clothing." These entries occurred annually or semiannually until 1863. Even more frequently, Omohundro paid Hinton to "make market." In 1855 he gave her money to buy fruit "for pickles and preserves." In 1856 Omohundro paid her for "making childrens cloth[es]." In 1858 Omohundro paid Mrs. Brown, a midwife, to attend to Hinton in the birth of her fifth child, who was still-born. A few days later, Omohundro paid for the child's burial, and then for Mrs. Brown to return to visit Hinton. In 1862 Omohundro gave money for Hinton to purchase cornmeal, brandy, a sausage grinder, and other kitchen items. In 1863 he paid a woman named Caroline to do Corinna's washing. In 1864 Omohundro paid Mrs. Murphy for nursing Corinna's infant child.[2]

What are we to make of these purchases—the fancy goods, the mundane necessities of life, the intimate and emotional labor of other women? In certain moments, Omohundro's purchases seem to reinforce popular, stereotypical representations of concubines: the expensive jewelry, the multitude of fashionable clothing and accessories, and the household finery. At other times Omohundro's cash outlays reveal the *work* required of a concubine: the household management, the childcare, and the emotional toll of such reproductive and sexual labor. Either way, all of Omohundro's purchases survive in the archive and reach us through his penmanship, his paper, and his perspective. Before Omohundro's death, Corinna Hinton's voice doesn't survive in a single record. Even after his death, her surviving words are sparse and mostly filtered through lawyers and government officials.

What does it mean that Corinna's story survives because of Omohundro's *purchases*—the purchase of her body and labor, the purchases for her, and the purchases she made with Omohundro's money? How can we read past Omohundro's rote notations of commodities for cash to understand what the same purchases meant for Hinton? What did it mean to Hinton to put on kid gloves, a diamond ring, and silk stockings before going to the shops of Richmond to buy fabric and ready-made clothes for herself, her children, and the men and women whom the father of her children enslaved and sold? How did Hinton understand her labor in Omohundro's kitchen, as she pickled and preserved fruit, baked bread, and dispensed rum to visiting slave traders? What did it mean for her to serve tea in her tea set in the house next to the slave jail? How did Hinton process the death of her stillborn child?

None of these questions are easy to answer, as details of Hinton's life appear only through her encounters with Omohundro and, later, the court system. Yet this lack of immediate evidence directly from Hinton's hand should not preclude attempts to understand her life on its own terms, as well as the lives of those like her. Women such as Corinna Hinton are too often viewed only from the perspective of the men who enslaved, commodified, and sexualized them. The archive is full of examples of white men who fulfilled their own fantasies of power through attempts to dominate black women's bodies. While it is important to document and analyze what ownership and mastery meant for these men, it is equally important to entertain the same situations from the women's perspective. Failure to do so too often results in statements such as "many of these fancy girls . . . often ended by falling in love with their men, and vice versa." What evidence exists that "fancy girls" loved the men who enslaved them, outside of gendered assumptions that time, children, and financial support must translate into love?[3]

This is an attempt to tell Corinna Hinton's story without recommodifying her person. There is no evidence that Hinton would have understood herself as a "fancy girl." Indeed, being categorized into a representative, marketable "type" was a form of violence itself. While there is no doubt that white men commodified and sexualized enslaved women's bodies in the slave market, it is worth asking what the experience of the slave market, and labor within it, meant to enslaved women, and to understand them, to the best of our ability, as individual women rather than as an undifferentiated group of bodies onto whom white men projected their fantasies. Though categorized by slave traders and potentially others around her as a "fancy," Corinna Hinton lived and labored both within and outside of this label. Light-skinned and enslaved, Hinton had to navigate a world that restricted the possibilities of her life by putting a price on her racialized and sexualized body, but her sense of self—her soul value—could not be defined by the moniker "fancy." What follows is an experiment in interpreting the life of Corinna Hinton both inside and outside of the market in her many overlapping and entangled identities.[4]

8 January 1858: 1 pair Earrings for Girl Jane & stockings 2.50

In order to understand the experiences of enslaved women who were sold for their sexual availability, it is necessary to first define and then deconstruct the identity slave traders tried to place on them. What was a "fancy" to a slave trader, and why was she so valuable? Nearly all slave traders, including Omohundro, described some of their "stock" as "fancy." Just as traders noted the going prices for "prime male field hands," they also created the type of the "fancy girl." With this designation, slave traders erased individual identities and replaced them with an ideal form. To mark a woman a "fancy girl" was to disregard her bodily integrity and personal sanctity, to deem her a marketable commodity available for sex and white male pleasure. This designation could be either implicit or explicit—conveyed directly in language or indirectly through visual markers, euphemisms, and innuendo.

The term "fancy" suggests extravagance, indulgence, and lust. Webster's 1841 dictionary defined "fancy" as, first, "the faculty by which the mind forms an image or a representation of anything perceived before; the power of combining and modifying such objects into new pictures or images; the power of readily and happily creating and recalling such objects for the purpose of amusement, wit, or embellishment; imagination," but also as "taste," "inclination," "love," "false notion," and, significantly, "something that pleases or entertains without real use or value." According to slang dictionaries, "fancy" could also mean "the favourite sports, pets, or pastimes of a person" and, interestingly, "the paramour of a prostitute is still called her fancy-man," or "a fellow kept by a prostitute." Finally, "fancy pieces" were "women of pleasure, doxies, &c."[5]

Nineteenth-century Americans used "fancy" in a number of contexts. A "fancy ball" was "a ball in which persons appear in fancy dresses in imitation of the costumes of different persons and nations." A "fancy store" was one that sold showy, ornamental objects and other "fancy goods" that were "in distinction from those of a simple or plain color or make." A "fancy stock," meanwhile, was "a species of stocks which afford great opportunity for stock gambling, since they have no intrinsic value, and the fluctuations in their prices are artificial." To the buyers and sellers of "fancy girls" or "fancy maids," then, these were women who were expensive, ornamental, and rare. They showed off a man's wealth and good taste but were of little true value. "Fancy" referenced the gamble and thrill of purchasing such a woman; the "fancy girl" was, to her purchaser, the embodiment of all those "images" of the mind, a combination of the presumed sexual availability of black women with the privileging of white skin in a pretty "imitation" of a white woman who could be "readily and happily" recalled — and then discarded — "for the purpose of amusement" with little thought to the woman herself.[6]

Particularly when communicating with one another, slave traders could be quite candid about the value they placed on a "fancy," and slave traders' letters are inundated with the casual violence of the term. John J. Toler, a trader who moved between the Richmond and New Orleans market, reported to his colleagues on one occasion, "Mr. D[ickinson] & Hill sold a no 1 Fancy the other day for $1300," and later noted, "Mr. H[ector] D[avis] sold a brown skin fancy to day for $1600 and a litler [sic] one with a child that said she was a seamstris [sic] for $1500." And then again, in the same month, Toler wrote, "they [sic] were three Fances [sic] sold yesterday at thes [sic] figures namely $1550 dollars $1680 dollars & $1650 dollars." Another trader who frequented the Richmond market, Philip Thomas, used similar language to write to his associate, noting, "I bought . . . [a] 13 year old Girl Bright Colour nearly a fancy for $1135 she can be sold for $1325. Zach bought a Fancy at $1325."

Thomas wrote the word "Fancy" in bold, oversized letters so that it jumped out from the page at the reader.[7]

Calculated marketing and desire for profit motivated slave traders and drew them to enslaved women whose sexuality they could exploit. Confident they could profit from their customers' sexual fantasies and dreams of mastery, traders saw "fancies" as a solid investment. Philip Thomas wistfully wrote his business partner, "I wish all we had were Eliza & Mariahs," referring to two "fancy" women he had purchased. Thomas was sure that "fancies" guaranteed high profits, so he was incensed when his agent, Calhoun, sold Eliza "low," writing, "Tell Calhoun I shall give him fits when I see him for selling Eliza as low as $1200 She was worth at least $2000." Thomas planned to capitalize on Eliza's sexuality, and Calhoun had not followed his employer's orders. Richmond auctioneers D. M. Pulliam & Co. similarly tried to lure traders in by promising, "Fancy girls would sell exceedingly well just now." Pulliam followed this statement with an enticing, "Hoping we hear from you soon."[8]

While slave traders rarely made explicit what constituted a "fancy," they could be pressed to do so, especially in court. In May of 1847, Louisianan Mansuel White initiated a legal suit against Hope H. Slatter, a slave trader based out of Baltimore. White had given a man named Buckner H. Payne money to purchase a slave from Slatter's agent in New Orleans, James Blakeley. Payne told Blakeley he wanted "a nurse for his family" and selected a fourteen-year-old "mulattress slave" named Mary Ellen Brooks. Payne said he was going to take Brooks to see his wife and a physician before purchasing her. Soon after, Payne purchased Brooks, but within a month the enslaved woman was dead.

The legal case surrounding Brooks's death at first flirted with and then made explicit the sexual violence inherent in her sale. Both parties to the case called multiple witnesses to attest to Brooks's health at the time of her sale, as well as the price they assigned to her. Witness after witness used similar, vague language in reference to the "type" of enslaved woman Brooks was. Slave trader Frances Jump claimed he "gave her a mattress to sleep on, as usual with house servants. She was pretty and intelligent, and well suited for a house servant." C. M. Rutherford testified that "there are cases where girls of that description would command a higher price." S. F. Slatter, Hope Slatter's son, allegedly called her "a small, delicate thing," while Blakeley described her as "a very pretty girl, a bright mulatto with long curly hair and fine features—she was about fourteen years old."

A doctor hired to do a postmortem examination described her as a "yellow girl." *Delicate, pretty, bright, intelligent, yellow, house servant, mulatto, fine*—this was the language of the "fancy trade."[9]

Part of Blakeley and Slatter's defense was to impugn Payne's motives. Their attorneys repeatedly asked questions about Payne's marital status at the time of Brooks's purchase, and whether or not his wife was in New Orleans with him. One of the questions the defense asked witnesses was "Is Mr. B. H. Payne a man of family . . . ?" When witnesses confirmed that Payne was married, Blakeley eventually became more explicit in his accusations, saying, "Ellen Brooks was a fancy girl." Someone in the room must have asked what Blakeley meant by fancy, because the minutes next note, "witness means by that a young, handsome yellow girl of fourteen or fifteen with long curly hair." Shortly after his revelation, Blakeley asserted that Payne actually had "no wife at the place where he lived," thereby implying that when Payne took Brooks to show his wife, he was actually raping her. Blakeley continued, "The death of the girl had been hurried by improper intercourse between him and said girl and that he had been informed by the girl."[10]

The focus of the extant minutes quickly moved on from this reference to "improper intercourse," but the language Blakeley used merits examination. While he used and defined the term "fancy," and while he acknowledged some level of unacceptable "intercourse," he did so in the context of a court case where hundreds of dollars were at stake. Blakeley also claimed that he had learned of this "improper intercourse" from Brooks herself, implying that Brooks either left Payne's house and sought him out for help or that he visited her after her sale. If Brooks really did turn to Blakeley for relief, her actions reveal a great deal about her desperation and the lack of allies available to her. Significantly, nowhere in the court records does the word "rape" appear.

The woman in question, Mary Ellen Brooks, exists in the testimony only as a lost investment to be recovered and as an object of sexual commodification. Fourteen years old and incredibly ill, she suffered for a month in a bedroom where Payne imprisoned her. She had no one to turn to for companionship other than a woman Payne hired, Ann Edwards, to nurse her back to health. After her passing, a doctor—an "expert" in the "pathology of consumption"—performed an autopsy on her body, which he described before the court alongside the traders who dissected the price of her various physical attributes. Brooks appears exposed in the archive in this same way, a poignant reminder of the ways in which the archive of slavery can be "a death sentence, a tomb, a display of the violated body."[11]

Even if Blakeley had not used the term "fancy," the language of his and others' testimony still revealed how they saw and categorized Brooks. Slave traders held just as many fantasies of domination as their customers, and it is telling that Blakeley described himself as Brooks's would-be savior, the man to whom she revealed her tribulations and abuse from Payne. Traders were notorious among the enslaved for their sexual violence against enslaved women. Escaped slave John Brown recalled the "dreadful fate which awaits the young slave women who are sold away South, where the slave-pen is only another name for a brothel."[12] In some cases, this was nearly the literal truth. Isaac Franklin, onetime employer of Silas Omohundro, speculated, "The old Lady and Susan [two enslaved women] could soon pay for themselves by keeping a whore house," though he was mainly concerned with his and his associates' pleasures, and continued that the brothel should be "located and established at your place, Alexandria, or Baltimore for the Exclusive benefit of the concern [sic] & [its] agents."[13] Lexington trader Lewis Robards also drew on images of the brothel to sell enslaved women. He kept two separate jails, with one dedicated entirely to the sale of "fancy" women.[14]

Those traders who did not specifically use the term "fancy" still recognized the value that buyers placed on the sexual and reproductive labor of young enslaved women. Walter Johnson writes that enslavers "imagined who they could be by thinking about whom they could buy."[15] When potential purchasers encountered a "fancy girl" in the slave market, they placed their own desires on enslaved women's bodies, fantasizing about sex, domination, and rakish challenges to social mores. To purchase a "fancy" was to make a personal statement in front of slave traders and the other white men and women present.

Thus abolitionist Calvin Fairbank recalled his 1842 purchase of Eliza, a "fancy girl" "only one sixty-fourth African," as a manly competition for mastery between himself and another bidder, a "short, thick-necked, black-eyed Frenchman from New Orleans." The two men attempted to outbid one another until the price reached $1,485. The auctioneer, in an effort to drive prices up, exposed Eliza's breasts to the crowd and cried, "Here is a girl fit to be the mistress of a king!" Egging on the competition between the two men for his own financial gain, the auctioneer continued, "Ah! Gentleman, who is going to be the winner of this prize?" When the Frenchman lost the bidding war, Fairbank, imagining himself as hero, announced that rather than keep Eliza, he was going to free her. While Fairbank likely embellished the tale, including such tropes as a conniving white mistress jealous of Eliza's beauty and the oversexualized Frenchman, his emphasis on the bidding war between himself and his antagonist is nonetheless indicative of the public performance of mastery during "fancy sales."[16]

Fairbank's account of Eliza's auction reveals much about abolitionist portrayals of the slave trade and southern society in general. Abolitionists focused on the image of the enslaved woman, whose person was subject to the physical and sexual violence of the master. Abolitionists "compiled excruciating evidence" of physical and emotional suffering at the hands of slaveholders, all of which, Amy Dru Stanley argues, was "meant to incite a visceral response [in the reading public] and played upon the cult of feeling dominant in Victorian America." The sale of Eliza represented slavery's perversion of the northern ideal of family life. Eliza's father had placed his own flesh and blood for sale in order to satisfy his financial debts. Father and auctioneer profited from the public marketing of Eliza's sexuality, while bidders hoped to purchase domestic affection and reproductive labor for a cash value.[17]

Tales of the "fancy trade," whether real or apocryphal, played into abolitionists' likening of southern life to prostitution. As a metaphor for the slave system, prostitution "denoted both economic relations and sexual exchange" as well as "racial subjugation." Abolitionists contrasted this with northern life, where free labor allegedly separated the private household from the marketplace. While many abolitionist authors did not go as far as Fairbank in describing scenes "at which civilization blushed, and angels wept," nearly every abolitionist account of slavery referenced the sexual exploitation that underwrote the entire system. For formerly enslaved women, addressing rape and sexual violence was an effort to "resist the misappropriation and to maintain the integrity of their own sexuality," even if literary and moral convention kept them from being too explicit in details. Elizabeth Keckley, for example, wrote, "Suffice it to say, the he [an unnamed white man] persecuted me for four years and I—I—became a mother." In Keckley's hyphens and pauses were the unspeakable details of rape, which she conveyed only through ominous silences.[18]

Along with language, slave traders used material signifiers to inform audiences who was "fancy" and who was not. While all enslaved people could be subject to sexual violence, these accessories and clothes marked certain women as valuable primarily, if not only, for sexual labor. Clothing was a key part of slave traders' efforts to commodify enslaved property. Similar or identical outfits "masked differences among the slaves; individual pasts and potential problems were covered over in uniform cloth" when they were "dressed as ideal slaves." Slave traders thus dressed women sold for sex in particular ways that matched the traders', and their customers', fantasies.[19]

Before an auction or private sale took place, enslaved people were commonly forced to wear new and often identical outfits, which the traders called "sale outfits." These outfits were inexpensive and utilitarian, but new and clean. For some women, however, slave traders purchased more costly items. Omohundro, for example, spent a great deal more on clothing "fancies" than he did other men and women. For women such as Maria Johnson, Jenny, Columbia, Sally, and Ellen, whom Omohundro labeled as "fancy" in his sales book, he purchased more expensive shoes, earrings and other pieces of jewelry, gloves, and stockings. On a few occasions, Omohundro gave Corinna money to purchase dresses for certain enslaved women, meaning that in many cases it was Corinna who directed the placement of the physical markers that conveyed the women's "fancy" status before sale. One aspect of Hinton's reproductive labor was thus to "dress" other women to be commodified and sold in a highly sexualized way. Perhaps Corinna believed the more money Omohundro made in the fancy trade, and in the slave market in general, the greater the chance that she would live a comfortable life and that she and her children would be safe from sale.[20]

Other traders dressed some enslaved women in hoopskirts or in richer fabrics. While short entries in account books do not describe the appearance of these items in detail, it is likely that such accessories and fabrics looked more expensive. Enslaved women wearing stockings and hoopskirts approximated potential purchasers' image of fashionable white women, with the key difference that these women were enslaved and thus considered sexually accessible. Fashionable dress highlighted the "racial mystery" of light-skinned enslaved women that allowed white men "the chance to transgress social mores while remaining perfectly safe in their own social positions." Women such as Mary Ellen Brooks were erotically dangerous for their racial ambiguity and the taboo of sex across the color line. Yet it was ultimately safe for a man like Payne to purchase a woman like Brooks because she was not, in fact, legally considered white, and as her owner raping her was a legal impossibility.[21]

9 June 1860: Cash to Corinna for Market 50.00

While female sexuality was a highly successful avenue for making money on the auction block or in private sales, traders could exploit sexual and reproductive labor in other ways. When enslaved women were not sold, traders could Rely on their work to cut costs in their jails, boardinghouses, and personal homes. Brown wrote that in the slave pen, "the men were separated from the women, and the children from both; but the youngest and handsomest females were set apart as the concubines of the masters, who generally changed mistresses every week."[22]

Omohundro "set apart" at least two women as his enslaved concubines, and each woman performed critical domestic and socially reproductive labor for his household and his adjacent business. Born in 1807 in Albermarle County, Virginia, Omohundro had found employment as an agent of the well-known slave trader Rice Ballard. Ballard was a member of the most successful slave-trading firm of the 1830s, Alexandria, Virginia's Franklin & Armfield, a firm with noted engagement in the sale of enslaved women for sex. Operating as the company's contact in Richmond, Ballard and his agents roamed the Virginia countryside looking for enslaved people to purchase, and then sent them on to Isaac Franklin in New Orleans or James Franklin in Natchez. Being an agent may not have commanded the most respect or financial reward, but many of the next decade's prominent slave traders got their start in the business working for larger firms such as Franklin & Armfield. For his work for Ballard, Omohundro earned a $10 commission on each individual purchased as well as training in the business practices of the trade.[23]

During his time with Franklin & Armfield, Omohundro came into contact with his first enslaved concubine, a woman named Louisa Tandy, who was fifteen years his junior and who fit traders' description of a "fancy girl." In 1838, when she was sixteen, Tandy gave birth to Omohundro's first son, Littleton. Shortly after, Louisa and their son moved to Cincinnati, Ohio, at Omohundro's behest. In a tactic he would later repeat with Corinna, Omohundro installed Louisa and the children in a house, appointed a white male acquaintance to check in with her, and reported to neighbors that Louisa was his white wife. He then annually visited Louisa, Littleton, and the four additional children they had together, spending a week or two each visit, for the next ten years. He gave Louisa an allowance of $12,000 a year and paid for the children's schooling, otherwise leaving Louisa on her own.[24]

Despite living in a free state and regardless of what Omohundro told his Ohio acquaintances, the question of race continued to plague Louisa and her children. Louisa Tandy was reportedly "coppery" and her skin tone became a source of gossip in the neighborhood. Omohundro attempted to put an end to any rumors by explaining to his friends that Tandy had "no African blood in her, but rather West Indian." Adam N. Riddle, a lawyer Omohundro appointed to manage his affairs in Cincinnati, initially believed Louisa was "slightly mixed" but this "explanation made by Silas removed that impression." The Omohundro children, too, faced questions while attending Hughes High

One half of a pair of undated images owned by Silas Omohundro and inherited by his children. The woman could be Louisa Tandy, Martha Tandy, or Corinna Hinton. Courtesy of Rene Tyree.

School as white pupils. The parents of other students reported to their teacher, John M. Edwards, that their mother was a "colored woman." Not sure of the truth, Edwards ignored these reports and the Omohundros' race "never came up in any way affecting [their] standing in the school."[25]

While Omohundro was still in contact with and traveling to visit Louisa Tandy, Corinna Hinton gave birth to her first child, appropriately named Silas Omohundro Junior. At the time of his namesake's birth, Silas Omohundro had left the employ of Franklin & Armfield and was working as an independent trader in Richmond. In 1846 he obtained a license to keep a "private house of entertainment" in the slave-trading district of the city, which he operated in conjunction with a slave jail.[26] Through these businesses in the marketing of human bodies, Omohundro gradually accumulated a fortune. In less than twenty years in the slave market, he purchased property in Richmond, a farm in Henrico County, Virginia, and real estate worth more than $33,000 in Pennsylvania. He filled his home with paintings, books, and

Accompanying image of Silas Omohundro, undated. Courtesy of Rene Tyree.

mirrors; he dined with expensive silver and glassware; slaves dressed him in fine suits and hats; he wore a gold pocket watch. Outside of the enslaved individuals he regularly sold, Omohundro held in slavery seventeen men and women who waited on him and helped him operate his jail. Though they were not included in his estate inventory, he also owned seven more enslaved people: Corinna and his children, property he preferred to classify as family. They, too, helped him run his business.[27]

Corinna was between fourteen and seventeen years old when she had her first child with Omohundro, who was forty-two at the time. Raping Corinna was, for Omohundro, part and parcel of legal ownership, and likely an act he had committed before. Enslavers had full "use" of those they enslaved. It is within this context that we must consider Corinna's life. In 1849 she was the enslaved fourteen-year-old mother of an infant son, with little possibility of escape. Corinna may have recognized the freedoms Silas possessed and the legal and social disadvantages she faced as an enslaved woman.

Corinna's "core experiences," as Marisa Fuentes writes, were "shaped by sexual violence and impossible choices, [and] are not fully elucidated by progressive notions of agency." Allying herself with Silas gave Corinna material comfort and a greater possibility of achieving freedom for herself and her children, but such potential benefits came at a cost.[28]

After receiving lessons in reading and writing with a Mr. Cawfield, a teacher Omohundro had hired, Hinton signed her name "Mrs. Corinna Omohundro" on multiple occasions. Calling herself Omohundro's wife, however, does not necessarily mean that Corinna loved Silas or viewed their relationship as a consensual, affectionate union. While it is important, as Annette Gordon-Reed points out, not to homogenize enslaved women's experiences by assuming every instance of sex between a white man and an enslaved woman was coercive, it is equally crucial to consider the legal and social constraints within which Corinna operated. As Saidiya Hartman has asked, "How can rape be differentiated from sexuality when consent is intelligible only as submission?" Do the Omohundros' six children, or the affection Silas evidently felt for their offspring, lessen the violence of their relationship, or show how few choices Corinna had?[29]

Is it even possible to understand their relationship in the absence of legal consent and personhood? Focusing on whether or not Hinton "consented"—whatever that term, firmly grounded in the "conventions of liberal agency," may mean in the context of nineteenth-century chattel slavery—distracts from the deeply rooted structural challenges that limited the possible in her day-to-day existence. As the evidence exists now, it is impossible to say with certainty what Corinna Hinton felt toward Silas Omohundro. Rather than debating and projecting meaning onto her inner life, her story is better served by recognizing the impossible choices she regularly faced, and the ways in which she navigated and challenged constraints of race and sex.[30]

One of those impossible choices was Omohundro's expectation or order that Hinton assist him in provisioning his slave jail and managing his boarding-house. With no legal wife, and with Louisa Tandy hundreds of miles away in Cincinnati, Omohundro needed someone to perform and oversee others' domestic labor. In Corinna he found a capable household manager who performed the socially reproductive labor necessary to the functioning of his home and business. Yet because Corinna was not his legal wife, he gained all of this without the corresponding economic responsibility a legal marriage to a white woman entailed. Omohundro could demand labor from Corinna as he would from a legal wife, but no laws required him to provide for her and their six children together, nor did Corinna have legal protection from abuse. Omohundro could sell Corinna and their children if he so desired or move them to a distant location and eventually cut off financial support, as he had with Louisa Tandy. As an enslaved woman, Corinna had no recourse against mistreatment; she depended on Omohundro's good will for her and her children's safety and support.[31]

Despite, or perhaps because of, her tenuous position in Omohundro's life, Corinna played an active part in Omohundro's success, taking on the role of his household manager. Antebellum authors placed the responsibility of prudent home management on women, emphasizing the importance of domestic economy in the overall financial success of a family. Catherine Beecher wrote that women were "agents in accomplishing the greatest work that ever was committed to human responsibility," as a "prosperous domestic state" was the foundation to a prosperous home, community, and nation. According to Beecher and writers like her, as Omohundro's wife, Corinna took charge of the household's well-being in the broadest sense. By 1863 this household included six children: Silas Jr., Alice Morton, Colon, Riley Crosby, George Nelson, and William Rainey. While not the legally married, white wife and mother of Catherine Beecher's imagined audience, Hinton performed the same type of work without the attached social reward of respectable domesticity. She cared for their children, provided food for Silas and his dependents, clothed the family, oversaw the work of enslaved laborers, maintained the cleanliness of the household, and managed the money necessary to perform such tasks.[32]

Hinton combined socially reproductive labor within Silas's household with his businesses. She provided clothing for the slave jail, assisted in "dressing" enslaved women, and managed his boardinghouse. Jacqueline Jones observes that "if work is any activity that leads either directly or indirectly to the production of marketable goods, then slave women did nothing *but* work. Even their efforts to care for themselves and their families helped to maintain the owner's workforce and to enhance its overall productivity." In the case of Corinna and women like her, there was no distinction between laboring for her family and laboring for her master; they were one and the same.[33]

From the framed kitchen in the rear of Omohundro's jail complex, Corinna assisted in or oversaw the running of his kitchen, preparing meals, pickling fruit, and making preserves. She kept his kitchen stocked, decided what supplies were necessary, and informed Omohundro what she needed to purchase, whether it was chicken, brown sugar, or eggs. Like many women in slaveholding households, Hinton likely had the help of other enslaved women in this work. One woman in particular, Patsy Clark, served as Corinna's assistant.[34]

Omohundro's Jail and Board Book, which spans from 1851 to 1861, is a good example of the money Omohundro made off of the socially reproductive labor of Corinna and the other women he enslaved. The slave jail, "Negro yard," or "depot" as it was known in New Orleans, was a common feature of the slave market. Slave traders visiting other cities to purchase and sell "coffles" of enslaved people needed somewhere to imprison the people they enslaved. C. F. Hatcher of New Orleans advertised his "depot" as "prepared to receive and accommodate from two to three hundred slaves" while James White claimed in his newspaper notices that he could "board" slaves.[35]

In a roughly ten-year period, Omohundro jailed 1,902 people in his jail. These enslaved men, women, and children stayed in the jail anywhere from one night to one year, depending on the whims of their enslavers. During the time period the Jail and Board Book covers, Omohundro made $6,250.57 off of jail fees alone, which ranged from 30¢ to 40¢ a night and included the fee for using the jail as well as basic rations. To jail so many people required domestic labor: preparing food, distributing it, washing linens, and tending to sick prisoners. Occasionally, if the jail was full or an enslaved person required additional attention, Omohundro paid other jailers or individual women to imprison individuals. One woman, Dicey Thomas, Omohundro hired on multiple occasions to "board" slaves.[36]

Many enslaved people were in Omohundro's jail while the trader who had purchased them traveled the Virginia countryside and the auction rooms of Richmond looking to purchase more people before going farther south. Omohundro took advantage of such situations, regularly selling itinerant traders supplies they would need for the overland journey: lamps, buckets, silverware, cups, food, and clothes. He made $1,076.50 off of food sold to visiting traders, which was generally in the form of bacon and bread. The bread, which the women Omohundro enslaved presumably made at least part of, sold at 35¢ a loaf. Between 1851 and 1861, Omohundro sold 4,290 loaves of bread. He also sold clothing items to traders using the jail, which he calculated separately from the outfits of the enslaved men and women about to be sold. This side business, which occasionally included specific sewing tasks or yards of fabric, brought him $425.07.[37]

The traders as well as the people they enslaved needed domestic labor while in Richmond, and many of the city's traders offered accommodations to men whose permanent residences were elsewhere but who spent a significant amount of time there, buying, selling, and watching prices. Corinna managed Omohundro's boardinghouse, which was located next to the slave jail. Omohundro's associate Robert Lumpkin also kept a boardinghouse

May 12 Board bill for J.E. Dobbs and Ferguson + Elder   328.00
  "   1 Fine Umbrella   8.00
  "   2 Trunks   at 15⁰⁰   30.00
         2 Old Trunks   at 5⁰⁰   10.00
         1 Pair blankets   20.00
         1 Carpet bag   10.00
         1 Kunlet   5.00
         1 Kit   5.00
         To Washing from Dec 7th 1862 to 1st April 1863 3¾ months at 5⁰⁰ 18.75
         1 Gallon Brandy   20.00
         1 Hat   14.00
         1 pair Shoes   9.50
         2 Reams Letter paper   40⁰⁰   80.00
         1 Gal Brandy   20.00
         Drayage   .50
         to Cash lent   10.00
                                                               $2533.95

Entry from Silas Omohundro's General Market and Account Book noting
"Mrs. Omohundro's Bill." Silas Omohundro Business and Estate Records, 1842–82,
Library of Virginia.

alongside his jail, as did C. F. Hatcher, who noted, "I can also accommodate
the owners with good board and comfortable rooms on reasonable terms."
A shared domestic space in the boardinghouse provided a central location for
traders to socialize while they waited on enslaved property to sell or negoti-
ated a purchase. Traders could form or solidify business relationships, evaluate one another's trustworthiness, and exchange market information.[38]

Omohundro paid for the boardinghouse license and the rent of the building, but Corinna handled most of the day-to-day responsibilities, allowing
Omohundro to focus on selling enslaved people and on the jail. He labeled
some of the boarding bills in his general account book "Mrs. Omohundro's
bill," but it appears that he settled most of the boarding accounts himself.
From 1851 to 1861, the boardinghouse brought in a total of $1,934.30. While
not as much as the jail, it was not an inconsequential amount, and it afforded
both Silas and Corinna other, immaterial benefits. Silas could make strategic business connections with his guests and Corinna could market her
sewing and culinary skills. While Omohundro gave a significant amount of

money to Corinna to pay her bills and costs associated with the boarding-house, she made some money of her own from the enterprise. How much profit she kept from the boardinghouse is unclear, but it's likely she claimed some, particularly for extra labor above the boarding bill. Omohundro also paid her for other, smaller tasks throughout the year. Sometimes, rather than giving her money, he loaned sums to her, ranging anywhere from $50 to $600. The act of lending implies that Corinna had her own income with which to repay him, plus interest.[39]

Hinton was not alone in her position as a female boardinghouse keeper. With few employment opportunities open to them, women often took their domestic skills to the urban market, hoping to sell what husbands, fathers, brothers, and other male family members counted on for free. The presence of young men, and men traveling, in the city provided ready customers for boardinghouse keepers and other women with domestic skills to market. Boarding was a viable employment option for women with few resources. Many did not even own the property on which they boarded customers.

In Richmond, census takers recorded forty women who ran boarding-houses in 1860. Only five of the forty owned any real estate. The rest rented houses and paid the rent with their earnings from boarding clients. The strict designation of boardinghouse in the census excludes women who rented out rooms, ran taverns, or, importantly, handled the day-to-day functioning of boardinghouses and inns to which their husbands' or enslavers' names were attached. Census takers, for example, did not designate wives as employed even if their husbands had day jobs in addition to owning some sort of lodging establishment. Census takers certainly did not list Corinna Hinton as the operator of a boardinghouse, even though they did include her as a (unemployed) head of household next door to Omohundro's residence.[40]

Yet Corinna was employed in crucial, if usually unwaged, work, mone-tizing domestic labor for Silas's customers. Slave traders boarding at the Omohundros' typically paid a dollar for each night they stayed, though fre-quent customers appear to have received discounts and the price did rise over time. The fee for staying one night generally included a meal, but laundry, excessive amounts of alcohol, and inviting friends over to supper cost extra. In 1862, for example, two boarders paid more for fifteen weeks of laundry, a gallon of brandy, and a handful of personal items Corinna had purchased for them. Intriguingly, the bill also includes the line "to cash lent 10.00." Corinna evidently let customers borrow her money on occasion; it is unclear whether the amount included interest.[41]

Corinna's labor in the boardinghouse increased her contact with visiting traders, who could stay as long as four months, as well as the visibility of her relationship with Omohundro. Yet the fact that Omohundro was the father of Hinton's children likely surprised none of her boarders, some of whom had enslaved concubines who boarded with them. For instance, trader A. Wilson brought "Miss Emily" to board with him off and on in 1851, while C. S. Skidmore brought "Miss Susan" to supper with him. The presence of these women was recorded in a very different manner from the enslaved women who stayed in Omohundro's jail, whom he entered into his record book as simply "Girl Mary" or "Negro woman."[42]

Robert Lumpkin was quite explicit in his willingness to board enslaved concubines with traders in his "hotel." Julia Wilbur, a northern reformer, visited Richmond in 1865 with, among others, Harriet Jacobs, and explored the slave-trading district of the city. Lumpkin told the women that, before the Civil War, he "did Board *white gentleman* & their *colored mistresses*" in his "*Hotel*." Lumpkin lived with Mary, a woman he enslaved. They had six children together and may have legally married in 1866. Like Omohundro, Lumpkin sent his children north for an education, to Mrs. John C. Cowles' Female Seminary in Ipswich, Massachusetts. Lumpkin reportedly feared "that some financial contingency might arise when these, his own beautiful daughters, might be sold into slavery to pay his debts, [so he] kept them, after their education had been completed, in the free State of Pennsylvania, where they would be safe." Lumpkin was equally open with Wilbur about his relationship with Mary, telling her he had "an elegant house in Philadelphia" where Mary lived and his children went to school. According to Wilbur, Lumpkin "seemed to think it would be a recommendation in our eyes [to] have us know that he has a colored wife (only he is not married) & has 5 children," but Wilbur and her companions remained unimpressed.[43]

Not far from Lumpkin and Omohundro was more evidence of the sexual economy of slavery in a strikingly similar household. Slave trader, auctioneer, bank president, and Omohundro family friend Hector Davis, one of the most influential slave traders in Richmond, lived as husband and wife with a woman he enslaved, Ann Banks. Banks was the daughter of an enslaved woman named Matilda Banks and a man named Sheldon Hansbury. Born on 11 July 1830, Banks was likely sold to Davis as a fancy girl. She was twenty years old when her first child with Davis, Audubon, was born. Three more children, Virginia, Matilda, and Victorine, were born between 1853 and 1858. The Davis children, like their mother, were listed as white in government records including the census, marriage certificates, and death certificates. Banks and her children spent much of their time in Philadelphia.[44]

The previous owner of Lumpkin's slave jail, a man named Bacon Tait, also had children with a woman of African descent. Like Omohundro, Tait had once been an agent of Rice Ballard; it is possible that the two men worked for Ballard at the same time. In an 1839 letter to Ballard, Tait wrote that he had "not [sat] at table in a private house with [white] Ladies for more than twenty years." By the late 1840s Tait was sharing his dining table primarily with one free black woman, Courtney Fountain. Around 1860 he moved Fountain and their children to Salem, Massachusetts, where they passed as white.[45]

Another associate, William Goodwin, the man who jailed Solomon Northup while he was in Richmond, sent his enslaved concubine, Betsy Barbour, to Detroit, Michigan. By the time of Goodwin's death, he had enslaved children and grandchildren residing in Detroit. He purchased a home for them there and instructed his executors to pay Barbour $150 annually. Trader R. H. Dickinson, too, had an enslaved concubine and children. After meeting Lumpkin, Julia Wilbur reported she "went into Dick Dickinson's, saw his colored family."[46]

In addition to enslaved concubines, slave traders also brought their legal wives with them while attending to the slave market, but they tended to stay in separate lodgings outside of jail complexes such as Lumpkin's. The white wife of Lexington trader Michael Hughes, for instance, accompanied him "down the river with his negroes" to Natchez. Hughes and his wife lodged with a friend or at the City Hotel, while Hughes's lesser partner, Salem Downing, stayed at the Forks of the Road, tending to business in less refined circumstances. Similarly, Margaret Bynum Glen, the wife of North Carolina trader Tyre Glen, made several overland trips with her husband to Tennessee and Alabama. Glen noted in his account book in 1838 that the expenses listed were for "self [and] family." Half of "Mrs. Glens expenses" alone came to $406.89, suggesting the family traveled in relative comfort. When Glen traveled on his own, he paid smaller sums at taverns and boardinghouses, such as his payment of $15 to "Mrs. Mulder" in Alabama in October 1838. The next year, while accompanied by "Lady and servant," Glen "paid Mrs. Mulder for bord [sic] $182.19." White wives had boardinghouse keepers and enslaved domestics to attend to their daily needs in rented lodgings, where they were less exposed to — but not ignorant of — the sexual economy of slavery.[47]

Within the area around Locust Alley in Richmond, women such as Corinna were inundated on a daily basis with traders' attempts to commodify enslaved women's sexuality. If the men's letters are any indication, they made frequent, crude references to sexual exploitation and its marketability. One visitor to the Richmond market, G. W. Eustler, assured his friend and sometimes trading partner Elias Ferguson that an enslaved woman, Sal, he had sold to trader and auctioneer R. H. Dickinson, was still available to him as a sexual commodity. Dickinson, Eustler explained, told him that Ferguson "might have it Once a day any time you called for it as long as she was there." For his part, Ferguson informed a friend, "you wanted to know if the yellow woman had been here to see you she was here this evening." That Corinna interacted regularly with slave traders in the boardinghouse likely exposed her to unwelcome attention in a market where sexual violence was the norm.[48]

23 December 1862: Dimont [sic] Ring Give to Corinna 100.00

In the life of Corinna Hinton Omohundro, the neat divides between public and private, and sex, family, and money, disappeared. Economic forces brought Corinna to Omohundro in the most brutal of ways, and this uncomfortable mix of the intimate and the economic would continue to influence her life as long as she was enslaved. Caught within the sexual economy of slavery, the clearest means of achieving freedom for herself and her children meant returning to the slave market as facilitator rather than person for sale.

Through her business association with a slave trader, Corinna thus gained access to money with which she could potentially distance herself from slavery. One way in which she did so was through her strategic deployment of material goods. As Stephanie Camp has shown, "When women adorned themselves in fancy dress of their own creation, they distanced themselves from what it felt like to wear slaves' low-status clothing." Though Omohundro paid her bill, Hinton went to stores such as Chiles & Cheney and selected for herself particular dresses and accessories. Putting on these outfits, or the jewelry Omohundro gave her, allowed Hinton to dress above her legal status and distinguish herself from other enslaved people. Perhaps, walking down the streets of Richmond in kid gloves, breastpins, and a diamond ring, Hinton could momentarily imagine what it was like to be free. With her light skin and expensive dress, she could play with the racial ambiguity that traders so valued in "fancy girls" but use it in this case to her own advantage. For a few fleeting seconds, Hinton could blend in with the other free, wealthy, "respectable" matrons of Richmond.[49]

Or perhaps, rather than blending in with, Hinton dressed in open defiance of middle- and upper-class white women. Richmond residents frequently commented on crossing paths with enslaved men and women dressed in "Northern and European finery" who "challenged the prevailing codes of deference simply through their sense of fashion." Hinton was almost certainly wealthier than many of the city's white workingmen; she almost certainly dressed more fashionably than their wives. That an enslaved concubine could afford such finery upset hierarchies of race and class, making a mockery of supposedly well-defined lines between slave and free, white and black.[50]

Selecting dresses to purchase or making decisions about what to buy for the household gave Corinna some freedom of choice and a modicum of independence, but the money came from, and linked her to, Omohundro. Particularly when she shopped at stores where she had book debt, her ability to make purchases depended on his financial reputation. Family was a crucial determinant of whether an individual was worthy of credit, and Corinna was no exception. If "rank . . . mattered more in placing individuals within the wealth structure of the city than did gender," then the bookkeepers of Richmond's Chile & Cheney's clothing store, who often extended her credit, must have seen her not as an individual enslaved woman but as either Omohundro's enslaved woman or, given her manner of dress and her light skin tone, his wife. Purchasing on credit, rather than enhancing her autonomy, linked Corinna once more to the slave trade.[51]

Outside of keeping accounts at Richmond stores, Hinton also received money from Omohundro in the form of paper banknotes. Paper money was the easiest form of payment in the local economy of which Corinna was a part. Omohundro frequently specified in his account book that he gave "Cash to Corinna." Only rarely did he record "Gave to Corinna in gold." "Cash to Corinna," despite its potential for autonomy, ultimately tied her back to the financial economy of the slave trade. Though paper money, unlike book debt or promissory notes, was in many ways anonymous and could be wielded equally by men and women, enslaved and free, the availability of cash, for Hinton, was grounded in the success of the slave market and profits from the men, women, and children she fed and clothed before they were sold. Corinna's finances and credit-worthiness, no less than Omohundro's, rested on the backs of enslaved human beings and the shackles and bills of sale that held them in bondage.[52]

The limited forms of freedom that came with cash and material goods are a poignant reminder that economic wealth did not automatically lead to independence and the ability to claim control over one's own body. Despite her clothing accounts, despite her diamond ring, and despite her cash in hand, Corinna Hinton was still Omohundro's slave, and her status, as well as that of her children, was always at risk. This was never clearer than at Omohundro's death, when his estate entered a lengthy court battle that lasted over a decade. At the core of this litigation was Hinton's identity within the Omohundro household: was she a "fancy girl," or was she Omohundro's wife?

Silas Omohundro died in Richmond in 1864, as the institution that had made his fortune fell apart around him in the midst of the Civil War. In his will, which was witnessed by Richmond mayor Joseph Mayo, Omohundro was more explicit than many men who had families with enslaved women, acknowledging Corinna's children as his own. He never specifically called Corinna his wife, however, referring to her only as "my woman," which clearly conveyed his sense of ownership of her, and "a kind, faithful, and dutiful woman to me and an affectionate mother." This description could have applied to the qualities he valued in Corinna as wife or as slave.[53]

In the will, Omohundro did officially free Corinna and their children together, though by the time of his death the failure of the Confederacy seemed likely and the future of slavery uncertain. Omohundro willed that Corinna receive the entirety of his personal estate, as well as her choice of real estate in Philadelphia or Richmond, out of which she decided to remain in Richmond. Omohundro directed the Philadelphia property and any personal items Corinna did not want to be sold by his executor, Richard Cooper, with the proceeds invested and paid to Corinna semiannually. Additionally, Corinna purchased three women, Lavenia, Polly, and Mariah, and one boy, Tom, from Omohundro's estate for over $16,000. While many enslaved Richmond residents purchased family members to keep them safe, there is no evidence that Corinna was related to any of these individuals. On the other hand, she may have feared that the three women and Tom would be sold in the division of Omohundro's estate and hoped to protect them through the purchase. Again, Corinna's actions leave no easy answers to questions of identity, resistance, and community.[54]

At Omohundro's death, Corinna thus appeared poised to inherit a significant sum of money. The appraisers of his estate, fellow slave traders N. M. Lee, Robert Lumpkin, and N. B. Hill, valued his Richmond property at $84,060. This sum included the price of his house and jail, the people he enslaved, and his household furniture. To this the appraisers added

$60,650 worth of real estate and farm equipment in Henrico County and, later, $26,000 from the sale of Omohundro's two homes in Pennsylvania.[55]

It was not court officials in Virginia, where wills such as Omohundro's were fairly common, but those in Pennsylvania who raised questions about the legality of Hinton's ties to Omohundro. In the 1850s Omohundro had, like Hector Davis and Robert Lumpkin, purchased property in Pennsylvania and sent his older children to be educated there. Between 1857 and 1859, Omohundro sent Silas Jr. and Alice Morton Omohundro to Lancaster and then Philadelphia, placing them under the care of Hinton's sister, Eliza Cheatham. Omohundro regularly sent Cheatham and his children money and paid for a tutor, Mary Davis, to educate them.[56] In 1866, as Omohundro's executors sold his Pennsylvania real estate and the sale entered the Lancaster County Orphan's Court, several court members claimed that the state was due a collateral inheritance tax because Corinna and her children were not Omohundro's legal heirs.

Corinna's title as Mrs. Omohundro was at stake. Was she to be considered Omohundro's wife, who ran his household and raised his children, or his illicit concubine? Corinna stubbornly defended her right to be called Omohundro's widow. In many ways, this was a battle she had been fighting since her first child with Omohundro was born. When she hired washerwomen to perform the least desirable forms of household labor, when nurses tended to her children, and when she dressed in expensive jewelry and fashionable clothes, Hinton made a bid for the class status her legal status as enslaved denied her. She had borne and raised his children, managed his household, and provided the domestic and socially reproductive labor necessary for his financial well-being. In other words, she had done everything that antebellum advice literature expected of a wife. In return, Hinton wanted the legal benefits that the status of wife afforded, and this was a claim she continued to pursue in litigation over Omohundro's estate all the way from the Lancaster County Orphan's Court to the Supreme Court of Pennsylvania.

There was plenty of evidence from Omohundro and Hinton's acquaintances in Pennsylvania that appeared to work in Hinton's favor. While their children were in Lancaster, Silas and Corinna visited the city six times, staying each time for a week to ten days. Silas introduced Corinna to several neighbors as his wife, and one claimed he "never thought she was his slave." A. W. Rand, who was briefly the children's caretaker, later testified in a court proceeding over Silas's estate that "Silas Omohundro and . . . Corinna Omohundro lived together as man and wife. She was introduced by him in society as his wife in conversation, in presence of [myself] and others, and in presence of their children he called her wife and on every occasion acknowledged her as his wife both in public and in private. They were looked upon and regarded as man and wife by those with whom they associated." In Pennsylvania, where no one knew Corinna's background or what kind of "businessman" Omohundro was, it was easy enough, given her presumably light skin tone, for Corinna to be viewed as a free white wife.[57]

The judges of the Pennsylvania Supreme Court, however, believed that "the proof [of Hinton's status] should come from Virginia" and not Pennsylvania because "that [Silas] should call [Corinna] his wife in this state is not strange. He could not indulge in the practice of concubinage with her in this state as he had done in Virginia, without submitting himself to reproach, and perhaps to punishment." Though one witness had optimistically postulated that Omohundro "may have purchased [Corinna] with the view of taking her to a free state, and marrying her there," the judges ultimately saw Silas's actions as emblematic of a slave society's lax morals and nefarious sexuality. They drew on long-standing abolitionist portrayals of the slave states as depraved and immoral to rule against Corinna, arguing that while Silas may have called Corinna his wife in Pennsylvania, it was only because northern society would not tolerate the degraded sexual practices of Virginia. In drawing this distinction, the court rebuked Silas, not necessarily for engaging in sex across the color line, but instead for engaging in sexual relations outside of wedlock. Hinton thus had to pay a collateral inheritance tax on the Pennsylvania property, because, not being his wife, she was not Omohundro's legal heir.[58]

In the midst of these battles over the legality of her relationship with the father of her children, as well as additional court battles with the estate's executor in the Richmond courts, Corinna Hinton stopped signing her name Corinna Omohundro, because in 1867 she became Corinna Davidson. Her second partner, Nathaniel Davidson, was a white Union veteran from New England who had resigned his army commission to report on the war for the *New York Herald*. Corinna and Nathaniel combined their business interests after his work as a war correspondent was done, opening adjoining shops in Richmond. Nathaniel sold coal and wood, while Corinna took her socially reproductive labor into the market once more, operating a bakery and confectionary. She also continued to take on boarders. The Davidsons likely needed the extra income; in the end, not much materialized from Omohundro's will. Davidson was involved in Corinna's courtroom struggles over her inheritance and thus knew of her past as enslaved concubine and "fancy girl."[59]

A job offer in the early 1870s gave Nathaniel and Corinna a chance to start over in a new city. Davidson began working for the *National Republican*, a newspaper based out of Washington, D.C., of which he was managing editor by 1878. In the nation's capital, Corinna could reinvent herself again. To those who knew her in D.C., aside from her husband and her children, Corinna was the wealthy, white wife of a successful newspaper editor and then appointee in the quartermaster general's office (who also happened to be an advocate of Spiritualism). She was also the mother of, by nineteenth-century standards, six extremely accomplished children. The surviving male children all secured well-paying jobs in major northern cities. Riley embarked on a career in newspapers with help from his stepfather. Colon also stayed in D.C., where he worked as an apothecary. William earned a law degree and moved to Chicago, where his work as an attorney allowed him to buy a house in Hyde Park and keep a live-in maid. The youngest Omohundro son, George, also moved to Chicago, where he temporarily worked for his sister's husband before returning to the D.C. area to work as a factory manager. Corinna's only daughter, Alice, married Pennsylvania native and industrial executive Edward C. Street. Alice, like all of her siblings, was taken for white by census takers and married a white spouse. Edward Street, who was eager to collect Alice's inheritance, knew of his wife's past in slavery, but the wives of the Omohundro sons may never have known their true family history.[60]

Corinna Hinton Omohundro Davidson died in 1887, a year after Nathaniel Davidson. Her youngest son, George, became the executor of her estate. George had been barely two years old when Silas died; Nathaniel had been more of a father to him than Silas. Did George remember Richmond? Did he remember the slave jails and the Devil's Half Acre? When he laid his mother to rest, what did he truly know of her life? What did he tell his children about their grandmother and grandfather? That they were enslaver and fancy girl or loving husband and wife? What did Corinna's daughter, Alice, tell her own daughter Corinna about her namesake? Could Corinna's children even imagine the fourteen-year-old girl whom a middle-aged Virginia slave trader bought with banknotes and promises thirty-some years ago? Could they reconcile the father who brought them candy and apples with the father who tore so many other children from their fathers? Can we?[61]

The internal dynamics of the Omohundro family, a complicated tangle of sex, money, and slavery, while foreign and distasteful to modern sensibilities, were an inherent part of the antebellum slave system. After all, as Friedrich Engels noted, "the word *familia* did not originally . . . refer to the married couple and their children, but to the slaves alone. *Famulus* means a household slave and *familia* signifies the totality of slaves belonging to one individual." Engels, in critiquing women's subjugation under capitalism, sought to remind readers that the bourgeois family was sullied by its resemblance to ancient slavery. He sought to make visible the historical and political development of the seemingly natural—the family.[62]

Perhaps George Fitzhugh would have found something to admire in Engel's history of the word "family." While abolitionists argued that southern slave society encouraged prostitution, illicit sexuality, and the breakdown of the family, slavery's proponents attempted to reverse these abolitionist attacks on southern society by arguing that the same were actually symptoms of free society, and particularly of the free market, where everything had a price. Fitzhugh, one of slavery's staunchest defenders, claimed, "Woman is a false position there [in the free states]," because the free market eroded women's sanctity in the home and "[threw] her into the arena of industrial war [and] robbed her of her own sex."[63]

Rather than likening it to prostitution, Fitzhugh likened slavery to the ideal of southern marriage, because of the paternal bonds each relationship allegedly contained. He extolled "the intimate connexion and dependence of slavery, marriage, and religion," calling the trio the "pillars of the social fabric." In fact, to Fitzhugh, "wives . . . are slaves; not in theory only but often in fact."[64] To condemn slavery, Fitzhugh suggested, was to condemn the presumably natural hierarchy of man and wife. Fitzhugh used abolitionists' criteria to reverse their critiques, praising modern slavery by tucking it back into hierarchies that middle-class readers would have regarded as natural and unquestionable. In doing so, Fitzhugh unwittingly gave credence to both Marxist and feminist interpretations of marriage and the household.[65]

In the sexual economy of slavery, family, household, and market collided together in ways that confound easy classification. Abolitionists could use this collision to make northern readers uncomfortable; proslavery advocates could use it to cover markets with the patina of male-female hierarchies. The market could be the household and vice versa, with slave traders capitalizing on domestic ideals by selling people as commodities prepared for household roles: as potential concubines, mothers, and daughters. In enslaved people, enslavers hoped to turn domestic affection and sexual attraction into a commodity, whether in the person of a "mammy" or a "Jezebel." They did so using the kind of labor that was often unpaid in the North. And in some cases the family truly was, as Engels put it, "the totality of slaves belonging to one individual."[66]

In Silas Omohundro's case, his biological family consisted largely of people he enslaved. In Corinna, Silas had found—at least in his imagination—the ultimate "capricious, delicate, diffident, and dependent" wife that Fitzhugh claimed to "worship and adore." In the purchase of "fancy girls," enslavers were drawn to the control they felt they could exercise over an enslaved woman. Perhaps they wanted to play the role of, as Fitzhugh put it, "a lord and master, whom she should love, honor, and obey." A "fancy girl" was doubly dependent, both "wife" and slave, "family" in both senses of the word. To say that enslaved people could be biological family or seen as family by enslavers is not, of course, to argue that Fitzhugh's positive assessment of slaves as paternal dependents is accurate. Rape may have led to an enslaver holding his biological children in bondage, and commodity fetishism may have led enslavers to imagine affection and desire in the purchase of "fancy girls," but, if anything, these examples are more akin to Fitzhugh's portrayal of a brutal, profit-driven free-market society than to his idyllic, paternal South.[67]

Corinna's position as mother, slave, de facto wife, domestic manager, and human capital put her in charge of the *family economy* in every sense. She entered the slave market as an object of exchange and navigated a complex existence at the intersection of the slave trade's financial, domestic, and sexual economies. Potential buyers assigned her monetary value based on her sexuality, her ability to reproduce and labor in the household, and the liquid wealth that holding her bill of sale signified. Her eventual purchaser, Silas Omohundro, valued her for all of these things as both a slave and a wife. Through involvement in his business, Corinna reentered the slave market not as object but as facilitator. She took the domestic and socially reproductive labor for which she was valued and attempted to use it to her own economic advantage, in turn contributing to the success of the institution—and the man—who enslaved her. Her life story adds one more link to the extensive chain of credit tying cotton producers in the U.S. South to bankers in New York City and beyond: the reproductive labor of free and enslaved women.

CHAPTER TWO

Seamstress

Hector Davis Account Book
Chicago History Museum

10 September 1859
paid board negro at old woman's 3.25

28 April 1860
Hector Davis Clothing a/c to Mrs. SN Davis
For 12 vests . . . 12
" 22 shirts . . . 8.80
" 15 suits clothes . . . 75

25 January 1862
Clothing a/c gave Va Isham to buy calico &c. 20.00

"Va Isham." "Miss Patterson." "Mrs. Solomon Davis." "Mrs. White." "Old woman." In brief but frequent notations, Richmond slave trader Hector Davis recorded the labor of women in his account book. He, or his clerks, noted women who sewed clothes, birthed babies, tended the sick, jailed enslaved people, and ran errands for him. Davis and his clerks named some women specifically; some women they did not. Some were free, some weren't. Some, such as Mrs. White, were white women hiring out the labor of enslaved women for their own profit. Others, such as Virginia Isham and Miss Patterson, constructed garments for the enslaved people Davis sold. The pages of his accounts contained the names of his business partners' and agents' wives, as well as his nieces and female kin—with the exception of his own daughters and their mother, an enslaved woman named Ann Banks. Davis and his clerks designated other women only by their sex—"old woman," "woman," "negro woman"—erasing their individual identities but recording the monetary value of their body, their labor, or the products of their labor.[1]

Davis regularly did business with and relied on the labor of women. Whether they were neighbors, acquaintances, wives, daughters, sisters, mothers, concubines, and/or slaves, women regularly interacted with the business of the slave trade, particularly in connection to the socially reproductive labor required to wash and dress enslaved people before sale. Some of this work was compensated and some was not. Jane Glen, for example, sewed for her slave-trading brother in North Carolina. J. J. Toler in Virginia ordered a woman named Mary to make him a new dress for an upcoming sale. Hope Slatter in New Orleans factored the price of clothing into his calculations of profit and loss on each sale. Hopkins Nowlin purchased two yards of "domestic," silk, thread, three spools of cotton, and needles. The list goes on: calico, gingham, linsey, buttons, flannel, yarn, thimbles.[2]

While Davis and his associates often turned to women for work, they deemed the details of such work less valuable information to preserve. Davis structured his accounts according to the racial and gender hierarchies of the society in which he lived; they reflected his preconceptions of how race related to types of work and the value thereof. Hence, Davis recorded the full names and accounts of his white customers but left incomplete the work and identities of "negro woman" and "old woman." Even the passive constructions of many of Davis's entries work to obscure women's labor. Many entries, for instance, simply read "paid for sewing."

Hector Davis made brief notes of his female associates' labors, but many other traders left no surviving records or preserved only the most legally and financially pertinent documents: bills of sale, bills of exchange, promissory notes, and similar financial paper. Yet Virginia Isham, Miss Patterson, and Mrs. S. N. Davis were obviously not the only women to sew for slave traders, even if others are difficult to locate and nearly nonexistent in the secondary literature. Lack of material does not mean lack of significance; the nature of these women's labor obstructed its broader survival in the records. Everything from the construction of the archive to the construction of a sentence pastoralizes these women's labor as much as the sentimental fiction and prescriptive literature of the antebellum era.[3]

Working within while questioning the limits of archival knowledge about socially reproductive labor, this chapter considers how slave traders used fabric and physical appearance to market enslaved laborers. It looks specifically at women's role in preparing enslaved people for sale and making "sale outfits," moving from preparation of the body to the construction of fabric and then the fashioning of outfits. Using the fragmentary information available about the needlewomen in Davis's accounts, it explores how slave traders, with the help of women's socially reproductive labor, manipulated markers of physical appearance to appeal to potential customers. It also considers how race and gender structured who performed what work and for what compensation.

10 September 1859: paid board negro at old woman's 3.25

Slave traders placed great importance on the way enslaved people appeared for sale, expending significant time and money to alter their physical bodies. The forced journey from the markets of Richmond to those of New Orleans, for example, whether overland or coastwise, took a heavy physical and mental toll. In order to make high profits, slave traders worked to erase the violence of this travel with rich foods, careful grooming, and strategic costuming. Traders and those they enslaved or employed, in other words, performed socially reproductive labor to create new characters for the "coerced theatricality of the trade."[4]

This socially reproductive labor could take place in a variety of locations, ranging from individual households to private, commercial slave jails where enslavers "boarded" enslaved people before sale. Some of these jails, such as Silas Omohundro's, were of a considerable scale. Others were smaller or structures not built specifically for that purpose. Consider, for instance, the "old woman" who "boarded" several enslaved people for Hector Davis. While historians would not define her, and she likely did not define herself, as a professional slave trader, she was a member of Davis's network of female laborers. She confined, fed, and potentially nursed some of the people Davis sold, likely within her own home.

Upon enslaved men and women's entry into a formal slave jail, slave traders and their assistants removed shackles and chains (at least temporarily) and ordered people to move, heal, and rebuild muscles after the journey from upper to lower South. Women prepared fattening foods such as bacon and butter for people to eat in the pens so they would appear healthy and strong. Some of these women were hired out, as was Susan Boggs, whose female enslaver hired her out to work in a trader's jail. Slave traders also ordered enslaved people to comb their hair, shave their beards, and wash their skin. Sometimes, traders used blacking to darken hair, greased enslaved people's skin with oil, and performed other such tricks to mask any imperfections. Former slave Moses Roper recalled, "I had to grease the faces of the blacks every morning with sweet oil, to make them shine before they are put up to sell." Roper also reported that during this time he and other enslaved individuals "were treated very well . . . in order to make us fat."[5]

As Moses Roper's recollection suggests, traders sometimes selected individual enslaved men to oversee preparations for sale. Marcus Rowland selected Roper for this task, while New Orleans trader Theophilus Freeman relied on an enslaved man named Bob. William Wells Brown, in his fictional work *My Southern Home*, drew on his experiences in the slave market to create the character of Pompey, an enslaved man whose job it was to "fit them for sale." While men seem to have orchestrated some of the washing, shaving, and oiling, particularly for enslaved men, they were not alone in their efforts.[6]

In his 1835 description of Franklin & Armfield's jail compound in Alexandria, Virginia, E. A. Andrews succinctly noted the physical spaces set aside for food preparation within a larger jail setting, noting, "Near the yard in which the women were confined, was the kitchen, where the food of the slaves was prepared. Here everything appeared neat and clean, and the arrangements for cooking resembled those which we usually see in penitentiaries." Andrews's passive sentence construction prevents us from learning who prepared the food in the kitchen, but he likened the workspace to that of a prison and placed it in close proximity to the part of the jail designated female.

Women also assisted in washing before sale. New Orleans slave trader John Hatcher described the process in 1843: "They [the slaves] generally come from the ship board dirty & before dressing them up anew they are put aside in a room where they can wash themselves. It is made the duty of a trusty woman to attend to them and in case any of them have their menses upon them not to let them wash but keep their dirty clothes on until they are well." In this extraordinary account, which survived only due to the subsequent death of one of the women Hatcher's employer sold, a slave trader allowed a glimpse into the quotidian bodily policing and social reproduction of enslaved women as commodities.[7]

Whether this "trusty woman" was enslaved or free is unclear, but it was her job to oversee the transformation of weary enslaved women, who had not bathed during their arduous passage via steamboat from Virginia to Louisiana, into clean, attractive, and healthy potential housemaids, cooks, field workers, and nurses. Before the "trusty woman" could order the women to dress "anew," she had to make sure that their bodies were clean and therefore appeared healthy and attractive to potential purchasers. After that, the washerwoman laundered the enslaved people's clothes "every week or ten days." If women were menstruating, Hatcher ordered the "trusty woman" not to let them change from their dirty clothes into their new ones. An enslaved woman who was menstruating could thus not attend to her bodily functions, but was forced to remain in soiled linens until she ceased bleeding. While enslaved women's ability to reproduce was central to their value in the slave market and usually a matter of warranty in a bill of sale, the physical evidence of the ability to reproduce—menstrual blood—was not something that traders wanted purchasers to see when the enslaved women were lined up in the sale rooms.[8]

The slave trader, Hatcher, policed and scrutinized this most personal matter, but through the words and actions of a woman he trusted. As Hatcher stated, he "never inspects the linen himself," thereby not troubling himself with women's matters. Instead, the enslaved women's linen was "put in a tub and sent out to be washed, the only way he has of knowing anything of the linen being stained is from the washer woman who washes the linen." Hatcher reported that he "knows this is the practice at the slave depots in Baltimore & has heard it was customary at Richmond." Male slave traders outsourced the traditionally feminine task of laundry to either enslaved women or free women in the neighborhood whom they paid. In addition to their domestic labor, the slave traders relied on the expertise of these women to identify and report "unnatural discharges" when they returned with the laundered clothes.[9]

> 28 April 1860: Hector Davis Clothing a/c to Mrs. SN Davis
> For 12 vests . . . 12; 22 shirts . . . 8.80; 15 suits clothes . . . 75

Once the slave traders, enslaved male assistants, and "trusty women" had done their best to transform the physical beings of the enslaved men and women into healthy and attractive commodities, they turned to physical adornments—the clothes and accessories that would convey particular messages to potential purchasers about the value of the people for sale. E. A. Andrews also observed this process at Franklin & Armfield's jail compound, describing the "tailor's shop, where were stored great quantities of new clothing, ready for the negroes when they set off upon their long journey to the south." Andrews found the clothing "well made, and of good materials; and in the female wardrobe considerable taste was displayed. Each negro, at his departure, is furnished with two entire suits from the shop." Solomon Northup remembered similar preparations, noting, "We were then furnished with a new suit each, cheap, but clean. The men had hat, coat, shirt, pants and shoes; the women frocks of calico, and handkerchiefs to bind about their heads."[10]

The new suits and frocks had both symbolic and monetary value for the slave traders, who charged either the sellers or the purchasers for the outfits and relied on the clothes to visually aid the likelihood of sale. Anthropologists explain that dress "conveys messages when members of a society who share a given culture have learned to associate types of dress with given, customary usage." As a tool of slave traders, dress told potential customers that the enslaved person in question was for sale and without a distinct personal identity. One slave trader highlighted the standardized nature of the outfits traders gave to slaves when he described a man wearing a "blue suit such as traders generally dress negroes in."[11] Dressed alike "in the trader's window-dressed version of slavery," enslaved people were meant to appear clean, orderly, and malleable to whatever identity the purchaser envisioned for them.

While most enslaved men wore "blue suits," slave traders did occasionally designate particular dress for enslaved men they intended to sell as a specific type of laborer. In addition to "blue suits," for example, J. M. E. Sharp purchased two "fancy suits" from N. C. Folger & Co. These suits may have been meant for men to be marketed as butlers or coach drivers. Women's outfits, too, had some level of variety. Frocks and dresses appeared far less frequently in slave traders' account books, suggesting that they were more often handmade than purchased at a store; visual representations of slave auctions often show women's dresses in varied, colorful patterns. The dress of "fancy women," in particular, was more likely to be made by hand. Middle- and upper-class women relied on dressmakers into the twentieth century; accounts of "fancy" women's garments more closely approximate the clothing of a lady of leisure than the utilitarian dress of enslaved laborers.[12]

In contrast to the "coarse stuff, an appropriate, simple uniform" of most of the enslaved people, women sold for sex might be dressed in "a dark bombazine gown, which set off her waist and shoulders to great advantage," a white apron, and an "abundance of lace-knots and gay ribands, somewhat coquettishly displayed on a cap of similar whiteness." A visitor to New Orleans similarly saw "a handsome quadroon girl, gaily dressed and adorned with ribbons and jewels . . . in a show window, to attract attention." Mary Boykin Chesnut remembered seeing the auction of such a woman, "a bright mulatto with a pleasant face. She was magnificently gotten up in silks and satins." "Fancy" women, then, were adorned in "fancy" dress that suggested luxury, novelty, and ornament. An enslaved woman dressed in silks and bombazines did not produce value by laboring in the field; enslavers called on such women to provide more intangible benefits.[13]

Slave traders factored the cost of clothing into their assessments of profit and loss, hence Davis and other traders' notations about thread, calico, suits, and dresses in their account books. Davis, for example, spent anywhere from $200 to $500 each month in his clothing account, amounts which went to everything from fabric to shoes. Slave traders and the agents they employed might negotiate the details of who was to bear this considerable cost when they agreed upon wages or commissions. As an employee of slave trader Elisha Cannon, agent J. W. Boazman agreed to "furnish said slaves with board, clothing, and medicine." If a trader or agent could not sell an enslaved person for a high enough price, they could lose the investment made on clothing. New Orleans trader James Blakeley used such an alleged loss to convince customers he was trustworthy and selling Mary Ellen Brooks at a fair price; he claimed he would "sell her [Brooks] for $600 thereby losing her clothing and shipping expenses."[14]

Jailers as well as traders profited from clothing the people they imprisoned, charging customers for each item they provided. In a legal suit over an unpaid jail bill, Archibald Lilly, a trader who traveled between Charleston and New Orleans, explained, "Expenses are incurred for clothing for his [the enslaved man, George's] use and bought during the said period [in the jail]. The plaintiff [J. J. Poindexter, the jailer] supplied them. The clothing consisted of a blue suit such as traders generally dress negroes in and cost from $10 to $12." George's enslaver, Mrs. Giles, complained that she had not wanted Poindexter to purchase new clothes. Lilly claimed he did not know if Giles "directed [Poindexter] to furnish the clothing charged for" but that the man "did need the clothing cap shoes [and socks]." Clothing thus served practical, symbolic, and economic purposes: "sale outfits" clothed and advertised enslaved bodies while bringing the trader additional money.[15]

Given Mrs. Giles's complaints, it is no surprise that not all slaveholders trusted the professional traders and jailers to add the cost of clothing to their sale commission. In some cases, slaveholders provided their own "sale outfits." In such instances, white women often played a role in decisions about the appearance of the clothing. Martha E. Twyman, for example, was the wife of a Virginia doctor who directed her family in how to clothe the enslaved women they sold. Twyman was very aware of the additional profits that came with sale outfits, noting that if she "dressed them [the enslaved women] up more becomingly, they will sell to better advantage." In 1848 Twyman's brother Jonathan took an enslaved woman named Aggy to professional traders in Richmond on their behalf. Twyman wrote Jonathan detailed instructions, noting, "I have made her a good calico dress, white cape and apron, [and] a good full underdress." She ordered Jonathan to make sure Aggy put on her new outfit and cleaned her teeth before leaving the house. In 1855 Twyman asked her sister, Frances, to purchase "pretty gray mouslains [sic] and shawls" as well as "neat bonnets, white aprons, undersleeves and collars." Her husband was to get her "bleached domestic cloth" and "black calico." With these items, she made her own sale outfits for enslaved people to be sold from her deceased father's estate. Twyman deemed her outfits superior to those they might receive in Richmond, noting that if the enslaved people were "dressed up there by men" they "would most probably dress them fine, but not with taste." As a white woman, Twyman believed she had a superior eye for both the style and quality of dress that would catch the eye of purchasers.[16]

Whether they were slave traders or individual slaveholders, antebellum southerners had plenty of options to choose from when selecting "sale outfits": machine-made textiles from the northern United States, Europe, and even some factories in the southern states; precut pieces of garments waiting to be sewn together; and ready-to-wear clothing, shoes, and hats. Ready-made men's clothing was available by the 1810s, and while most ready-made women's clothing would not be widely accessible until the early twentieth century due to the form-fitting requirements of women's clothes, some basic items such as shifts could be purchased. Yet ready-to-wear apparel did not automatically replace the importance of hand-sewn clothes for Davis and his fellow slave traders. Rather than embracing manufactured clothing entirely, Davis selectively purchased ready-made items when it was more convenient, while on other occasions he purchased fabric and paid individual women to construct garments. Davis's clerk left few details about the items of clothing, so it is difficult to say for certain why Davis preferred to buy an outfit in some cases. The clothing account usually contains only statements such as "paid for clothing" and "paid for sewing" with no information about the types of clothing purchased or sewed.[17]

The extent to which slaveholders adopted machine-made fabrics and ready-made clothing for use on plantations varied considerably by era, region, and plantation size. Helen Bradley Foster, for example, finds that store-bought cloth was uncommon on many southern plantations, with "overwhelming evidence that most cloth and clothing was homemade, and the evidence for this mode of manufacture comes from every slave-holding state." Thus, many plantations included weaving rooms, which were predominantly female spaces. With so much of their clothing made at home, many of the formerly enslaved people whose WPA narratives Foster analyzed considered store-bought fabric and apparel a desirable luxury.[18]

Seth Rockman emphasizes that, even as weaving rooms persisted on some plantations, "Negro cloth" manufactured in the northern United States was popular from the early nineteenth century onward. Marketed specifically at the supposedly distinct needs of slaveholders, "Negro cloth" encompassed a variety of fabrics, ranging from cottons to woolens, both brightly colored and plain in appearance. Some northern manufacturers even based their business on the "southern market" for such cloth and competed for the business of planters and southern merchants. By 1845, for example, "seventeen of the forty Rhode Island textile manufactories listed in one directory specialized in Negro cloth." Rhode Island continued to hold a place of prominence in the manufacture of textiles marketed to slaveholders, though mills from Massachusetts to Pennsylvania also made similar cloth.[19]

Northern manufacturers, such as the Hazard brothers of Peacedale Manufactory in Rhode Island, supplied cloth as well as "clothes ready made" to both planters and southern merchants. "Ready made" items included shirts, pants, vests, jackets, and frocks. While planters sent lists of enslaved people's measurements to northern manufacturers, the manufacturers fit these individualized numbers into standardized categories, meaning that the "ready made" items required further customization. Enslaved seamstresses generally performed the work of fitting standardized sizes to individual bodies, as well as cutting and sewing garments from uncut fabric.[20]

Advertisements from both Richmond and New Orleans reflected this wide variety of "Negro cloth" and "negro clothing" available. Levy's, a store Hector Davis frequented, advertised carrying "Negro Clothing by the piece or yard, comprising Kerseys, plaids, Tweeds, Full Cloths and various other goods suitable for Negro Clothing." Another merchant specified that he carried "Negro clothing . . . cut large," both of which suggest that stores carried pieces to vests, shirts, and pants that had already been cut (generally the most difficult part of constructing a garment) but not sewn together. Bissell, Austin, & Co., Louisiana merchants, similarly advertised "negro clothing—5000 yards kerseys and linseys; 2000 do Louisiana Osnaburgs—150 ready made suits for sale." Though they occasionally referenced dresses or women's clothes, the majority of advertisements for "negro clothing," "servants clothing" or "plantation clothing" were for men's and boys' clothing—namely, "coats, pants, vests, and shirts," as well as suits. Slave traders, too, were more likely to purchase ready-made men's clothing than ready-made "frocks."[21]

The provenance of cloth and ready-made clothing could become a point of sectional pride and a marketing tactic. Many advertisements specifically mentioned purchases made in "New York," "Philadelphia" or "the North," as well as a few references to "English negro cloth." Others, however, carried fabrics produced in the South, including "Maryland Plaid Linseys," "Staunton Jean," "Louisiana Osnaburgs," and "Kentucky Jean." Several merchants emphasized that their ready-made clothes, in varying states of completion, were of "southern manufacture." P. A. Hebrard advertised his "ready-made Negro Clothing" as "of the best material, and cut to fit each individual, at as low prices as articles of inferior quality of Northern manufacture." Hebrard's customers, who could fill out printed order forms with enslaved men and women's measurements, could feel confident they were getting a bargain while simultaneously supporting a southern business.[22]

In Virginia, Simpson and Miller advertised in both Staunton and Richmond their "stock of superior READY-MADE CLOTHING . . . manufactured *by us*" with "a large stock of NEGRO CLOTHING and Boy's Clothing always on hand." Other merchants mentioned ready-made items of "*Richmond manufacture*, gotten up in the best manner, both as regards workmanship and style." Tailor and merchant E. B. Spence gave perhaps the most impassioned plea in favor of southern textiles, emphasizing that his was "STRICTLY A SOUTHERN MANUFACTURING HOUSE" that compared "in every respect with clothing made in Northern cities."[23]

Whether the cloth was Kentucky Jean, linsey from Rhode Island, or osnaberg from the Manchester Manufacturing Company in Virginia, women played a significant role in the manufacture of early nineteenth-century clothing, both for the slave market and outside of it. At the same time that middle-class reformers were advocating women's place in the home, industrial capital pulled poorer women into the market to fill the needs of textile manufacturers, who "simplified (or deskilled) clothing construction to its most basic components." Manufacturers used the same domestic ideology that advocated wealthier white women staying in the domestic sphere to justify paying poorer women less than men, imagining that all women were legally and economically dependent on a male breadwinner for most of the necessities of life, even if that was far from reality.[24]

The "Negro cloth" and "Negro clothing" with which Richmond merchants stocked their stores thus passed through a variety of female hands from start to finish. Southern planters did not adopt the same sexual division of labor for enslaved men and women that they enforced in their own households, so enslaved women picked as much cotton as, or more than, enslaved men did. These bolls of cotton eventually reached the female mill hands, piece-workers, and seamstresses who helped transform the cotton into manufactured cloth or took home precut fabric and stitched it together, returning ready-made garments to be shipped to the "southern market." That all of this production took place out of sight of the eventual purchaser further veiled the importance of women to its completion. In other cases, manufacturers sent the precut fabrics to southern merchants, who could hire their own pieceworkers to finish the product before marketing it as "ready made." Finally, some merchants sold the unfinished pieces, which the purchaser could take back to their home for female relatives or enslaved women to finish for free. The success of ready-made clothing relied on many modes of production, and many forms of women's labor: wage earning and enslaved; in the mill and in the home; on the plantation and in the city.

25 January 1862: Clothing a/c gave Va Isham to buy calico &c. 20.00

Virginia Isham purchased calico from a store in Richmond on Hector Davis's behalf and then constructed dresses from it. Isham also purchased ready-made shirts for some of the men in Davis's jail. Mrs. S. N. Davis sewed shirts, vests, and other clothes for Hector Davis. Davis's agents purchased shoes from some Richmond retailers and took enslaved men and women to be "dressed" at others. That Davis and other slave traders simultaneously purchased ready-made clothes and paid women to sew outfits for them reflects the uneven reach of ready-made items in the nineteenth century, as well as the continuing importance of local needlewomen for constructing, finishing, repairing, and altering clothes.

When purchasing "Negro cloth" and "Negro clothes," Davis preferred four Richmond retailers: John Greentree, Julius Levy, Moses A. Myers & Brother, and Moses A. Waterman. Davis kept an almost monthly account at Myers & Brother in the late 1850s, spending anywhere from $7.75 to $416.88 in a given month. Omohundro also patronized Waterman; he paid $14.75 for "dressing 2 boys Turner & William" there in 1860. With thirty-two recorded payments for clothing in Davis's two account books, Myers & Brother received the greatest portion of Davis's patronage of a retail store. Davis entered eighteen payments for clothing to M. A. Waterman, fifteen to Julius Levy (one of which was made specifically to "Mrs. Levy"), and six payments to John Greentree and Brother. Davis nearly always went to John C. Page for shoes, and had a running monthly account with them. He frequented John Thompson for hats.[25]

While none of the merchants depended solely on slave traders for business, they did acknowledge that slave traders formed a significant portion of their clientele. Lewis B. Levy's store, located near the slave-trading district of Richmond, devoted particular attention to clothing for slave traders, listing four prominent traders as references in advertisements. Occasionally traders' agents or enslaved assistants took individuals to such stores for dressing. One dry goods storeowner, his grandson later recalled, even brought his customers' enslaved women to his house, where "the women and girls came into the back room and were dressed by my old mammy Mary, who was a stout mulatto woman." Mary "dressed" enslaved women in ways similar to Corinna Hinton, though in a very different context.[26]

In New Orleans, the mercantile firm N. C. Folger & Co. was a favorite provider of cloth and ready-made clothing. They marketed "blue satinet round jackets," "blue satinet pantaloons," "white cotton shirts," "kersey Monkey Jackets," and "knit suspenders," among other items meant for enslaved laborers. A number of slave traders were indebted to Folger for unpaid book debt. J. M. E. Sharp, for example, owed the merchant $281.50 for "9 Blue suits, shirts, & drawers," "9 undershirts," "10 pairs socks," and other pieces of clothing for men and boys. These were the "sale outfits" Sharp ordered the people he sold dressed in, and the same outfits for which he charged his customers an additional fee. Similarly, Charles Lamarque owed Folger $127.90 from a protested promissory note. When trader and jailer L. M. Foster filed for bankruptcy in 1860, his debts included an impressive $2,439.75 due N. C. Folger & Co.[27]

When traders needed these store-bought clothes fitted or sewn together, they turned to women, because in the popular imagination, seamstresses were always women. Davis could have done the work himself, had one of his agents complete the task, or asked the men he enslaved to sew for him. That he did not was a reflection, not of men's natural inability to sew, but of the gender ideology of the era. In those same monthly recordings of his clothing account, Davis noted payments for sewing only to individual women. He paid wives of his agents, enslaved women, and unnamed needlewomen for individual items of clothes as well as unspecified sewing.

Richmond had plenty of women willing to sew for money, and they encompassed a wide range of skill and professionalism. Nineteenth-century authors usually portrayed needlewomen as an undifferentiated mass of unskilled laborers struggling to survive, and historians have in some cases followed these authors' lead. Yet the experiences of needlewomen ranged from the impoverished seamstress of Mathew Carey's polemics to highly trained, economically independent dressmakers and milliners.[28]

That "seamstress" was gendered female by the nineteenth century was not a given. Until the eighteenth and nineteenth centuries, men dominated clothing production. Male tailors made apparel for both men and women by hand; the first milliners were men. Though early modern women still controlled household production of textiles, men dominated production of clothing for the market and fought women's entrance into the fashion trades. Only with the popularity of the mantua in the late seventeenth and early eighteenth century did women gain access to dressmaking, as constructing mantuas did not require the kind of technical skill that male tailors' guilds jealously protected. Without a built-in whalebone bodice, the looser fitting mantua was also cheaper and thus available to a wider clientele, creating more business for dressmakers. Historians of women's employment note that at the same time women were entering needle trades in larger numbers, trade guilds and popular opinion limited or closed off access to other professions once open to women.[29]

By the nineteenth century, then, women were so closely related to needlework in the popular imagination that sewing became a "natural" ability of women rather than a skill that required considerable knowledge and training. While some needle-based professions, such as dressmaking and millinery, continued to require professional training or apprenticeship into the late nineteenth century, the growing availability of ready-made men's clothing and the accompanying simplification of clothing production lowered public perceptions of sewing as a skill. Marla Miller argues that "as early as the second quarter of the nineteenth century, the notion that plain sewing was most appropriately performed by working class women was firmly planted."[30]

Seamstresses, literally those who stitched seams, received less training than dressmakers, as they did not have to cut and fit garments. Nonetheless, seamstresses still had to possess considerable craft knowledge. They had to know, for instance, how to space stitches on skirts so that the skirt hung properly. Sewing was also tedious and uncomfortable work, requiring women to sit for hours hunched over fabric. Seamstresses worked in a variety of contexts that reflected the piecemeal transition to ready-made clothing. While some seamstresses worked for mantua makers, others performed outwork, picking up cut fabric to stitch together at home and return to a manufacturer or store. The first five wards in New Orleans, for example, included twenty-five women who identified as pieceworkers.[31]

Richmond tailor and merchant E. B. Spence employed between seventy-five and one hundred seamstresses who constructed the "ready made" clothes he sold in his shop. In one of his advertisements, Spence specifically noted the "worthy females" whom he beneficently employed, "who might otherwise suffer for the necessaries of life." Here Spence countered popular tropes of impoverished seamstresses who performed low-paying, degraded work by describing himself as the women's savior from hardship and far worse forms of labor. Though these women's labor supplied Spence's store and increased his profit, he saw himself as the one who was doing them a favor, thus distancing his business from moral concerns about underpaid seamstresses. In New Orleans, Hebrard's "Louisiana Plantation Clothing Manufactory" also turned to disadvantaged women, in this case those in New Orleans's "various asylums." Like prisoners forced to work in garment construction, the asylum residents upon whom Hebrard depended had little choice in becoming needlewomen.[32]

As can be seen regarding the needlewomen of the New Orleans asylums, relying only on official government records when locating women's work can yield inaccurate results. Hector Davis paid Miss Patterson thirteen times between 1857 and 1858 for "sewing" and "making clothes," but Patterson did not appear in the census or city directory as a seamstress. With no additional information about her, we do not know how often she sewed for pay or what role Davis's compensation played in her household's finances. Had Davis not employed a fairly meticulous clerk, we would not even know that Miss Patterson worked with needle and thread.[33]

Mrs. S. N. Davis was another woman whose labors are preserved in Davis's records. Mrs. S. N. Davis was almost certainly Anna Davis, the white wife of one of Davis's agents, English-born Solomon N. Davis. In 1859 Hector Davis paid Solomon N. Davis $600 for "services 1 year." Solomon Davis must have advertised his wife's needle skills to Hector, for, beginning that same year, Hector intermittently paid "Mrs. S.N. Davis" in his clothing account. In January 1860, for example, Hector paid Anna Davis $4.80 for twelve shirts, meaning that each shirt cost him 40¢ to have Anna Davis construct. When Davis's clerk recorded what items Anna Davis sewed, he usually noted shirts, but for Davis and his partners she also sewed "suits," which varied in price throughout the year. Between March 1859 and May 1860, Davis paid Ann Davis $1,012.20 from his clothing account. On the 1860 census, Anna Davis had no occupation.[34]

Without consistent details about what Hector Davis paid Anna Davis per item of clothing, it is difficult to compare the price of her work to Davis's other options for acquiring clothing. From account book entries that do specify rate per piece, however, Anna Davis's fees were on a par with or less expensive than the price of buying a ready-made outfit. Merchant E. Morris of Richmond advertised "Negro Clothing, from $4 to $5 a suit" in 1855. Two years earlier, Keen, Chiles, & Baldwin advertised "50,000 dollars worth of ready made clothing must be sold in sixty days" including "negro suit at $5." Prices in New Orleans at the same time were noticeably higher. N. C. Folger charged $12.50 for "blue suits" in 1860. In 1859 and 1860, Hector Davis paid Anna Davis anywhere from $4 to $5 a suit, making her prices at least as good as those of local retailers. Additionally, Anna Davis could make custom alterations according to Davis's particular needs, and the quality of her work may have been superior to that of items quickly and cheaply produced in larger quantities.[35]

Since all of the stores at which Davis usually shopped sold ready-made as well as precut items, it is likely that part of Davis's purchases were precut items that he then employed other women to sew together. Though it is possible that Anna Davis cut the fabric herself, she certainly constructed the same items — suits, shirts, and vests — that Richmond dry goods stores advertised as available for purchase in precut form. In the case of other women, the account books give no clues about the type of sewing they performed.

Other slave traders' accounts leave similar questions about the nature of needlewomen's work and what led traders to compensate some women for sewing but not others. There was no clear divide between women who were family members and those who were not. North Carolina slave trader Tyre Glen, for instance, recorded payments to his sister, Jane Glen, and his mother for sewing. In 1830 Tyre paid Ann Glen $2.50 for clothing one enslaved woman. This was the first of several entries "on acct to Mother." He also recorded payments to Jane for sewing shirts.[36]

Yet Caroline "Carrie" Charles, the daughter of slave trader Israel Charles and sister of slave trader John H. Charles, received no compensation for her socially reproductive labor. Her father purchased enslaved people in and around Greenville County, South Carolina, while her brother sold people in the "west," including New Orleans. Carrie contributed to the family business by sewing outfits. She reported to her sister in 1858 that her father was "very busy buying negros he has bought 14 since brother left." In turn, she was "very busy" with "cloth and clothing to make for the negros," writing, "I do not do much work it takes the most of my time to think how to have the work done." Though Carrie felt herself "very busy making clothing," a close examination of her letters reveals that, in fact, the women her father enslaved did most of the work. "I make Sophia do a good deal of sewing," Carrie confided to her sister, "I dont [sic] know what I would do were it so she could not help." Feeling "their [sic] were so many idling about," Carrie explained that she "tr[ied] to keep them busy at something." Her position as a slave trader's daughter allowed her to perform managerial tasks while enslaved women such as Sophia performed the tedious work of stitching seams.[37]

Even though Carrie may have directed more domestic labor than she performed, she felt entitled to claim it as her own and to have a voice in her male relatives' business. She instructed John how to manage the clothing, writing, "You will find [the calico dresses] marked on the inside of the body." John felt that Carrie could comprehend the intricacies of his business and often shared information with her and asked her to pass requests along to their father. Having discussed matters with her brother and contributed materially to his business, Carrie felt confident enough in her knowledge of the slave market to claim that John "has sold seven at very good prices."[38]

Similarly, Richmond slave trader John Prentis relied on his wife, Catharine, to clothe the men, women, and children he enslaved. Catharine had to sew two suits of clothes for each person to be sold. John noted in a letter to his brother, "She [Catharine] has had a fine job of work makeing all the clothes for my people two suits a peice. Our room was a compleat taylors shop for 10 or 12 days." Prentis recognized Catharine's contribution to his business, just as John Charles seems to have trusted his sister's comprehension of market matters. These men's faith in their female family members illustrates underlying tensions in the ideology of domesticity. Even as prescriptive literature and popular commentators discounted the economic significance of household labor, it continued to play an important role in men's day-to-day lives, and these men were not incapable of recognizing that.[39]

If free white women's sewing appears in the archive of the slave trade only in small, fleeting glimpses, that of free black and especially enslaved women is even harder to locate. Nonetheless, if we ask particular types of questions and attend carefully to the details of fragmentary records, we can still uncover telling examples of African American women's work. Take, for instance, Hector Davis's many payments to Virginia Ann Isham. She appears again and again in Davis's account book as receiving payment for various types of labor but most often for needlework.

While Davis's account books initially give no indication of Isham's legal status, upon closer investigation of his estate records it is clear that Virginia Ann Isham was an enslaved woman whose husband, William, Davis enslaved and relied on for assistance in his jail. Isham was born in the 1820s in Virginia. During the time when she worked for Davis, she was also caring for her only child, a son born in 1845. While Davis did not enslave Virginia, he likely knew of her through William, her husband and his slave. The identity of the person who enslaved Virginia is unclear; she may have been hiring herself out in the city or even to Davis. What is clear is that by at least 1857, Hector Davis entered into a financial agreement with Virginia Isham, selling the clothes she fashioned to traders or individual slave owners who used his auction room or jail. From July 1857 to December 1860, Davis paid a total of $1,376.37 to Isham. By January 1863, with inflation caused by the war, this number jumped to $2,980.56.[40]

Davis's clerk did not always record the exact reason Davis paid Isham; but when he did, it ranged from "clothing negroes" to buying ready-made items such as stockings and sewing supplies such as scissors and calico. At times he made payments to her account, implying that the clerk who kept Davis's books could give her book credit rather than pay her in cash. This would have been a significant loss of autonomy for Isham, since she would have had to go to Davis or his clerk each time she wanted ready money. She may have had other sources of income; at one point Davis loaned her money.[41]

Other slave traders who did business with Davis knew the Ishams also. On several occasions visiting traders paid Virginia Isham, through Davis, for midwifery. William Isham received payments for running errands and attending enslaved people who were ill. The Ishams were thus a familiar sight around Davis's property, coming in and out of his office to receive payments and deliver supplies. Virginia could be seen about the jail, attending to pregnant enslaved women while William administered medicine to those who were sick.[42]

Though they were familiar with Davis and his business associates and received some compensation for their work, Virginia and William were still enslaved and at a significant disadvantage. Davis punished William for an unknown offense in 1862, sending him to stay at Sidnum Grady's slave jail for several days. If William asserted too much autonomy or displeased Davis in his services, Davis could mete out physical punishment as he saw fit. Virginia had no power to intervene as she saw her husband locked away in a jail very similar to the one they both worked in on a daily basis.[43]

In the sewing business, too, Virginia Isham had little leverage. The arrangement favored Davis significantly; she received only one-fourth of the profits he made by selling the products of her labor, and Davis paid a higher price for clothes sewn by white women such as Anna Davis. One week in December 1859, for instance, Davis paid "Mrs. SN Davis" $50 for sewing while

Isham received $10. Anna Davis's average rate was 40¢ per shirt and $5 per suit of clothes. Isham does not appear to have had any set rate per piece. Virginia Isham could not turn to the law or an influential husband to assist her in achieving a better rate; Anna Davis could.[44]

Despite these disadvantages, Virginia Isham made extra money for her family by sewing for Hector Davis. The quantity she received depended largely on the rise and fall of the market in slaves. The more enslaved people Davis dressed and sold, the more money Virginia Isham made, and the closer she came to buying freedom for herself and her family.

Davis's account books provide an in-depth case study of one enslaved woman's sewing in the slave market; enslaved women's needlework survives in other archival material as well. When Alexandria slave trader Joseph Bruin jailed sisters Mary and Emily Edmondson, the women later remembered that Bruin ordered them to sew calico "show dresses" to wear upon their sale, performing labor toward their own commodification. Hector Davis's associate Elias Ferguson asked his partner, John J. Toler, to have "Mary" make a hoop-skirt for an enslaved woman they were about to sell. Toler was unmarried, so Mary, if Toler was anything like his friends, was likely an enslaved woman. Ferguson was in desperate need of the hoopskirt as a marketing tool; he urged Toler to "tell her [Mary] to make it by to nite."[45]

Corinna Omohundro was responsible for clothing all of the enslaved men, women, and children in Silas Omohundro's slave jail. From 1856 until his death in 1864, Omohundro recorded in his account book semiannual or annual payments made to Corinna for "negro clothes." These payments ranged from $200 to $400. When "dressing" the hundreds of men, women, and children who passed in and out of Omohundro's jail each year, Corinna used a mixture of ready-made clothes, precut clothes, and fabric. In some entries Omohundro recorded purchases of bolts of fabric, while in others he noted cut but not sewn pieces. He paid $16, for example, for "2 Pieces Domestic 89½ yards for Negro Shirting" as well as $5 for "cloth & cutting for Wyatts coat." In one instance, a seamstress had to cut and then sew the shirts; in the second example, she had only to sew the precut pieces together.[46]

Some of the other women Omohundro enslaved likely helped Corinna with sewing, but no evidence of this remains. Other than paying Corinna for "dressing" or for "Negro clothes," Omohundro recorded few details. Unless the woman doing the "dressing" was Corinna, he usually did not note who performed the labor. In one exceptional case he recorded $5 paid for "clothes from Matilda for William, Wyatt & Joe." Usually, though, Omohundro's passive sentence construction makes it difficult to determine the exact nature of Corinna's work and which women performed what parts of garment construction.[47]

An enslaved woman's ability to sew could also bring additional value in their sale. Slave traders regularly advertised enslaved women as seamstresses, and potential purchasers regularly requested enslaved women with sewing abilities. Slaveholders wanted enslaved women who could sew for their family as well as the other people they enslaved. Enslaved seamstresses could perform a variety of tasks, from repairing damaged clothing to constructing entirely new garments. Some slaveholders even paid for enslaved seamstresses to further their skills. Sue Petigru King wrote that she sent a young woman she enslaved to "school to learn to sew." Enslaved women skilled with a needle benefited slaveholding families, saving them the cost of hiring a dressmaker each time they wanted a new outfit. Enslavers could also hire out enslaved seamstresses and keep the profits for themselves. These seamstresses may have accrued some benefits from their skills, such as the ability to make extra money on the side.[48]

Some advertisements included specifics about a needlewoman's skill set. An anonymous advertisement in the Richmond Dispatch extolled the virtue of a "likely young woman," for sale, "a very superior cutter and seamstress." Though not included in the census or city directory as a dressmaker, this unnamed woman possessed the abilities of the most skilled needlewomen, cutting fabric. And she was not the only woman thus trained—another advertisement in the Richmond Dispatch from 1853 proclaimed, "The Ladies of Richmond in particular, and the public in general, have now an opportunity of purchasing the most valuable Ladies' Maid ever offered for sale in the United States. She is a finished seamstress, tailoress, mantuamaker; cuts and fits with unequalled elegance and precision, every garment of ladies' or gentlemen's attire." These women's skills are a clear reminder that not only enslaved men performed skilled, artisanal work.[49]

Potential purchasers similarly sought out enslaved women with sewing skills. W. B. Davidson placed a wanted advertisement in the Richmond Dispatch proclaiming his need for a "No 1 seamstress," while an anonymous advertiser requested to hire "by the month or year, a good nurse or seamstress." While some purchasers wanted women with specific needle skills, others tended to conflate all work done within the household, asking, as did the advertiser above, for women who could simultaneously sew, nurse, and clean. Some Richmond residents, also like the previous advertiser, did not want to purchase an enslaved needlewoman but to hire her out. Hiring agent E. D. Eacho, for example, advertised for hire a "seamstress" who could "work with fine muslins and linens" as well as "starch and iron them in a fine manner."[50]

The man who purchased Mary Ellen Brooks, the young enslaved woman who died shortly after her sale as a "fancy girl," came to the New Orleans slave jail of Hope Slatter asking for "a bright mulatto" to "wait on his wife and do the sewing for a small family." Brooks had already been sewing while imprisoned, having been put to work darning one of the agent's coats. As became clear later in the court case, Brooks's sewing abilities likely had little to do with what made her attractive to her purchaser. He had no wife in the city and purchased the young woman for sex, not to sew for a small family. Brooks's case hints at the propensity of slave traders, as well as their clients, to conflate socially reproductive and sexual labor.[51]

In some cases, "seamstress" served as a synonym for "fancy girl." Whether in private letters or public advertisements, traders associated certain domestic skills, such as sewing, with sexual availability. One Lexington slave trader emphasized the connection between intimate spaces, domesticity, and sexuality by jailing his "very handsome mulatto women" not in a sparsely furnished cell but in a house with all the trappings of an aristocratic parlor. A visitor described the rooms as "not only comfortable, but in many respects luxurious. Many of the rooms are well carpeted and furnished." Within, the "mulatto women" sat "at their needlework awaiting a purchaser." The scene could have been one from any plantation house, save for the fact that these women were not entirely white, and their enslaver could order them up from their sewing to "turn around to show to advantage their finely developed and graceful forms."[52]

The same themes of feigned domesticity and illicit sexuality came through in the language of advertisements for some young enslaved women. Robert Lumpkin described a seamstress he sold as "raised by one of the best housewives in Virginia." Another Richmond resident described a seamstress as "a likely MULATTO GIRL, aged fourteen years," while an unnamed "Southern gentleman" visiting the "Cary St. Jail" asked specifically for a "light colored" "good seamstress." Itinerant trader John J. Toler often conflated the two, in one case using "yellow wimmen" and "seamstress" interchangeably. When it came to young, light-skinned enslaved women, sewing abilities, whether imagined or real, represented the qualities a white enslaver valued in a "fancy girl." They saw sewing as a feminine task that took place in the privacy of the household; decorative or "fancy" sewing such as embroidery was a marker of white female gentility. These men expected "fancy girls" to perform the sexual labor of wives, but they did not explicitly admit this in print, or even verbally to slave traders. What they did instead was ask for enslaved women whose appearance, demeanor, and skills approximated that expected of a white woman of the leisured class. Though it seemed innocuous on the surface, men in the know understood the underlying message in Phillip M. Tabb's advertisement of a "very genteel" "first rate seamstress."[53]

IT SHOULD BE NO SURPRISE, then, that when designing the banknotes of his newly formed Traders' Bank of Richmond, Hector Davis chose to use the image of a woman engaged in cloth production to represent industry. Davis contracted with the American Bank Note Company to print plates for his bank's currency around 1860, but only small bills were ever printed. The $20 and $50 plates, though never used at the time, survived, and were employed in the twentieth century to print notes for collectors.[54] The design of these notes, almost certainly influenced by Davis, reflects the era of their creation as well the worldview of the bank's mastermind. The $20 note features two vignettes, one on either side of the bill. Uniting the two vignettes is a portrait of Henry Clay, who evidently earned Davis's admiration. He was perhaps a southern man after Davis's own heart: a slaveholder who also supported internal improvements and the Second Bank of the United States. To the left of Clay is an engraving of an African American man picking cotton. To the right is the image of a well-dressed woman, reclining comfortably in a chair, with one hand resting on a spinning wheel. Behind her, in contrast to the potentially old-fashioned spinning wheel, looms a factory with smoke billowing from two stacks.[55]

The woman at the spinning wheel was originally the work of artist Christian Schussele. Schussele was born in Alsace and studied lithography, among other artistic forms, before immigrating to the United States in 1848. Settling in Philadelphia, he was known for his works of historical import. Owen Hanks, one of the founders of the American Banknote Company, completed an engraving of Schussele's image around 1859. Given Schussele's interest in American history and culture (he later completed "Men of Progress," an homage to American inventors), the woman was likely an allegorical representation of industry. Women's socially reproductive labor signified production, even in an era of burgeoning manufacturing.[56]

Together, these images tell a uniquely southern version of progress. Though thoroughly invested in the "premodern" slave system, Davis recognized the importance of "modern" internal improvements, finance, and manufacturing. The images in the collage—an enslaved field hand, Henry Clay, a spinner, a factory—could seem contradictory on a banknote conceived by slave traders, but they were in fact links in the same chain. Traders such as Davis and the directors of the bank sold enslaved laborers to cotton planters, using Clay's internal improvements, including railroads, banks, and turnpikes, to facilitate the process in an efficient and economic manner. Using the same infrastructure, planters sold this cotton to textile manufacturers for a profit. All of these monetary exchanges rested on the backs of enslaved laborers who grew the cash crop. The banknotes themselves, had they been printed, would likely have been composed partly of cotton.

In the forefront of it all was a woman at the spinning wheel, a symbol of feminine labor and domestic economy. More prominent than the factory, she suggests that even manufacturing could not supplant the importance of women's work at home, the foundation of the broader economy. Yet the factory, too, housed women workers and the products of their labor. The Traders' Bank note thus showcased a range of labor that women could and did perform: picking cotton, textile production and construction based in the home, and textile production in factories. Factory work was compensated with wages; work in the home could be compensated or not, depending on the context and for whom it was performed; picking cotton was almost never compensated work for women laborers before the Civil War. Taken together, these various iterations of women's work illustrate the ways in which the development of capitalism in the antebellum United States relied on many forms of labor, wage based and not. Just as Hector Davis and his fellow slave traders depended on many different types of women workers to clothe the people they enslaved, early capitalism, too, benefited from businesses' ability to draw from a vast pool of laborers, depending on particular needs. The extramarket ideological forces that restricted opportunity based on sex and race provided an extra boon to men such as Hector Davis, who could make a greater profit if he paid women less and paid enslaved women nothing or next to nothing. In the clothing industry, the invisible hand of the market was actually a very visible, tired, and female hand whose freedom depended on the meaning attached to its particular hue.

CHAPTER THREE

Concubine

> *I Josiah Cole hereby lease unto Sarah Conner of this city, a Dwelling*
> *house . . . situated on Gravier Street . . .*
>
> *New Orleans Feby 14th 1849 to Theo Freeman for Thirty Dollars on the*
> *1st day of March 1849 for value received*
> *Jno T. Hatcher & Co*
> *[Endorsed] pay to Sarah Conner or order. [signed] Theo. Freeman*
>
> *Sarah Ann Connor of the City of New Orleans hereby leases to William*
> *Schneider also of the same city the two story and attic brick dwelling*
> *known as 212 Gravier*

Antebellum New Orleans was one of the busiest commercial ports in the world, and home to one of the largest slave markets in the United States. The city's bustling commercial districts attracted visitors of all backgrounds, from cotton factors and bank agents to sailors and itinerant laborers. What tied many of these visitors together was their sex and their need for socially reproductive labor: they were men living away from the women who normally cooked, cleaned, and otherwise readied them for the day's work. Luckily for them, there were plenty of New Orleans residents ready to provide such care for a price, and many of them were women.[1]

In 1860 alone, census takers in Wards 1 through 5 of New Orleans listed 151 women renting rooms, 125 running boardinghouses, 514 seamstresses, 42 nurses, 320 laundresses, and 1,656 domestic servants. Given census takers' propensity to underreport women laborers, and the fact that they entirely excluded enslaved women from their records, these significant totals actually underestimate the number of women providing socially reproductive labor for money. These seamstresses, nurses, servants, and other workers came from a variety of backgrounds. Some were born in the United States, but many were not. Many were single, but some were married. They included young women in their early teens to octogenarians. They encompassed all skin colors and legal statuses. For all their differences, however, these women often performed similar work. What differed was the compensation they received for the work, which often depended not on skill level but on legal status and skin color. Hired-out enslaved women, for instance, had to hand over the money they made to their enslavers. If they were lucky, they could keep a portion, or perform additional labor on the side for themselves.[2]

Sarah Ann Conner occupied many of these different legal statuses and occupations during the course of her life, moving from slavery to freedom once and then repeating the process a second time. Legally, courts defined her alternatively as a slave, a concubine, and a free woman of color. Sometimes her associates described her as a slave, but other times witnesses thought she was a domestic servant or a landlady. Sometimes people described her as mulatto, other times as quadroon, occasionally as black, and at times as white. Throughout it all, Sarah Conner of course remained the same person; she performed the same labor and presumably kept the same general physical features. The only thing that changed was how others perceived and valued her and her labor. In Conner's status as an enslaved woman, her labor as a laundress was not her own. In her status as an enslaved concubine, others assumed her rental properties belonged to the white man in her life. The sexual economy of slavery meant that, even as a free woman of color, her right to her own body was never secure.

When the white men and women around her attempted to evaluate, describe, and make sense of Conner's liminal existence, they filtered the evidence in front of them through prevailing ideologies of race, class, and sex. Surrounded by the sexual economy of slavery, the white men who described her had difficulty understanding Conner outside of her social, economic, and sexual ties to white men. Based on the setting, the people around her, and their own conceptions of race, different observers came to very different conclusions about who Conner was and what rights she had to her own person and the proceeds of her labor.

White observers tried to fit Sarah Conner into the world as they saw it, but the ambiguities of Conner's life meant that she defied simple categorization. It is largely through their words, though, that evidence of Sarah Conner survives. Because Conner was likely illiterate, her words, like her actions, reach us through white intermediaries. In many cases their descriptions tell us more about their worldviews than they do about Sarah Conner. Yet glimpses of Conner survive despite the intentions of the men investigating her. This chapter sifts through the myriad portrayals of Conner to see what of her survives the violence of the archive.

I Josiah Cole hereby lease unto Sarah Conner of this city, a Dwelling house . . . situated on Gravier Street . . .

Many of the basic facts of Sarah Conner's life—where she lived, for instance—depended on who enslaved her, who held the piece of paper in his or her hand that conveyed legal ownership of Conner's body and labor. The first person to do so, the individual who enslaved her at her birth, lived in Virginia. While no material survives to testify to the early years of her life in that state, Conner consistently reported she was from Fairfax County. She remained there until 1837 or 1838, when her enslaver sold her to slave trader James G. Blakeley, a former agent, like Silas Omohundro, of Franklin & Armfield.[3]

When Blakeley forced her to New Orleans, Conner was just over twenty years old. She likely left siblings behind in Virginia, as well as friends, parents, and a sweetheart or spouse if they had not already been sold away, too. The men who traded in her labor and her physical attributes described her as "slight" at five feet and two inches and a "bright mulatto" with several scars on her right hand and breast. Her age and her appearance made Conner vulnerable to sale as a "fancy," the trade for which New Orleans was so infamous.

Travel writers, novelists, diarists, and writers of all kinds couldn't resist mentioning the presence of light-skinned enslaved women and free women of color when discussing New Orleans. While descriptions of (allegedly sexually available) light-skinned, mixed-race women had a long history in the Atlantic World, as Emily Clark points out, by the 1840s and 1850s the idea of the "tragic mulatto" was "an elaborate literary and commercial trope that served a complex array of cultural and political purposes" and one that was firmly tied in the public imagination to New Orleans. Through these narratives, New Orleans became famous as a site of sex across the color line and tragically doomed nearly-white women.[4]

Behind the sentimental novels and eroticized travel narratives were actual women who faced existences far more harrowing and complex than romanticized tales meant for the white reading public. Enslaved and free women of color faced sexual violence due to their skin color, were sold for sex, and lived, willingly or not, with white men without the legal protections of marriage. The racialized sexual economy of New Orleans encompassed both free and enslaved women of color and "tended to blur the boundaries of slavery and freedom for the women involved." Regardless of the women's legal status, white men "fetishized their willingness and their skin color." Conner's experiences illustrate how the sexual economy of slavery affected enslaved as well as free women, and how the commodification of their sexuality could circumscribe possibilities for women of African descent.[5]

Conner's initial sale in New Orleans may have been for sexual labor. On 17 April 1838, Jane Shelton of New Orleans purchased "a mulatress slave named Sarah Connah [sic] aged about twenty two years" for $1,100 cash. Yet Conner did not live with Shelton. Instead, Shelton said that she "hired out" Conner, "or, that is a gentleman vouched for her." Shelton's description is reminiscent of descriptions of enslaved women hired out as prostitutes. A resident of antebellum New Orleans noted the prevalence of young enslaved women who "engage [themselves] to be [a man's] bed companion," remaining "with him for a specified sum per month, which she pays to her master. The amount paid these girls is usually from $12 to $20 a month." The anonymous commentator also claimed that some enslaved girls were chosen early to be "educated and instructed by their masters in a certain way" to attract a hirer. He or she noticeably left the question of these women's willingness to engage in prostitution unaddressed, assuming their ultimate consent.[6]

Historians of enslaved women "hired out" for specifically sexual labor have taken the women's positionality more seriously, considering it another form of sexual violence. Some slave-owning men and women "sold or leased out the women they enslaved for the express purpose of concubinage and/or prostitution despite the state's [Louisiana's] official prohibition of such transactions" and gave no thought to the willingness of the enslaved individual. Historian Diana Williams contends that such practices were the actual foundation of the infamous New Orleans quadroon balls, rendering them "a capitalist innovation in a newly constituted and rapidly 'Americanizing' society of citizens" "rather than a vestige of a more racially fluid, seigniorial Latin culture." Such gatherings may "even have served to democratize access to 'fancy women,'" since "hiring" a "fancy girl" for a certain period of time was economically attainable for a wider swath of white male residents than purchasing one would have been. The idea of quadroon balls, then, can be seen as the extension of the slave trade's sexual economy. Alexis de Tocqueville described one of the balls he attended as a "sort of bazaar," explicitly linking the sexualization of black women's bodies to a commercial arena.[7]

Whatever her ties to the "gentleman" who "vouched for her," Conner did not live with the woman who enslaved her, and in her distance from Shelton, she found space to work for money of her own. A common thread running through the documents relating to Conner's life is her desire to earn enough money through domestic work to purchase her freedom. According to multiple witnesses, she repeatedly expressed her desire to purchase herself, to which one friend cautioned her that "if she had any such idea she had better keep it to herself." Despite this advice, Conner did have a unique right, for the slave states, to purchase her freedom under Louisiana's Civil Code. While a Spanish colony, Louisiana had recognized *coartación* as the legal right of enslaved people to purchase their freedom after paying their enslaver an established price. This price remained constant over time and was subject to outside appraisal. *Coartación* thus acknowledged enslaved people's ownership of personal property so that they could earn the amount needed for self purchase. While American control of Louisiana lessened the rights of *coartación*—most onerously, that self purchase could be made only with the consent of the enslaver—certain provisions of the Spanish law remained, however restricted. Conner could still enter into a legally binding contract with her master or mistress for her freedom, though it now had to be in writing. She could also sue directly for her freedom. All of this depended, however, on her mistress's compliance, Conner's "honest conduct," and the price of self purchase. Conner's desire to buy her freedom meant that she needed money.[8]

One of the few ways for Conner to earn this money, as an enslaved woman, was through socially reproductive labor. Only a year after her arrival in New Orleans, acquaintances reported that Conner began renting a handful of rooms on Burgundy Street, furnishing them herself and then renting them out again to "two or three gentleman." How she acquired the resources to rent the lodgings is unclear, but some of the funds may have come from extra work performed on her own account while hired out, such as doing laundry. While renting rooms, Conner took in laundry, an enterprise in which she later employed two or three other enslaved women. Though laundry was one of the most physically demanding and least attractive forms of labor, it was one of the few options before Conner.[9]

Subletting furnished rooms was a means of generating income that other enslaved women and free women of color took advantage of. Though it required enough money to rent the physical space and furnish it, the renting of rooms was less regulated than running a boardinghouse. There were plenty of men, white and black, in the city looking for ready-made domestic spaces and household labor, and Conner found multiple male boarders who appreciated her work ethic and the quality of her lodgings. She was also able to build a network of friends among the working women of the neighborhood. These were the women with whom she confided her plans of purchasing her freedom and turned to in times of trouble. One of Conner's neighbors, a free woman of color and midwife named Celeste Powell, for example, served as Conner's security when she signed court bonds.[10]

Another free woman of color, Melissa Tarrington Garrison, lived with her brother and his wife "on Canal Street . . . right around the corner from where Sarah lived." The two women became "intimate," and Conner "was with habit of consulting" Garrison about important matters. Foremost among these was Conner's labor toward her freedom. Garrison knew that Conner kept the money she earned for herself in the care of another woman, whom Garrison described only as "a griffe woman." This woman acted as Conner's private deposit bank, storing her money in "a mahogany box" until Conner accumulated enough to purchase her "liberty." That Conner trusted her money to a fellow woman of color is significant. Conner must have trusted this woman implicitly, more than she felt she could trust a male companion or her boarders, who would have had access to any money she stored in her rooms. Conner was willing to reveal the location of her savings to Garrison, suggesting a deep level of trust between them as well.[11]

Perhaps Conner also discussed with Garrison, Powell, and the "griffe woman" her encounters with the white men whose gaze she seemingly could not escape. While working, she received visits from "a Doctor . . . who appeared to be her friend or chere amie." The doctor could have been the man to whom she was hired or one of Conner's renters. There were other men who were also interested in Conner. One, Mark Davis, was a Virginia slave trader who spoke with Jane Shelton about purchasing her. Another slave trader, Theophilus Freeman, had his eye on Conner and would eventually approach Shelton about her. In Conner's status as an enslaved woman, her body was always under the scrutiny of white men and women who evaluated her physical person for the profit it could bring them, whether economically or emotionally. When Davis saw Conner, he imagined what purchasing her could mean for him; he assigned value to her height, her proportions, and her skin tone. Try as she might to work her way out of slavery on her own terms, Conner was forever subject to the speculating eye of men and women like Davis and Freeman.[12]

Conner turned to Garrison for further support when she made the potentially risky decision to enlist one of these men, Freeman, as a broker for negotiating her freedom. Garrison later recalled, "In the month of July 1841 . . . I saw said Sarah hand to Theophilus Freeman of said city the sum of $950 for the purpose of purchasing the freedom of said Sarah; such was the mutual understanding between said Sarah and said Freeman." Garrison claimed that she understood Conner's role to be that of Freeman's client, not the subject of a sale. Freeman was acting on Conner's behalf and said "that he would return to said Sarah the balance on $700 or $750."[13]

Why Conner could not buy herself directly from Shelton is unclear, and Shelton changed her account of the transaction multiple times. In 1848 Shelton claimed that "at the time she sold the said Girl Sarah to Freeman, [she] did not stipulate that Sarah should be free, nor did she care anything about it." Yet when questioned in court in 1850, Shelton changed her story, testifying "at the time she sold Sarah she sold her to be free, such was her intention in selling her [Conner] it was understood when she sold Sarah to Freeman that she was to be free; witness told Freeman she would not sell Sarah any other way."[14]

It is more likely that Shelton's original statement was accurate. Conner may have known that Shelton felt indifferently toward her and thought her chances of obtaining her freedom would be better if Freeman were involved as her "agent," a seasoned broker who could make a financially advantageous purchase on her behalf. Freeman allegedly convinced Shelton to sell Conner "very low," either because Shelton did want Conner to be free or because Freeman drove a hard bargain.[15]

For Freeman's perspective, a less reliable narrator is difficult to find, and his subterfuge was never clearer than when it came to Conner's emancipation. Whether or not Freeman intended to emancipate Conner, if or when he did, and whether the potential emancipation meant anything to Conner's day-to-day experiences, are issues to which the archival record provides only conflicting answers. Freeman was willing to do just about anything to protect his economic interests, and this often meant lying to courts, creditors, and customers. He knowingly sold free men of color as slaves, stabbed business partners in the back, and hid assets from creditors. Freeman's ruthless business tactics and his propensity for deceit make his motivations for working with Conner in 1841 difficult to tease out.

Freeman later alleged that "he made the purchase with the funds of said Sarah and for her benefit." Though he wrote a bill of sale noting "I Theophilus Freeman have this day sold to Sarah Conner herself to herself all the right title & interest which I purchast of Jane Shelton," Freeman failed to properly register this emancipation. Louisiana law classified slaves as real estate, and to be legally binding, the transfer of property, even in one's self, required a notarial act signed, witnessed, and registered in the conveyance office of the city. Therefore, whether she knew it or not, all of Conner's labor had not, in fact, brought her freedom.[16]

Freeman might have truly agreed to purchase Conner in order to free her, or perhaps he had done so in exchange for her sexual and domestic labor. Freeman had no other clear incentive in 1841 to free Conner, and he was not a man who did a favor expecting nothing in return. Freeman's name is re-membered today primarily for his involvement in the sale of Solomon Northup, a free man from New York whom two men, James Russell and Alexander Merrill, kidnapped and sold as a slave. While in Freeman's jail, Northup recounted repeated instances of Freeman's cruelty, including his sale of a young girl, Emily, from her mother because, as Freeman put it, "there were heaps and piles of money to be made of her . . . when she was a few years older. There were men enough in New-Orleans who would give five thousand dollars for such an extra, handsome, fancy piece as Emily would be, rather than not get her." Freeman may have initially been inter-ested in Conner for similar reasons.[17]

Whether legally free or not, Conner lived in many ways as a free woman while with Freeman between 1841 and 1845. She operated her own busi-nesses and kept the profits of her labor. She also traveled extensively, visit-ing several northern cities with Freeman in the early to mid 1840s. Only a month after Freeman purchased her, he had Conner accompany him on a trip to New York City, Philadelphia, Washington, D.C., and Baltimore. The purpose of Freeman's northern excursions is unclear, but he may have been meeting with bankers and factors involved in both his slave-trading business and his work with John Goodin & Co. Or, more nefariously, he may have been contacting men such as Alexander Merrill and James Russell, whose kidnapping victim Solomon Northup had reached Freeman's jail only two months earlier.[18]

The pair traveled first to Philadelphia, spending several weeks there be-fore moving on to New York City. In New York, Conner and Freeman stayed at Mr. Blanchard's Globe Hotel, where they remained for over a month. While there, Freeman met with several of his slave-trading associates, including Mark Davis (who had considered purchasing Conner), Lewis N. Shelton, and John L. Harris; many slave traders frequented New York for business. After returning to Philadelphia for "some time," Freeman and Conner stopped in Washington, D.C., before "getting on the cars going South" in Baltimore. Given later descriptions of Conner's skin tone, it is likely she passed as white in the North, possibly introducing herself as Freeman's wife. In these north-ern cities, Connor could move about freely and present herself as a well-to-do white woman.[19]

Only two years later Conner again traveled north, this time without Free-man but still with his support. In Freeman's words, he "sent" her to Cincin-nati, where she spent part of her time boarding with Fanny Preston. Preston was a "mulatto" woman born free in Virginia about fifteen years before

Conner. Though the census taker recorded no occupation for Preston, it is likely Conner was not the only boarder she took in to earn money. She also worked part of the time as a nurse.[20]

When not staying with Preston, Conner could have lodged at the Dumas Hotel, an African American owned and operated boardinghouse popular with black visitors to the city, as well as a station on the Underground Railroad. The Dumas Hotel was no less famous for housing the enslaved concubines of southern enslavers. Levi Coffin knew "many instances of white men bringing their yellow children from the South to our State [Ohio] to be set free." Coffin had personally advised "two good-looking young white men from [Mississippi]" who brought "with them mulatto women, whom they claimed as wives. They wished to purchase land and settle in Ohio, and having been referred to me for advice respecting a suitable locality, they called on me." Coffin accompanied the two men to the Dumas Hotel, where the women were boarding.[21]

That Freeman claimed he "sent" Conner to Cincinnati is telling. While it is possible to interpret Conner's travels in the North as the advantages of allying with Freeman, her actions must always be considered within the power dynamics of a society built around race-based slavery. Feminist historians have questioned the validity of equating female sexuality with agency, particularly in histories of slavery. In a society where racialized sexual violence was condoned and even encouraged, finding "agency" or opportunity in sex between women of color and white men is dangerous. Conner's experiences with Freeman are a stark reminder of this. Despite the fact that Conner traveled extensively with Freeman, it was only through her own actions that she later became legally free. Even then, her freedom was constantly at risk of being, and in fact was, revoked. Moreover, legal freedom from Freeman did not mean that Conner was free from his power and influence.[22]

This was never clearer than when Freeman fell into debt in 1844. Perhaps unbeknown to Conner, Freeman had recently escaped a lawsuit in Richmond after agreeing to pay, but not actually paying, his former partner Goodwin a settlement of their joint business. He had at least two other cases pending against him in court, and one of his businesses, John Goodin & Co., officially failed on 18 January 1844. As a member of the firm, Freeman was liable for $149,888.72 in outstanding debts. Freeman claimed he owned $97,450.79 worth of John Goodin & Co.'s assets, but this was still not enough to satisfy the creditors.[23]

What happened next is murky and varied significantly according to who was testifying. One of the suits pending in the parish court against Freeman was that of *William H. Williams v. Theophilus Freeman*. In March 1843, Williams, a slave trader based out of Washington, D.C., obtained judgment for $14,890.50 against Freeman. Williams certainly transacted business with Freeman, and the New Orleans–based trader may truly have owed him almost $15,000. Yet Williams never pursued the debt's payment. In fact, he transferred all rights in the judgment to Freeman's friend and business associate Junius Amis. Amis acquired the judgment on 13 April 1844, and, according to Freeman's creditors, did so without paying a cent to Williams. Amis then allegedly asked the courts to seize some of Freeman's property in order to pay the debt.[24]

When the sheriff went in search of Freeman's property, the property he seized was Sarah Conner. Along with Conner, the sheriff seized another woman Freeman enslaved, Elizabeth, and her child. It is difficult to comprehend how Conner must have felt as Sheriff Samuel Powers took her, a supposedly free woman, out of her home in order to sell her for Freeman's debts. Even if Freeman, as his creditors alleged, had orchestrated an elaborate plan to protect Conner and preserve his assets, how confident could she have felt, knowing that Freeman had also told her she was free? Conner's control of her own body was never secure; Freeman and the white men and women around her constantly used her physical being as a bargaining chip, counting on the value she embodied to bring them revenue, secure them loans, or forestall the payment of debts. Elizabeth and her child, seized alongside Conner, would have had even fewer reasons to hope a sale would not occur. Freeman had never made any promises of freedom to them.[25]

Shortly after Powers's arrival, Freeman signed a bond allowing Conner to stay in his possession until the sale. But the sheriff returned soon enough, and took Conner, Elizabeth, and Elizabeth's child to the City Exchange to be sold to the highest bidder. In the midst of the raucous crowd at the City Exchange, Powers led Conner to the auction block. Did he drag her, or push her, or did she go willingly? As the men in the crowd undoubtedly leered at the young woman's form, how did she react? Did she stare disdainfully back at them, or did she avert her eyes, refusing to acknowledge the scene around her? The auctioneer undoubtedly extolled her physical virtues, probably making lewd sexual references. As he and the audience members attempted to commodify her person, to see her only as a sexual object to be possessed, how could Conner have felt, as she waited and hoped that Freeman's plan would succeed?[26]

As the bidding came to a close and the auctioneer announced, "sold," the highest bidder was none other than William H. Williams. Her new "owner," however, had no interest in keeping Conner for himself; he had assumed a different judgment against Freeman in exchange for Conner's purchase. At least, that was what Freeman's creditors later argued happened. And it is difficult to understand how, if this was not the case, Conner returned to life as usual after Williams purchased her, not going with him to Washington, D.C., or moving out of her house with Freeman. Freeman's creditors were less concerned with what became of Elizabeth and her child, and so their fate was not recorded in any surviving legal documents.[27]

Conner must have breathed a substantial sigh of relief after her harrowing experience at the City Exchange, where the freedom she believed she had purchased with the proceeds of her own labor was only one bid away from disappearing. Did she resent Freeman for allowing things to go so far and for putting her at such risk in order to save his own skin? But the worst was yet to come. John Goodin & Co.'s finances still had to be settled, and neither partner was having an easy time collecting debts. In August, John Goodin surrendered his assets to the courts, declaring insolvency. Six months later, Freeman did the same.[28]

According to law, Freeman attached a schedule, or inventory, of his property to the bankruptcy surrender. The contents of the schedule came under significant scrutiny during the protracted court proceedings surrounding Freeman's debts. Freeman claimed to possess $137,991.73 in total assets, including notes and drafts from a number of slave traders. Other than "a residuary interest in certain claims and property transferred to Geo. W. Barnes & F. Jordan as collateral security for amounts due to them," and a "buggy in the possession of Wm. H. Williams," Freeman did not include any land, enslaved people, or other physical property in the schedule. Likely because of the glaring absence of enslaved property in the inventory of a slave trader, Freeman's creditors argued that he had illegally transferred title to most of his property prior to filing for bankruptcy in order to protect the majority of his assets from seizure. One of the people who was concealing Freeman's property, they argued, was Sarah Conner.[29]

As Freeman attempted to delay impending financial disaster, Sarah Conner decided to act to legalize her freedom. On 11 April 1846, Conner filed a petition with the First Judicial District Court asking the court to recognize and make legal her informal emancipation. In her petition, Conner identified herself as "a free woman of color" and recounted her story from bondage to imperfect liberation, emphasizing her domestic labor as the basis of her manumission. While a slave of Jane Shelton, Connor "had by her industry and good fortune for a series of years accumulated about the sum of seven hundred dollars and was anxious with her to obtain her freedom." In her account, Conner stressed that it was *her* labor, and *her* money derived from that labor, which led to her freedom. While she acknowledged that Freeman transacted the sale with Shelton, she emphasized that it was "made with the funds of your petitioner and for her benefit." Conner recognized the significance of the purchase money being her own. Moreover, Conner "ever since that time . . . has been in the actual enjoyment of her freedom undisturbed by the said Freeman or any other person." Realizing she could not completely conceal her ongoing connection to Freeman, she added, "although she has been occasionally in his service."[30]

Conner's petition arrived in court five years after the initial sale because, as Conner stated, "she has been informed that since the date of these acts the said Freeman has become embarrassed and unable to pay his debts." Conner told the court she had "in consequence thereof become very solicitous that her freedom should be beyond all doubt or question secured to her and that there should be some public evidence upon the records of the county that she is a free woman and that *confirmation* of the said private act should be obtained." Conner believed herself to be free but knew that only the power of the courts could make that freedom recognizable by law. She had already learned what happened when she relied on Freeman's private word to protect her.[31]

There are several ways to interpret Conner's actions. On the one hand, it is possible to understand them as an assertion of independence and as an aggressive pursuit of her freedom. Having been duped by Freeman once and subjected to the auction block, Conner took matters into her own hands and turned to an authority above Freeman. Freeman could have continued to stall or make excuses about her formal emancipation, or perhaps Conner had not realized the real danger she was in until the sheriff seized her.

Alternatively, Conner could have filed the petition at Freeman's bidding. If Conner was a free woman, she could own property and thus shield some of his assets from creditors. She could also buy and sell enslaved people for him. This was the interpretation Freeman's creditors put before the courts. To them, Conner was nothing more than a pawn or, depending on their objective, a source of revenue. Whatever she did, they claimed, had surely been done at Freeman's insistence. Freeman may indeed have recognized the benefits of having a free concubine, but if that was the case, why had he not freed her earlier, before he filed his surrender? Maybe he truly believed Conner would be safe despite his debt proceedings, or maybe her freedom was not of great import to him.

When confronted with the idea of formally emancipating Conner, Freeman offered no opposition. He answered her petition, stating, "He cannot deny any of the allegations in said petition. He has not at any time claimed the said Sarah as his slave and has no purpose of ever doing so." Maybe, at this moment, the advantages of Conner's legal emancipation crystallized in his mind. Finding no opposition from her legal owner, the judges initially had an easy decision to make. On 13 May 1846, Judge A. M. Buchanan decreed Conner free and ordered Freeman to pay court costs. Whatever the motivation behind Conner's petition, the end result was to her benefit. With her emancipation recorded in the city's deed books, she was no longer subject to seizure by the sheriff and sale on the auction block. Freeman, the man with whom she lived and slept, could no longer leverage her body for credit or offer it as payment of debt. Or so it seemed for a time.[32]

New Orleans Feby 14th 1849 to Theo Freeman for Thirty Dollars on the
1st day of March 1849 for value received
Jno T. Hatcher & Co
[Endorsed] pay to Sarah Conner or order [signed] Theo. Freeman

In this and subsequent suits over Conner's legal status, Louisiana's court system called on friends, neighbors, and acquaintances to define Conner's ties to Theophilus Freeman. Though Conner consistently argued she had never been Freeman's slave, her word was not enough to prove her freedom. Instead, her freedom depended on the testimony of various witnesses who arrived at different conclusions about Freeman and Conner. Whether others defined Conner as a wife, slave, domestic servant, concubine, or a combination of these had dire consequences for maintaining her freedom and retaining the fruits of her labor.

In court records, their associates most often—but not consistently—described Conner as Freeman's concubine. Mark Davis, who had known both parties before they knew one another, testified that Conner "did live with . . . Freeman as his concubine." His selection of the term "concubine" had connections to Louisiana law as well as popular discourse. According to Article 1468 of the Civil Code, "Those who have lived together in open concubinage are respectively incapable of making to each other, whether *inter vivosi* or *mortis causa*, any donation of immovables, and if they make a donation of movables, it cannot exceed one-tenth part of the whole value of their estate. Those who afterwards marry, are exempted from this rule." A married man keeping a concubine "in the common dwelling" constituted grounds for a wife to claim separation. The existence of concubinage as a cultural practice, though discouraged by legal restrictions, was nonetheless acknowledged in the Civil Code. While the Civil Code made no explicit reference to who could be a concubine, as Article 1468 could technically apply to any sex or race, the application of the law often worked against the rights of concubines of African descent.

In addition to the law, cultural understandings of concubinage appeared regularly in print, from travel literature and novels to New Orleans newspapers. Some editorialists decried the immorality of the city's inhabitants and their willingness to engage in concubinage, particularly concubinage with women of color. One anonymous author shortly after the Civil War reflected on the importance of marriage, noting that there were "two classes of persons who are exempt from its joys"—those who were "deaf and dumb, lame, blind or idiotic," as well as "fast" men who kept a "fast horse and a concubine." The author chastised this latter sort, who, "too economical to marry," would die wifeless and alone.[33]

Here the author implicitly compared the reciprocal obligations and expenses of legal marriage with the relative "economy" of concubinage. According to Article 121 of the Civil Code, husband and wife owed one another "fidelity, support, and assistance." Article 122 further specified that the husband was obliged to "receive her and to furnish her with whatever is required for the conveniencies of life." A man owed no such legal obligations to a concubine, though he most often still received the benefits of her domestic labor.[34]

Legislative resistance to an 1847 effort to criminalize concubinage evidenced the futility of the above author's advice. Though he or she would likely have applauded the so-called concubine bill, the bill found little support in the state legislature. The proposed bill aimed to make concubinage a criminal offense with three to twelve months imprisonment for anyone convicted. Rather than seriously consider forbidding the practice, the legislators "discussed [the bill] amidst considerable merriment." After a brief laugh, they tabled the bill, where it presumably stayed. Concubinage was both common enough to invite policing and acceptable enough to continue legally.[35]

While applicable to all women, the designation "concubine" held particular connotations for women of African descent. Already subject to racist stereotypes about their sexuality, they were less likely than white concubines to receive the sympathy of a judge, jury, or reporter. Take, for instance, the law limiting donations to concubines. Louisiana law considered manumission a monetary donation to the enslaved individual. A donation to anyone proven to be a concubine was limited to one-tenth of the estate. Thus, if the executors of an estate assigned a monetary value to an enslaved concubine that exceeded one-tenth of the total estate, he or she could technically not be freed. Still enslaved, the concubine could therefore not receive an inheritance. While the law limiting donations technically applied to all concubines, "the Louisiana Supreme Court was more likely to allow donations exceeding ten percent to white concubines." Most importantly, the enforcement of the law did not bring a white concubine's freedom into question.[36]

Other acquaintances struggled to define Conner's ties to Freeman. A business associate of Freeman's, Lewis N. Shelton, noted first that he met Conner while she was "in the service of Theophilus Freeman." Though Shelton saw Conner and Freeman traveling and living together, he had trouble separating her roles as domestic manager and sexual partner. When pressed, Shelton could only say that he did "not know whether the plaintiff lived with Theophilus Freeman as a concubine or not. Saw her at his house as a domestic" and ended his testimony there. Shelton's description illustrates the murky division between enslaved domestic, domestic manager, and enslaved concubine. Conner was in Freeman's "service" in a number of ways; women of color in domestic service were at heightened risk of sexual assault from employers or enslavers who viewed them as sexually available.[37]

Whether the court viewed Conner as a concubine or a domestic had additional implications for Conner's economic status. When a woman had sexual ties to a man, her right to wages for her work was in question. A wife performed socially reproductive labor in exchange for the necessities of life; if a concubine lived "as man and wife" with a man, then her labor was presumably not paid in wages. The accusation of concubinage called into question a woman's claim to compensation for labor performed in the household. The tensions inherent in such reasoning occasionally came to the surface in women's petitions for compensation.

Doria Hauthe, a white domestic servant, petitioned the estate of Pierre Pereuilhet for back pay in one such instance. Hauthe had nursed Pereuilhet during a drawn-out illness that ended with his death in 1866. Hauthe claimed $2,875 in compensation for feeding, clothing, nursing, and otherwise caring for Pereuilhet. Pereuilhet's executor countered such a large claim on the estate by arguing Hauthe was Pereuilhet's concubine and thus not entitled to pay for her work. The estate's attorney argued, "The concubine is no more entitled to receive compensation for labor performed about the household than the legitimate wife would be if she performed such work. And can it be pretended that the wife who would come in Court and claim compensation for nursing her husband and keeping his house would find an attentive ear from any tribunal? . . . In what better light then can the concubine represent herself?" The law did not stipulate that a concubine receive a portion of the estate as a wife would, however. Calling her Pereuilhet's concubine denied Hauthe both the legal inheritance of a wife and the legal compensation of an employee.[38]

The position of concubine was a liminal one, recognized but not favored in law and society. The designation "concubine" could only limit an inheritance, not secure it. A concubine might receive room and board in return for her labor, but it was not required by law. Whether or not such labor was eligible for wages was debatable and not guaranteed. A concubine's claim to rights and compensation was nonexistent if she was enslaved; those claims were still weak if she was freed. Both before and after her legal emancipation in 1846, witnesses continued to describe Conner as Freeman's slave and concubine, unable to act as an independent economic actor in both senses.

Conner's presumed status as enslaved concubine led witnesses to state that Conner lived with Freeman when Freeman was in fact living with Conner. Such statements highlighted the dangers of Conner's nebulous status. Around the time of her self purchase, Conner left Burgundy Street for a four-room dwelling on Gravier Street, between Carondolet and Baronne, for which she paid her landlord, Josiah Cole, $50 a month. Conner's name was the one on the lease of the property, and she was the one who managed the rented rooms. Freeman collected some of the rent from his fellow slave traders, but he paid the same back to Conner. Thanks to a slave-trading tenant who did not pay his rent, a promissory note with the endorsement "Pay to Sarah Conner" in Freeman's handwriting is preserved in the archives. While Conner continued to work for her own benefit and independence, the sexual economy of slavery meant that others presumed she labored (for free) on behalf of Freeman. As a formerly enslaved woman, they viewed her predominantly through her (sometimes imagined) sexual ties to white men[39]

At 163 Gravier, Conner rented rooms to and labored for a variety of men, the majority of whom were slave traders, including W. J. Martin, Archibald Lilly, Francis Jump, George Reid, J. F. Goolsby, James White, D. M. Mathews, and, of course, Theophilus Freeman. The men to whom Conner rented would have found their four shared rooms furnished with mahogany or cherry bedsteads, marble sideboards, carpets and rugs, washstands, "looking glass," and chairs. When not in their rooms, they could have relaxed or dined in the common room, outfitted with a table and several "common chairs." From the kitchen, Conner or one of the enslaved cooks of her renters would bring the men meals as they discussed business, punctuating their remarks with spits of tobacco into one of Conner's two spittoons. People not renting from Conner could also pay to eat in the common room; slave trader L. H. Huddleston noted that he "sometimes ate there [at Conner's] but did not board there."[40]

While boarding with Conner, Freeman started using her rented building as a base of operations. The landlord, Josiah Cole, who described Conner as a "decent girl," agreed to let Freeman build "a shed . . . to use as a negro yard" on a vacant portion of the lot, adjacent to but separate from Conner's premises. Freeman paid no additional rent for use of the land but agreed to leave any improvements once the lease expired. This brought Conner into even closer proximity to the daily imprisonment and crude bartering over the price of enslaved people. The arrangement must have seemed perfect to Freeman: like many other successful slave traders, he could now offer room and board to his customers at Conner's residence, right next to his place of business. Conner called herself a seamstress in 1846; she likely also sewed for Freeman and potentially for the other traders in her household. In order to earn this money, Conner lived and worked where she could look out her window and see and hear the physical embodiment of the market in enslaved people.[41]

During this time, Conner decided to test another one of her rights as a free woman. Like several of the women in her neighborhood, including Celeste Powell, Conner purchased enslaved laborers. In May 1847 she purchased a twenty-six-year-old enslaved woman, Mary Ann, from Caroline M. Williams for $600. Shortly after, Conner made another purchase, this time going to the auction rooms of Bernard Kendig, a colleague of Freeman's. From Kendig she purchased an enslaved man, Lewis, but then decided to "swap" Lewis for a nineteen-year-old woman named Ellen whom Caroline Williams enslaved. Conner had now joined the ranks of the slaveholding class.[42]

Or had she? Freeman's creditors were later to claim that Conner only purchased enslaved people for Freeman's benefit. In other words, when Freeman was in financial trouble, Conner did business in his name. Though in court these creditors routinely misrepresented the facts of Conner's life, they may have been right in this respect. Conner only recorded the purchase of two enslaved people before a notary, and the only references to her purchasing slaves by private act occurred during the time she was with Freeman. The most damning evidence comes from Conner's own confused testimony in court, when she claimed in one suit to have purchased Ellen from Freeman's colleague Junius Amis and in a different suit to have purchased Ellen from Caroline Williams.

Maybe Conner purchased Ellen and Mary Ann for Freeman. Like his creditors later claimed, Freeman could have had Conner buy the women in name only, in order to protect his investments from the mounting claims of his creditors. Or perhaps Conner knew the women somehow, or took pity on them, or saw in them a situation like her own. Or, finally, maybe she purchased them for her own profit, because owning people was the surest route to upward mobility in antebellum New Orleans, and these women could assist in the physical work of cooking, cleaning, and caring for renters. What the justices, the juries, and the clerks of court—the men who allow us to glimpse Sarah Conner's existence—were interested in was not *why* she purchased Mary Ann and Ellen, or what the purchase meant to her, but that she purchased them and that her name appeared on a bill of sale given in exchange for money.[43]

Know all men by these presents that Sarah Conner and Theo. Freeman do hereby Lease unto L. D. Right one half of the dwelling house No 163 Gravier Street from 14th February 1847 to the 1st of November 1849

Even as Conner seemed to have cemented her claims to freedom and the proceeds of her labor in the parish court, the long reach of slavery's sexual economy would not let her go. Freeman's creditors had tired of his constant subterfuge as syndic, or manager, of his bankruptcy case and replaced him with A. F. Dunbar, one of the parties to whom Freeman owed the most money. Dunbar began a tenacious pursuit of the money owed him, hounding those who owed Freeman money as well as Freeman himself. Freeman, Dunbar alleged, had not only failed to mention significant property on the inventory of his remaining assets, he had also compelled several of his friends to institute legal suits against him in an effort to tie up his assets in court.[44]

Joining Dunbar in the escalating case against Freeman was Robert Mott, the attorney for another of Freeman's creditors, the Bank of Kentucky. Freeman had lost a previous debt case to the Bank of Kentucky, this one over a protested promissory note from 1844 for the sum of $1,225. The Bank of Kentucky, too, became frustrated with Freeman and alleged that his friends were instituting fraudulent suits on his behalf, specifically mentioning the suit of William H. Williams.[45]

In light of this ongoing struggle and Freeman's apparent inability to pay any of the money he owed, Robert Mott issued a writ of execution against Freeman. Mott requested that a "special search" be made for the enslaved property of Freeman, believing "they [were] being hid away and secreted." As a result of this search, on 20 April 1848 Sheriff John L. Lewis seized four enslaved people—Emmanuel, Isham, Mary Ann, and Ellen. The sheriff took them to the parish prison, as he had with Conner, to await sale at the insistence of Freeman's creditors. Where Conner had been two years early, Mary Ann and Ellen, the two women she enslaved, were in 1848. Yet Mary Ann and Ellen legally belonged to Conner, not Freeman, or so Conner attempted to prove. Several days after the seizure, Conner petitioned the Fourth District Court to return Mary Ann and Ellen to her. Conner claimed she was the "true and lawful owner" and called the sheriff's actions "illegal and oppressive."[46]

The Bank of Kentucky answered Conner's petition swiftly and decisively, using the sexual economy of slavery against her. Mott began by denying the legality of Conner even filing a legal petition, claiming that "the plaintiff is a slave, the property of Theophilus Freeman and cannot stand in judgment and has no right to file a petition." He went on to impugn Conner's motives by calling her Freeman's concubine. Freeman, Mott argued, "has been doing all his business in the name of [Connor] & been carrying on a considerable traffic in slaves, with his own money & for his own benefit in the name of [Conner] for the purpose of shielding his property from the pursuit of his real creditors." Conner's petition, he alleged, was in fact the work of Freeman, and thus fraudulent. As Freeman's concubine, it was easy enough for Mott to argue Conner was also his slave. Conner was a free woman of color sexually tied to a man who formerly enslaved her. For many, imagining Conner's labor and property apart from Freeman's control was difficult.[47]

The line between free concubine and enslaved concubine was vague and easily manipulated. Creditors as well as heirs often used the liminal position of formerly enslaved concubines to discredit their freedom and their right to property. Josephine Anna Sinnet was, like Conner, an enslaved woman, born in Virginia and sold to New Orleans, who became the concubine of a white man, Joseph Uzée. After Sinnet's death, Uzée's legal widow used Sinnet's sexual ties to Uzée as grounds for disinheriting Sinnet's children with him. Sinnet's estate, the widow claimed, was actually Joseph Uzée's property as there was no way Sinnet had acquired any property through her own labor.[48]

The widow, Frosine Uzée, told the Orleans Parish Court that Sinnet's emancipation was null and void because she had not met the requirements, being under the age of thirty and not a native of Louisiana. If, however, the court deemed Sinnet's emancipation valid, Uzée had a second line of defense: "But should said emancipation be declared to be legal, and she to have been capable of acquiring property and holding the same in her own right," her estate's claims were nonetheless invalid because "said Anna lived in open and notorious concubinage" and any acts of sale from Joseph Uzée to Sinnet were "without any consideration [payment] on the part of said Anna & is a donation in disguise." Sinnet's history of enslavement, her presumed inability to earn her own money, and her living with Uzée could disqualify her children from inheriting her estate.[49]

Because Sinnet was Uzée's enslaved and then free concubine, observers assumed that she did not work or have money of her own. While witnesses in the trial over Sinnet's estate repeatedly stated that she had "no means" to acquire property on her own, they simultaneously gave evidence of Sinnet performing labor that earned money. One witness first stated that he "never knew nor heard that Anna was following any trade or occupation by which she could make money. She lived in this house as the wife of Uzée." The same witness later stated, however, that he boarded with Sinnet and "came into the house to get my meals." Even though Sinnet had the help of her mother (an enslaved woman whom Sinnet hired) and later an enslaved woman named Harriet, she still managed the household for boarders, of which the witness was not the only one. That Sinnet rented to boarders and also sold sugarcane from the front of her house disappeared from witnesses' consciousness once they understood her as Uzée's concubine.[50]

Conner's work renting out rooms, sewing, and doing laundry similarly became invisible when Freeman's creditors argued that all of her assets and property, as well as her own body, actually belonged to Freeman. Conner's money saved in the mahogany box became Freeman's money, putting her freedom in question. Mott and Dunbar took this logic to its extreme and instituted separate suits in the Fifth District Court asking to reverse the decision granting Conner her freedom. Dunbar instituted the suit "for the purpose of subjecting Sarah Conner to be sold as a slave for the benefit of the creditors of Theophilus Freeman." Robert Mott, the bank's lawyer, similarly wanted "Sarah declared to be the property of the said Freeman & subject to the execution of these petitioners." To both of these men, and to Freeman's creditors in general, Conner was entitled to no special considerations as a free woman. On the contrary, both her history with Freeman and her skin color gave Freeman's creditors another avenue for pursuing their ultimate goal. Conner was only a vehicle for redeeming their pecuniary losses and finding revenge on Freeman.[51]

Yet Conner fought back. She answered the petitions of both parties with equal vehemence, averring "she never was the slave of Theophilus Freeman [and] although a title was passed by Mrs. Bennett [Jane Shelton] to said Freeman," it was only for the purpose of her manumission. Again, Conner used her history of labor and resulting financial independence, as well as her property rights, to argue for her freedom. She had, with her own money, "purchased & sold slaves & movables" since her emancipation, which she offered as evidence of her legal status. Other witnesses attempted to "prove that deft [defendant] had money of her own to pay for herself" despite the creditors' claims that Freeman had paid for her purchases. Melissa Tarrington Garrison, Josiah Cole, Mark Davis, and Conner's former boarders all testified to Conner's renting out of rooms, work as a laundress, payment of bills, and general economic competency. Finally, Conner pleaded, "having enjoyed her freedom for the last eight years she cannot now be reduced to servitude."[52]

The final question at hand was whether Conner's emancipation antedated Freeman's economic failure. According to the laws of Louisiana, creditors' claims to a debtor's estate took precedence over emancipations or the sale of slaves. Thus, if Conner had actually been emancipated in 1841 by private act, she was not subject to the claims of Freeman's creditors. If, however, her true emancipation had been in 1845, when the private act was recorded, or in 1846 with the judgment of the First District Court, then her freedom came after Freeman's bankruptcy and was null and void.

On 21 December 1848 the sheriff again traveled to 163 Gravier Street. Carrying the final judgment of the court in his hand, he found Freeman at home and handed him the same. When Freeman opened the paper, he discovered that Conner was again his slave and thus "subject as such to the execution in favor of Plaintiffs." The judge, A. M. Buchanan, decided in favor of the Bank of Kentucky and Freeman's creditors, reversing the judgment of 1846 and refusing a request for retrial. Buchanan based his decision on article 190 of the Civil Code, which stated that an "enfranchisement" made when the emancipator could not pay his or her debts was in fraud of the creditors and thus null and void. Buchanan believed the true date of Conner's emancipation to be the summer of 1845, when Freeman was "in a declared state of insolvency." Additionally, Conner was not thirty years of age at that time, which was also a violation of Article 185 of the Civil Code.[53]

According to the state of Louisiana, Sarah Conner was again a slave, despite Conner's vigorous protests otherwise. It was in the interests of those with economic power and social influence—the creditors, the bankers, the judge and jury, the slaveholders—that Conner's freedom was denied. How did Conner feel when she discovered her fate? In just an instant, her legal status changed from free to enslaved, from economic actor to object of the economy, yet the woman herself—her mind, her spirit, her physical being— had not. The only thing that had changed was how others saw her—but that was not a change without consequences.

Denied a retrial in the lower courts, Conner's lawyers appealed to the Louisiana Supreme Court. When the court met in May 1849, they reexamined her case, considered the decision of the lower court, and came to a different conclusion. The judges recognized that many of Freeman's actions were likely fraudulent, but held that, ultimately, "the action by the individual creditors, in this instance, [is] untenable." Though successful in one case, she had to endure two more years of uncertainty while her identical battle against A. F. Dunbar played out in the courts. Again, the lower court found against her and Conner appealed the judge's ruling. In 1851, when Conner's next appeal reached the Louisiana Supreme Court, the higher court's justices found for Conner a second time. Although they noted that Freeman's antedating Conner's emancipation paper was "ridiculous," they also held that this should not interfere with "any bona fide right, which Sarah the defendant has acquired previous to its true date." The justices also found something to admire in Conner's story, calling her an "industrious & thrifty woman" who had worked hard to purchase her freedom. All of Freeman's creditors had ultimately failed in their attempts to again reduce Sarah Conner to slavery.[54]

Mary Ann and Ellen, caught in their enslaver's legal troubles and battle for her own freedom, were not so lucky. After more than a year in the city jail, Mary Ann and Ellen, as well as Isham and Emmanuel, were sold by the sheriff at auction on 30 June 1849. Freeman was present at the sale, heckling the auctioneer and attempting to dissuade the crowd from making bids. No one paid him much mind. In fact, Conner's lawyer claimed that Conner had given up her interest in the suit but "Freeman would not permit her" to discontinue its pursuit. Conner, though legally free, still fell under Freeman's control. Freeman could have used multiple threats to compel Conner to obey him: physical and sexual violence, manipulation of her claims to freedom, economic ultimatums, or all of the above. If she alienated him, he might even recant his testimony about the private act in 1841.[55]

Though under pressure from Freeman, Conner was technically free (again), if that legal freedom meant anything to her after seeing how quickly it could be revoked. Perhaps hoping to live by the letter of the law to avoid further trouble, in 1849 Conner applied for the first time to remain in New Orleans as an emancipated slave. According to the Civil Code, newly freed slaves had to petition the parish police jury to remain in the state after emancipation. By the time Conner finally did so, her less-than-slavish behavior had earned her public notice. The Second Municipality Counsel tabled Conner's request. Undeterred, and by 1850 victorious in her case against the Bank of Kentucky, Conner tried again the next year. This time the Police Committee "examined minutely into the character of the petitioner, and [found] it not at all reputable." Likely Conner's arrest the previous year for unlawful assembly at a house on St. John Street with "sixteen colored women, mostly enslaved, and ten to twelve white men," among other things, factored into their decision.[56]

Despite this, Conner continued to reside in New Orleans, and in August 1851, Alderman Etter ordered her to leave the state within sixty days. Since police ignored most manumitted slaves who disobeyed contravention laws, Etter's order is illustrative of Conner's notoriety. Judith Schafer notes "after 1842, city police generally arrested only free people of color illegally in the state who attracted their attention by some inappropriate behavior." Conner was on city officials' radar. Etter's decision, made in the Recorder's Court for the Second District, warranted comment from the *Times Picayune*, whose author noted that Conner had "figured prominently of late in civil action before our tribunals, and is said to possess some property." The newspaper printed Etter's decision in full and made a point of noting the punishments for free people of color who did not leave Louisiana after being ordered to do so. A second arrest resulted in lifetime imprisonment in the penitentiary.[57]

Despite continuing legal trouble, in 1851 Conner again decided to try her luck in the court system. Days before Alderman Etter ordered her to leave the state, she filed a petition with the Second Municipality claiming that two white people, Charles Cammeyer and Mary Cunningham, had stolen a man she enslaved, Peter. Sometime that spring, Peter, whom Conner had purchased two years earlier by a private bill of sale, disappeared. Freeman, learning that Cammeyer had claimed a runaway enslaved man working at Mary Cunningham's property, convinced Conner that this man was in fact Peter. Whether Freeman truly believed the two men were one and the same is up for debate.[58]

Though it helped that Cammeyer had already served jail time, Conner's claim against him, within the racial hierarchy of New Orleans, was risky. Likely predisposed to question her honesty, one of the sheriffs investigating the case swore an oath against Conner and Freeman, citing Conner for perjury and Freeman for subornation of perjury, or inducing Conner to commit perjury. On 21 August 1851 the sheriff issued an arrest warrant for both. Conner and Freeman would have to prove that they made the complaint against Cammeyer and Cunningham in good faith.[59]

When the case reached the First Judicial District court, the prosecution focused their argument on Freeman. It was not Conner, they insisted, but Freeman who was important. A conviction against Conner meant a conviction against Freeman, whom they clearly believed was guilty. Freeman, after all, had run afoul of public opinion for nearly a decade with his never-ending litigation and still-unpaid debts. Several of the witnesses testified that Freeman had "antipathy toward Cammeyer," and one man even claimed that Freeman paid him $50 to testify against the alleged thief.[60]

The prosecution also made it clear that Conner and Freeman lived together, and submitted some evidence from Freeman's debt cases. Returning again to Conner's past as Freeman's "slave & concubine" they argued that, as Freeman's dependent in two senses, Conner could not act on her own but was an appendage of his will. Alderman Etter, who had ordered Conner to leave the state, also offered his own testimony. Etter, who seems to have harbored some antipathy of his own, claimed that Conner could "write her name & that he saw her do it [.] [S]he can read writing. This fact was not addressed on her trial." Etter's testimony countered Freeman's argument that Conner was not fully aware of the content of her lawyer's petition when she swore to it.[61]

The case aroused considerable interest from the reading public of New Orleans. News of Conner's legal battle with Freeman's creditors had made its way to Ohio, where it attracted the interest of abolitionists. A synopsis of the suit appeared in the *Anti-Slavery Bugle* in 1850. *State v. Sarah Conner*, meanwhile, was covered extensively in New Orleans newspapers with titles such as "The Case of Sarah Conner" and "The Perjury Case," which they claimed had "excited a good deal of excitement in the community." The authors of these pieces were less than kind to Conner, dredging up her past legal battles, her prior arrest, and her relationship to Freeman. They referred to her as "the notorious Sarah Conner" and "the celebrated Sarah Conner," drawing on tropes of the Jezebel to impugn her character. As a free woman of color who challenged white men in court, Conner elicited no sympathy from the newspaper's writers.[62]

The juries, both in the lower courts and when Conner appealed to the Supreme Court of Louisiana, similarly showed Conner no sympathy. After lengthy testimony from over a dozen witnesses, both courts decided that Conner had knowingly lied to the recorder's court to carry out Freeman's vendetta against Cammeyer. Etter chastised Conner for cohabitating with

Freeman, pointedly noting that she was "not, nor can she be, his wife, for a white person cannot, in this State, marry a person of color." Etter also denied that Conner, as her attorney had argued, was "in duress or in the fear of loss of life or liberty to compel her to make or swear to the affidavit against Cammeyer." In Etter's opinion, Conner was a "moral agent capable of committing a crime and responsible for her acts to the law."[63]

When it suited the racial status quo, then, Conner was a "moral agent," autonomous and answering only to herself, while in other situations Conner was merely "the tool of a white man." The pretzel logic of racism and the ideological maintenance of the slave system gave Conner scarce room to maneuver. Depending on whose purposes it served, Conner was slave, free, appendage, or independent actor. In countless situations, both as a slave and as a free woman of color, Conner's life and being became a venue for white men to carry out their ideological battles. Rather than being seen as an individual woman, Conner became the embodiment of concerns over white privilege, sexual license, and the maintenance of the institution of slavery. Though she was deemed an autonomous "moral agent" in the case against her, she was deemed only an avatar of Freeman in the state's case against him. He was convicted of subornation of perjury shortly after.

When Sarah Conner reached the bar of the Supreme Court for the last time in 1852, she heard her sentence for perjury. She had been more or less a constant presence in the state's court system since 1846, and now she faced her severest criminal charge. The judge declared her guilty and sentenced her to five years' hard labor at the state penitentiary. It is unclear, however, when or if Conner ever actually went to the penitentiary. No evidence survives of her being imprisoned in Baton Rouge, so it is likely that she somehow evaded her sentence.[64]

> *Sarah Ann Connor of the City of New Orleans hereby leases to William Schneider also of the same city the two story and attic brick dwelling known as 212 Gravier.*

After the infamous "Perjury Case," Conner appears to have finally moved beyond Freeman's grasp. Freeman's conviction likely aided her escape. Freeman moved to a different house on Gravier Street, this time between Rampart and Basin. His creditors continued to hound him throughout the 1850s, but Freeman, wily as ever, kept on in his business, though he was never quite as prosperous as before. Solomon Northup, making his way back through

New Orleans as a free man in 1853, reported, "from respectable citizens we ascertained he had become a low, miserable rowdy—a broken-down, disreputable man." His creditors attacked him in the courts, and prostitutes physically attacked him in his home. After 1858, when the parish court charged Freeman with assault and battery upon a woman named Susan McNally, Freeman disappeared from written records.[65]

Though the residue of Conner's association with Freeman continued to plague her in the form of legal fees, she did her best to move on. By 1860 Conner had escaped the court system with $500 of personal property still intact, and she continued to rent out furnished rooms. None of her renters were slave traders. Several were police officers and, ironically for a woman so harassed by the law, she began a long-term relationship with one of them. Smith Isard was a white police officer born near Cape May, New Jersey, in 1818. After serving for some time on merchant ships out of Philadelphia, Isard settled in New Orleans and found work as a police officer. Throughout his time in the city, Isard received public commendation for his work, eventually earning the rank of assistant to the chief of police. The *Picayune*, having dealt so harshly with Conner, praised Isard as "competent, intelligent, well-known and highly appreciated."[66]

This match, like Corinna Hinton's with Nathaniel Davidson, seems to have had more to do with emotion than coercion and limited opportunities. Conner continued to support herself through socially reproductive labor, taking on boarders who included two other Isards, likely Smith's relatives. She apparently had a good relationship with Isard's family; her will included bequests to his kin in New Jersey. Conner lived with Isard until his death in 1872, at which time he was working as a "special bank officer." The couple's impressive memorial at Cypress Grove Cemetery described Conner as Isard's wife, an interesting inscription for the late nineteenth-century grave of a free woman of color who kept her maiden name, even in death, and her white partner. While Corinna Hinton adopted the surname Omohundro, Conner chose not to adopt the surname of either Freeman or Isard. Though she had her status as Isard's "wife" literally carved in stone, she did not relinquish her identity as Sarah Ann Conner of Fairfax County, Virginia.[67]

Isard left his entire estate to one of his brothers, but he and Conner had come to a financial arrangement prior to his death. Isard's brothers and the executor of his will, fellow police officer Thomas N. Boylan, respected his final wishes. When the court's appraiser visited their house on Gravier Street, Boylan quickly "pointed out" $100 worth of wearing apparel "as the only [items] belonging to the late deceased in said residence." When the notary ignored him and tried to appraise the furniture, Conner protested vigorously. The notary reported that "all of the furniture and effects in said domicile being then and there claimed by one Mrs. Sally as her property and who objected and refused to the placing of seals thereon by the undersigned notary in his official capacity." Conner knew that the furniture was crucial to her success in renting out rooms, and she was not about to let the courts claim her belongings as part of Isard's estate.[68]

Furniture intact, Conner continued to earn money by creating living spaces for men who paid for domestic comforts in cash. She must have done fairly well, as she operated at least two properties. She decorated her own dwelling with lace curtains, silverware, silver pitchers and goblets, photographs, and at least three oil paintings ("School," "War," and "Ten Virgins"). Conner had the assistance of another mixed-race woman, of French descent, Rosa David, who had lived with her off and on for at least ten years. Conner even successfully petitioned the court for unpaid rent on a dwelling at 212 Gravier Street. It was one of her only successful suits, gaining her $500 in back rent with interest, costs of suit, and a lien on the tenant's personal property.[69]

And then she left New Orleans. For reasons that are unclear, sometime after 1880 but before 1892, Conner left New Orleans for Washington, D.C.. She had somehow come into contact with kin—probably nieces and nephews—after the end of the Civil War. In 1880 a young couple and their daughter from Virginia with the last name of Conner boarded with her in New Orleans. Maybe this reconnection precipitated her cross-country journey.

In Washington, Conner again built a strong network of female friends and accumulated a fair amount of property. She adopted a daughter, Mary Eleanor Carter. She also developed ties to the kin with whom she reconnected, including Andrew Conner and Alice V. Conner (she was less fond of their mother, whom she disinherited "because of her conduct to me"). She also formed relationships with other women in her new community, one of whom named her daughter after Conner. Her years of domestic labor finally allowed Conner to live a comfortable life. She owned at least two properties in Washington, a considerable amount of jewelry, a piano, and plenty of furniture, which had always been important for her line of work.[70]

Sarah Ann Conner, free woman of color of New Orleans, "notorious" to the Crescent City's population, died in 1892, at age 72, in the nation's capital, within a hundred miles of where she had been born. Her lengthy will testified to her wealth as well as her network of friends. Conner's bequests are notable for the number of items and cash that she left to women. Outside of Andrew Conner, Benjamin Henderson of New Orleans, and her executors, all of her belongings went to female kin and acquaintances, including her adopted daughter, Rosa David (who had resided with her in New Orleans), Smith Isard's female relatives, Alice V. Conner, and various female friends. A few bequests to residents of New Orleans revealed her continued connection to old acquaintances there. Conner requested that her body be sent back to New Orleans for burial next to Smith Isard, and she paid $200 for upkeep of the grave.[71]

Turncoat, heroine, prostitute, rebel—our mental image of Sarah Conner, however we paint the contours of her face, the glint in her eyes, the curve of her lips, haunts us. How do we remember her, how do we make sense of her life? To many, both contemporaries and historians, she existed merely as an appendage of Theophilus Freeman, an intriguing but inconsequential anecdote in the story of the slave trade or the life of an infamous slave trader. Yet she had a story of her own, a story that sheds more light on the nature of the slave trade than Freeman's does. Conner complicates the many dichotomous arguments historians make about slavery, neither resistant nor accommodating, neither seducing white men nor running from them in the North, never content being a slave but willing to enslave others. It could be— and has been—argued that Conner was any of the above. To antebellum New Orleans, she was the Notorious Sarah Conner. What will she be to us? Perhaps our answer says more about our own time than it does about hers.

CHAPTER FOUR

Housekeeper

> *Slave Manifest, Barque Cyane, December 15, 1848*
> *Lucy Ann Cheatem [sic] Female—21-5"3—Mulatto—John Hagan*
>
> *Will of John Hagan, February 15, 1856*
> *To Lucy Ann Cheatham . . . Ten thousand Dollars ($10,000) for services*
> *rendered me as a nurse while sick*
>
> *Lucy Ann Cheatham v. Her Creditors, May 11, 1863*
> *Ordinary Debts . . . Sampson & Keene [Furniture Dealers] due $469.50*

After the Civil War, Mary Lumpkin "went to housekeeping" in New Orleans, where her longtime friend Lucy Ann Cheatham lived and worked renting out furnished rooms. Lumpkin lodged with Cheatham for a time until she found a place of her own to stay. Though they had always kept in touch through letters, they must have had much to discuss during those days they shared a house. Perhaps they reflected on old times and all of the places they had previously "went to housekeeping."[1]

To "go to housekeeping" was to set up and run a household of one's own. When women "went to housekeeping," they assumed management of cooking, cleaning, washing, sewing, and otherwise caring for the inhabitants of a house. In this way, the household was a site of production: the production of current or future workers or citizens. By 1865 Cheatham and Lumpkin had kept house in varied geographic locations and in very different social and legal circumstances. Both women started their lives in Virginia, but their paths diverged from there. Cheatham spent most of her life in New Orleans; Lumpkin went from Richmond to Philadelphia before housekeeping in New Orleans and, finally, New Richmond, Ohio.[2]

It was in New Richmond, Ohio, that Lumpkin learned of her friend Cheatham's death in 1887. Cheatham's daughter, Frederika, wrote her the news before L. M. Dawson, the county clerk of court, asked Lumpkin to testify to her old friend's family situation. In the course of executing Cheatham's estate, the Orleans Parish Court requested that court officials in Ohio interview Lumpkin on their behalf. The court wanted to know about Cheatham's children, her children's father, and the various places in which she had kept house.[3]

This was no easy task. Lucy Ann Cheatham had lived a life that, while familiar to Mary Lumpkin, could have been a source of gossip to outsiders. Lumpkin had to be careful how she recounted the events of Lucy's life. So Mary Lumpkin told the county clerk a particular story about her friend Lucy Ann Cheatham, one that could have described the lives of many of the women of the era, and one that began in and was sustained through the household. She met Lucy through the domestic chore of sewing. The two maintained their friendship until Lucy met her future husband and followed him to New Orleans. They kept in touch via letters and yearly visits, when Lucy and her husband stayed with Mary and hers. Mary helped Lucy communicate with and send gifts to her family in the Richmond area. After the turmoil of the Civil War and widowhood for both women, Mary moved to New Orleans, where the two could visit more often. Through letters and shared experiences, the women forged a bond that sustained them through personal difficulties.[4]

When Lumpkin told Dawson that Cheatham "married" her husband, however, her language obscured the origins and nature of Cheatham's ties to the father of her children; namely, that he purchased rather than married her. Lumpkin knew the potential dangers this truth presented to Lucy's children too well, because Mary had also been enslaved. Mary's carefully crafted narrative disguised the fact that major events in her life and in Lucy's were in many instances not under their control. Neither woman was able to gossip about suitors and then select a husband of their liking. Neither woman had much say, while their enslavers were alive, whether they kept a household in New Orleans, Richmond, or somewhere else entirely. Lucy could not choose to stay with her relatives in Richmond rather than go to Louisiana. Nor could either of the women discuss the birth and future of their children without the concomitant, if perhaps unspoken, fear that the children would be sold away from them or never receive freedom from their fathers. Mary revealed none of these troubled elements of her life to the prying eyes of L. M. Dawson. The courts in New Orleans might not know that Lucy had been a slave, and Mary was not about to be the one to reveal that secret.[5]

Slave Manifest, Barque Cyane, December 15, 1848
Lucy Ann Cheatem [sic] Female — 21-5"3 — Mulatto — John Hagan

"Housekeeping" was part of a home, but housekeeping did not a home make, at least not in the sense that "home" took on by the mid-nineteenth century. As late as the 1830s, "household" and "home" meant essentially the same thing: a space where people ate, slept, and kept their things. Changes in the economy, the increasing popularity of sentimental fiction, and the social commentary of women such as Catharine Beecher gave new meaning to "home" as the century progressed, imbuing it with the sanctity of the family and imagining it as a private, domestic retreat away from the turmoil of public life. In many ways, nineteenth-century writers defined the home against what they came to see as its opposite: the boardinghouse and other rented lodgings.[6]

As Wendy Gamber writes, "if homes were private, boardinghouses were public. If homes nurtured virtue, boardinghouses bred vice. Above all, boardinghouses were creatures of the marketplace." A boardinghouse keeper polluted the alleged sanctity of the home by selling the domesticity a woman was supposed to give for free. The woman who made a house a home, sentimental fiction explained, was a loving wife, mother, daughter, or sister who presided over the family's decidedly private space with selfless love and affection. In contrast to the boardinghouse keeper, this woman's altruism and devoted care was what made the home sacred. If much of the literature of the era is to be believed, this care was hardly work at all. Rather than demanding physical labor, it was the natural role of women to care for a home and its inhabitants.[7]

The reality of the household was, of course, very different. Housework was just that—work—and a variety of women performed it, not just selfless mothers and wives. Overseeing and managing domestic labor, rather than doing it oneself, showed a woman's social status. Throughout the United States, wealthier families paid poorer women to wash, clean, and cook for them. In the slaveholding states, men and women purchased or hired enslaved laborers, mostly women, to perform domestic work. Potential slaveholders paid for "wanted" advertisements or visited slave jails in search of enslaved women with specific skills as housekeepers, laundresses, chambermaids, ironers, nurses, and lady's maids. In the South, "no white woman of any standing, nor who hoped to have any did her own housework." White families depended on the domestic labor of black women for both its material and ideological benefits. Enslaved domestics' labor maintained slaveholders' lifestyle, creating status and domesticity for white women.[8]

Domestic work also took place in what can more accurately be termed a "houseful," or "a coresidence of households that might or might not be related by family ties" instead of a "home." Many times, but not always, a boardinghouse keeper or landlady presided over a houseful. Property owners rented out part of their own house or offered space for multiple families to rent within the same structure. Single men, women, and families paid for space in hotels and boardinghouses or rented rooms, paying rent to a boardinghouse keeper, hotel proprietor, or property owner. In hotels and boardinghouses in the antebellum South, the domestic labor in these spaces was the province of both enslaved women and wageworkers.[9]

In some instances the housekeeper could simultaneously occupy a number of the above identities: enslaved, the mistress of the household, and the mother of the head of household's children. Enslaved women who ran the households of white men constituted a particular class of "housekeepers," overseeing as well as performing domestic chores, raising children, and in many cases contributing labor to businesses. The men who enslaved them called on these women to perform not only physical work but also the emotional labor of domestic caregiver. Corinna Omohundro, as we have seen, was an enslaved woman who had children with the man who enslaved her. As housekeeper, she performed the duties of a white wife without the attendant privileges and legal protections.[10]

As the histories of Omohundro, Cheatham, and Lumpkin suggest, within the sexual economy of slavery "housekeeper" was often code for a woman who performed sexual as well as domestic labor. Like "quadroon," "housekeeper" was a term with a long history that tied it to the Atlantic World. Emily Clark describes the way in which the *ménagère* of the French Caribbean translated to the *placée* of New Orleans. A *ménagère* was the housekeeper of a plantation who worked under a contract and whose labor could include "administering the budget, . . . managing the shopping, overseeing the preparation of meals, and supervising cleaning and laundry." Often a role occupied by a *mûlatresse*, the *ménagère*—always in popular discourse, if not in reality—was also the sexual partner of the white male plantation owner. After the Haitian Revolution, the *placée* gradually evolved as "a new version of the *ménagère* in New Orleans" with her "roots in the figurative and literal immigration of the Dominguan *mûlatresse* to New Orleans." Even as descriptions of *plaçage* came to dominate commentary about New Orleans, the figure of the *ménagère* did not disappear. In the 1851 case of Josephine Anna Sinnet, discussed in chapter 3, one witness described Sinnet as Uzée's "*ménagère* or mistress." In the confusion over Sinnet's position in Uzée's household, and amid witness's other descriptions of Sinnet as slave, housekeeper, concubine, and domestic, this witness felt the need to clarify what he meant by *ménagère*. He could also have used the language of *plaçage*; Only three years earlier, a newspaper report of a robbery included a description of a free woman of color, Ellen Faber, as "*placéing*" with a white man.[11]

Fiction and lore tended to glamorize the work of the *"placée"* and the *"ménagère,"* ignoring the very real physical and emotional labor they performed. Consider the case of an enslaved woman named Cynthia, whose story William Wells Brown included in a narrative of his time in slavery. While enslaved by a trader named Walker, Brown met Cynthia, a "quadroon . . . and one of the most beautiful women I ever saw." Walker purchased her "for the New Orleans market." On the way to New Orleans, however, Walker decided he wanted Cynthia to labor for him rather than one of his customers, so he "took her back to St. Louis, established her as his concubine and housekeeper at his farm and . . . had two children with her." It is significant that Brown, when writing of Cynthia, used the term "housekeeper" three times and "mistress" only once. Housekeeper, more so than mistress, conveyed the nature of the labor Cynthia would have to perform. In addition to sexual labor, Cynthia managed Walker's household while he was away trading and raised the four children she bore him. When Walker found a white housekeeper who could claim the title of legal wife and give birth to legal heirs, however, he sold Cynthia and her children back into the slave market.[12]

Domestic labor took place in private, intimate spaces, and it made domestic workers vulnerable to sexual abuse, especially as public discourse often associated domestic labor with sexual availability. To be both enslaved and a domestic was to be doubly exposed to such dangers. Even when an enslaved domestic was not a concubine or in any way sexually tied to her enslaver, many observers nonetheless assumed that she was. Recall how Lewis N. Shelton struggled to separate Sarah Conner's domestic labor for Theophilus Freeman from her sexual labor for him. He knew Conner was "in the service of Theophilus Freeman" but could not define their relationship beyond saying that he "did not know whether the plaintiff lived with Theophilus Freeman as a concubine or not. Saw her at his house as a domestic." In such cases, observers also tended to assume that the concubine or housekeeper was dependent on the male head of household, ignoring the labor that she performed to sustain said household.[13]

Like Conner, Martha Harris, a free woman of color residing in New Orleans, acted as housekeeper for slave trader O. B. Chapin. The exact nature of Harris's relationship with Chapin is difficult to determine from the testimony of Chapin's white male acquaintances. According to one, Chapin was "not a married man" and "a colored woman of the name of Martha Harris [has] taken charge of the House." Since he did not live with a wife, some of Chapin's acquaintances assumed that Harris's position as housekeeper extended to both domestic and sexual duties. Particularly when the man in question returned to a house managed by an enslaved or free black woman "at meal times and at night," acquaintances could easily imply that the relationship was not purely professional. The images of the *ménagère*, the "fancy," and the quadroon were so strong in the popular imagination that separating fact from fiction, and domestic from sexual labor, was difficult for many observers.[14]

Mary Lumpkin had to navigate these complicated and contradictory narratives about race, homes, and housework when she testified about Lucy Cheatham's life and her own. What was Cheatham's relationship to the father of her children? Where did she make her home? Who counted as her family? When speaking to the clerk of court, Lumpkin carefully recounted Cheatham's life as a series of respectable domestic situations. She met Cheatham, Lumpkin explained, when Lucy was "living with Mr. Betses." Hidden in that short statement was a secret history of sexual violence, family separation, and imprisonment. Cheatham was not merely "living" with "Mr. Betses," she was kept in his slave jail.[15]

"Mr. Betses" was William Betts, a slave trader and auctioneer based out of Richmond who also happened to be a commissioner of the Traders' Bank of Richmond. Betts was a longtime associate of Robert Lumpkin, the slave trader who enslaved and had children with Mary Lumpkin. Betts worked near both Lumpkin and Silas Omohundro in the slave-trading district of the city. It was likely through Betts's connection to Robert Lumpkin that Mary and Lucy first came into contact.[16]

Mary Lumpkin used domestic work to explain her initial relationship with Cheatham. Lumpkin reported to the clerk of court that Cheatham "used to do my sewing for me[;] that is how I became acquainted with her." At the time of their meeting, Mary Lumpkin had been Robert Lumpkin's enslaved concubine for at least two years. She already had two daughters by him, Martha and Anna, and was apparently no longer responsible for her own sewing. This sewing may have been for Lumpkin and their children or it may have been for the people Robert Lumpkin jailed and sold. As Lumpkin's enslaved concubine, Mary could order other enslaved women to perform domestic work for her. Yet Mary did not view Lucy as less than her or try to keep her distance from her in an effort to maintain hierarchy. Rather, the two women struck up a friendship. As Mary later recalled, "We Lucy Ann Hagan and myself were very intimate ever since I first became acquainted with her. She always confided in me since we first became acquainted."[17]

Brought together by sewing, Lucy and Mary became confidants. What did the two young women discuss? What did Mary tell Lucy about her life and ties to Robert Lumpkin? Evidence of the experiences of enslaved concubines is scant, and the rare and exceptional testimony of Mary Lumpkin provides some of the only concrete evidence of enslaved concubines finding comfort and solace in the company of women in similar situations. While it is but one example, it speaks to survival and coping strategies, and hints that it was more than a coincidence that so many of these women ended up living close to one another when they were free.

Yet, while they were enslaved, Lucy and Mary could not remain close physically. Lucy was soon to lose her confidant and find herself in a situation nearly identical to Mary's. Around 1848, John Hagan, one of Robert Lumpkin's business associates from New Orleans, made his annual trip to Richmond and purchased Lucy Ann Cheatham. What did Hagan initially think when he saw Cheatham? Was his plan to sell her in the fancy market in New Orleans, or did he immediately plan to keep her as his enslaved concubine?

In the words of Mary Lumpkin, Cheatham "left for New Orleans" on 15 December 1848. While Lumpkin presented this story to the clerk of court as a personal decision—Cheatham simply "went" to Louisiana when she was "very young"—the reality was much harsher. John Hagan purchased Cheatham and placed her on board the *Cyane* with sixty-five other enslaved men and women, all destined for the jails and auction rooms of Hagan or his New Orleans associates. Four other women and eight men accompanied Cheatham as Hagan's property.

Cheatham endured the *Cyane* for almost a month. During that month at sea, life for Cheatham could not have been pleasant. Just as enslaved women were at risk of sexual abuse on the overland journey to New Orleans, they faced similar risks at sea. Captains and officers, as well as any traders who might be on board, often selected several enslaved women and sequestered them in their private cabins. Before the *Creole* revolt, for instance, the ship's captain had ordered six enslaved women brought to his quarters for "housekeeping and maid duties." Again, sexual labor was disguised under the veil of domestic labor in the captain's transparent attempt to conceal his true motives. The names of two of the women the captain selected were recorded: Rachel Glover, who was about thirty, and Mary, a "mulatto" of around thirteen years. Lucy Cheatham's age and appearance were similar to Mary's; her experiences on board may have been as well.[18]

Will of John Hagan, February 15, 1856
To Lucy Ann Cheatham . . . Ten thousand Dollars ($10,000)
for services rendered me as a nurse while sick

Lucy Ann Cheatham first set foot in the Crescent City on 12 January 1849. She arrived as the designated property of John Hagan. The man who had purchased her was thirty-six. He was unmarried, and part of a family network of slave traders that spanned three states. Hagan had two brothers, Hugh and Alexander, with whom he worked buying and selling enslaved people. They had been active in the trade since at least the early 1830s, beginning their business operations in Charleston, South Carolina, and traveling back and forth to New Orleans. In the 1840s and 1850s the Hagan brothers strategically based themselves in the three major markets of the slave trade at that time: Richmond, Virginia; Charleston, South Carolina; and New Orleans.[19]

Hugh Hagan resided in Richmond, where he oversaw the purchasing of enslaved people to be sold in the New Orleans market. Hugh may have provided the Hagan brothers' connection to Robert Lumpkin, as he sometimes conducted business out of Lumpkin's jail. The eldest brother, Alexander, remained in Charleston, where he stayed until financial trouble drove him out in the 1840s. After this, the brothers used their mother Rosanna's residence in Charleston as a base of operations. They stayed with her during annual visits to purchase slaves and occasionally asked her to witness documents. Alexander reported that John "always leaves [New Orleans] in summer to purchase slaves at the north and he could not do without going." The Hagans also had assistance in Charleston from Rosanna's brothers, Hugh and Alexander McDonald, slave traders and bankers.[20]

John Hagan, the middle brother, settled in New Orleans around 1838. At the time of Lucy Cheatham's arrival, Hagan owned adjoining lots on Esplanade Avenue between Victory and Moreau streets. Hagan purchased the property from Hope H. Slatter, another slave trader with family connections to upper South slave markets. On Slatter's former land, Hagan maintained a slave jail as well as a living space. If not before, then upon her arrival in New Orleans, Hagan decided to make Lucy Cheatham his enslaved concubine, and he brought her to live with him on Esplanade.

According to Mary Lumpkin, Hagan did not make Cheatham his enslaved concubine until she was in New Orleans. Lumpkin heard four or five months after Cheatham's arrival that the young woman "was married." In Lumpkin's narrative of Cheatham's life, the sexual violence and exploitation of enslaved women inherent in the slave market were buried in the language of nineteenth-century domesticity. Did Lumpkin make this narrative transformation to protect her friend's painful history, to soothe her own psyche, or to keep her inner self protected from prying white eyes? Perhaps it was all of these factors that led Lumpkin to paint a strategic picture of Cheatham's life with John Hagan. Lumpkin told Dawson, "She wrote to me telling me about her marriage and she directed me to address her letters to Lucy Ann Hagan in care of (her husband) John Hagan." That was all Mary Lumpkin said on the matter.[21]

What could Lucy have told Mary in that letter? Could words convey the experiences and trials she had faced? Would she, too, have simply stated that she was married? Would those few words convey to Mary Lumpkin the reality of Cheatham's situation, given Mary's own life with Robert Lumpkin? There is only documentary evidence of Lucy Ann Cheatham's name, her age, her height, her skin tone, and her market value—all the matters that concerned those men who bought and sold her for profit. The apparent limits of the archive, however, should not prevent us from considering Lucy Ann Cheatham, and not just the men who purchased and sold her, as an individual person.

Perhaps after Cheatham arrived at the jail complex on Esplanade, she had a conversation with Hagan similar to the one Louisa Picquet had with the man who purchased her. On the boat ride to his residence, John Williams informed Picquet, a young enslaved woman, that she was to be his enslaved concubine. In Picquet's words, "Mr. Williams told me what he bought me for. . . . He said he was getting old, and when he saw me he thought he'd buy me, and end his days with me." Picquet bore Williams four children, ran his household, and nursed him before his death. Picquet remembered, "I did all the work in his house—nobody there but me and the children." Enslaved concubines, then, were not just kept by wealthy men. Picquet had no other enslaved women to assist her in her work or provide her company.[22]

Having separated from his legal wife, Williams relied on Picquet for many forms of labor. He had children from his former wife, as well as four with Picquet, and he needed Picquet to raise them. Picquet washed, cooked, cleaned, and otherwise kept the household in order. When Williams became ill, he relied on Picquet to nurse him. Beyond this domestic and sexual labor, Williams also clearly relied on Picquet for emotional labor. Williams wanted to "end his days" with Picquet—he wanted a companion. On their first day together, Louisa remembered, "He said if I behave myself he'd treat me well: but, if not, he'd whip me almost to death." Williams wanted the keeper of his household to "look bright" just as Theophilus Freeman wanted the people in his sale rooms to. Williams did not want a disobedient concubine; he wanted a pleasant, subservient one. To perform happiness and obedience was emotional labor, and the value of that labor was significant.[23]

Williams's proposition to Picquet—a choice that was not a choice at all—also illustrates the value of what Emily Alyssa Owens calls "affective objects" within the sexual economy of slavery. The market made enslaved women's "utterances like consent"—apparent if not true acquiescence—objects of value. Some slave traders eroticized the appearance of consent, submission, and deference, pursuing enslaved women as ways to exemplify mastery and virility in forms other than physical force alone. To quote Sharon Block, "A master did not have to rely on physical abilities to force his dependents into a sexual act" when his privileged position allowed him to place enslaved women in impossible situations, both physically and emotionally.[24]

An 1855 letter from slave trader S. H. Christian in Raleigh to Richmond trader R. H. Dickinson exemplifies this self-centered, competitive sexual violence. Christian wrote to Dickinson of an anonymous "girl" whose name was unimportant to Christian but whom he sought as a sexual conquest. Christian complained to Dickinson, "I never courted a woman white or black half as much" but he was "now fully convinced that I can do nothing with her at all." Rather than boasting of sexual conquest, Christian played the part of a spurned lover, claiming, despite evidence otherwise, "I cannot and will not abuse her—have been as kind as to one of my children." In his mind, Christian was the victim, believing the woman was "disposed to abuse me on all ocations [sic] and has exposed me to her associates in the city for even maken [sic] a proposition." To Christian, this was a game: he made a "proposition" and was disappointed the woman was not willing to play along.[25]

Hidden behind Christian's banter with Dickinson was a history of sexual abuse and an individual woman's agony. Before Christian, Dickinson had enslaved the unnamed woman and only later sent her to his colleague. She believed (likely correctly) that Dickinson had sent her away "for not gratifying" him after he "had made the attempt." She made additional complaints to Christian about Dickinson, which Christian "will not mention of course [I] do not believe them." Yet the woman would not be silenced. While Dickinson and Christian continued to pretend that Dickinson had obeyed her refusal of his "attempt," she accused Dickinson of giving her a sexually transmitted disease. Christian defended Dickinson, reportedly saying "that you [Dickinson] did not disease her." He, too, then "made the attempt" just as Dickinson had.[26]

The unnamed woman had been sexually assaulted by two men who enslaved her and who seem to have passed her and other enslaved women between themselves. She was deeply unhappy; as Christian callously complained, "she is always crying or in a bad umer [*sic*] never saw her smile. Just such a negro as I would not have to keep at any price." Just like Williams, Christian expected the woman he enslaved to perform the part of a happy and obedient concubine. Trapped between Dickinson and Christian, and refusing to pretend contentment, the woman surveyed her surroundings and turned to another trader named Golden for help. She complained to Golden of Christian's behavior, and he was happy to play the role of honorable savior. Golden told her that Christian "was no Gentleman if [he] would offer to sleap [*sic*] with her and that she was above such things." That Golden was potentially the most sympathetic ear that the woman could find speaks to the lack of options before her.[27]

Golden and the woman were a source of entertainment and gossip for Christian and Dickinson. Dickinson thought the woman was manipulating Golden for her own benefit, but Christian disagreed. "She has no secrets," he wrote Dickinson, "and will admit staying with Golden. You are mistaken about her not loving Golden she does love him no mistake." To Christian, within the sexual economy of slavery, this was what love looked like. An enslaved woman's desperate attempt to escape her two tormentors turned into, in Christian's words, consent, willingness, and desire.[28]

Even as he speculated about the woman loving his business associate, Christian was already recalculating how he could profit from her body. Since she refused to perform the emotional and sexual labor he required, Christian would get his value in another way: by sending her back to Dickinson to sell. He mused, "She does not know but what I intend to keep her and has no idea that she is to be taken back not the most distant." The woman had no control over where she was or whose control she would be under next. As she continued to be in a "bad umer," Christian apologized to his friend for the trouble and asked how to proceed, saying he "will offer her if you say so — set your price." As the unnamed woman disappeared back into the slave market, Christian awaited another potential enslaved concubine from Dickinson, writing, "If . . . you have another good girl and will send her by G [Golden] I will give a fair price for her."[29]

Had John Hagan "made an attempt" or a "proposition" with Cheatham? Or had he exercised his legal power over her body more directly, unconcerned with her response? Had Cheatham, like the unnamed woman, cried ceaselessly, or had she, like Picquet, followed her enslaver's orders, at least on the surface? Even as Picquet humored Williams for her own survival, she reported feeling relief when he died.

The name of Lucy's eldest child can provide some clues to her mindset. Her first and only daughter was born on 21 November 1850, around a year after Cheatham's arrival in New Orleans. When she named her first child, Lucy made a daring statement, though it was one that was never apparent to Hagan. John Hagan believed his daughter's name was Dolly, and he wrote as much in legal documents before his death. After he died, however, Cheatham and her daughter always wrote her name in full: Frederika Bremer Hagan. Cheatham chose to name her first child in honor of a Swedish reformer who had publicly criticized both slavery and women's subjugation.[30]

Though Bremer's most famous work concerning the United States, the two-volume set *Homes of the New World*, was not published until 1853 and 1854, her fiction was available to purchase in New Orleans. Additionally, Bremer actually visited New Orleans in December 1850, and local newspapers tracked her progress as she traveled south. She visited several of the city's slave jails, spoke with slave traders, and attended at least one auction. Cheatham could have met or glimpsed Bremer during her visit; at the very least she was aware of Bremer's political beliefs. None of the slave traders Bremer met were pleased by her presence. It may have been beyond her power to escape John Hagan, but Lucy Cheatham remained defiant in whatever ways she could.[31]

After the birth of Frederika Bremer Hagan, Cheatham had three more children, all boys. John Alexander Hagan, born in 1854, died only a year later. William Alexander Hagan was born shortly after, on 20 October 1855. The birth and subsequent death of at least one other son was difficult for Lucy. Mary Lumpkin reported that "Lucy Ann Hagan told me that she had two boys and but one girl and that she would like to have another girl. That was before one of the boys died then after that one died she said she had had three children and that she did not want to have any more."[32]

Cheatham had the assistance of other women when giving birth to and raising her children. A woman named Mary Wilson attended her in the birth of at least one of her sons. Wilson, who became a lifelong friend of Cheatham's, was likely Mary Nelson Wilson, the concubine of J. M. Wilson. Mary Wilson later remembered that "[she] had known her [Cheatham] since 1850. We were neighbors, and were quite intimate. . . . When I was first acquainted with her I was living on Esplanade St. between Royal and Chartres, she lived in the same block with me." In 1850, J. M. Wilson operated a slave jail at 15 Esplanade, not far from Hagan's compound. The 1860 Census included a Virginia-born "mulatto" woman Mary Nelson and her six children in Wilson's household. Tellingly, the census taker listed Mary as J. M. Wilson's "housekeeper." J. M. Wilson likely had children with another enslaved woman as well. On 19 April 1856, Wilson emancipated "Caroline Williams 27 years yellow complexion and her two children Alice and Valentine. The former aged five years and the latter aged eighteen months." Based on the behavior of Wilson's associates, he was likely emancipating his enslaved concubine and two children with her.[33]

Cheatham became close with at least two other women in New Orleans, Magnolia Phelps and Mary Wood, who are harder to locate in the records but who remained in contact with Cheatham the entire time she was in the city. She may have also known other enslaved concubines including Ann Maria Barclay, Louisa Peterson, and Sarah Conner. The business networks of slave traders were close. Nearly every slave trader in New Orleans had at one time or another roomed with, done business with, or served as a witness for, every other slave trader in town. As the enslaved concubine of Hagan's associate Henry F. Peterson, Cheatham likely met Louisa F. Peterson. Henry F. Peterson had served as a security for Sarah Conner for one of her court bonds, and he put Louisa Peterson at risk of sale when he and Conner failed to pay the same. Ann Maria Barclay, the enslaved concubine of another New Orleans slave trader, George Ann Botts, like Sarah Conner, had to fight to maintain her freedom despite Botts's emancipation of her in Cincinnati.[34]

Cheatham also remained in contact with Mary Lumpkin, both through letters and through physical visits. The two women continued to write one another regularly. Lumpkin remembered that she "corresponded with her [Cheatham] ever since she left Virginia up to the time she came back to Virginia on a visit in 1858 I think it was." Lumpkin's testimony is an extraordinary testament to the power of female friendship networks and the resilience of two enslaved women in the face of adversity. Not only did Cheatham and Lumpkin routinely exchange letters, they used their communication as a source of strength and resistance for themselves and other women around them.[35]

Resistance is often understood as the prerogative of men, associated with armed rebellion, physical violence, and flight. Yet as Stephanie Camp has pointed out, more subtle forms of subversion were far more common, and far more likely to be practiced by enslaved women. These acts were no less bold for their lack of violence or physical aggression. They are also often harder to pin down: How does one measure or interpret quieter rebellions? Studying enslaved women's resistance requires "creative approaches: a shift from the visible and organized to the hidden and informal, as well as rigorous attention paid to personal topics that, for enslaved women, were also political." In the friendship of Lucy and Mary, we have evidence of feminine resistance that is no less important for its apparent passivity. When Lucy wrote to Mary, she fought to keep ties with friends and family that John Hagan and the impersonal factors of the slave market had tried to tear asunder. Lucy refused to be isolated in New Orleans; she refused to lose touch with her kin in Virginia.

In fact, she used her position in Hagan's household, where she had some access to money and material goods, to assist her loved ones.[36] While John Hagan was busy buying and selling enslaved people, Lucy Ann Cheatham Hagan was busy writing and sending provisions to her mother and half-sisters, who were still enslaved in Richmond. Cheatham had somehow learned to read and write, and she put these abilities to good use. Her mother and half-sisters, however, either could not read or did not have the ability to send and receive letters. In order to contact them, Cheatham relied on her female friends. When she wrote Mary Lumpkin, Cheatham included messages, money, and clothing for her mother and sisters in her letters. Lumpkin recalled "Lucy's mother, after I became acquainted with her, got messages and letters in my letters from Lucy Ann Hagan, she received letters from Lucy Ann Hagan through me, and also bundles or packages, such as a dress to the old lady from Lucy. She did send some packages of her own clothes to two half sisters of hers," as well as "some money from Lucy Ann Hagan which she had sent to her mother." Trapped in a situation beyond her control, Lucy seized whatever benefits she could, and extended these to her family back in Richmond.[37]

Beginning around 1853, Cheatham also reunited with family and friends in person, taking her children on nearly annual trips to Richmond. Some years Cheatham accompanied Hagan when he traveled to Virginia to buy enslaved people. On these trips the entire family lodged at Lumpkin's jail. Mary Lumpkin remembered, "She [Lucy] came every other year and two summers in succession, the years the yellow fever was so bad, and she always stopped with me," adding, "I don't suppose her mother could accommodate her so well." More likely, John Hagan wanted to stay with his friend and business associate Robert Lumpkin rather than with an enslaved woman and her two children, whose domestic spaces were not legally theirs. That, however, was a detail that Mary Lumpkin did not share with the clerk of courts. During these visits, the Lumpkin household, next to the slave jail, was comprised of two slave traders, the enslaved women with whom they had children, and those children. What would an evening together at "home" have looked like for these women?[38]

Though Cheatham did not stay with her mother and half-sisters, her relatives came to visit her often while she was at Lumpkin's. What must they have thought, seeing Lucy staying as a guest in a house next to a slave jail? By that point, however, Cheatham's mother and Mary Lumpkin had become friends and saw one another even when Lucy was not in town. Perhaps Cheatham's family was accustomed to visiting Lumpkin's jail. They must have met, or at least caught a glimpse of, John Hagan as he made his business deals. Mary Lumpkin said, "While said John Hagan, Lucy's husband, was living he always came with Lucy Ann Hagan from New Orleans to visit Richmond Va and they always put up with me, that is visited me and they always roomed and slept together." Lumpkin emphasized the domestic, intimate ties of Hagan and Cheatham: they "roomed and slept together." Cheatham may not have been afforded the privileges of legal marriage in life, but Lumpkin, through her testimony, hoped to allow Cheatham and her children that respect in death.[39]

Lucy Ann Cheatham had been sharing a domestic space with John Hagan for around seven years when Hagan died on 8 June 1856. Her fate, to a large extent, rested on how Hagan managed his affairs in life and how he instructed others to manage them after his death. John Hagan wrote two wills before he died. In the first, Cheatham and her daughter were listed as his enslaved property. In the second, Cheatham and her two living children were included as free beneficiaries of the will. In the first will of August 1855, Hagan wrote, "It is my wish that my slave Lucy Ann Cheatham and her daughter Dolly, or any other children Lucy may have, be immediately emancipated and all expenses paid out of my estate." To his children, Hagan also willed the lot on Esplanade Street and $5,000 "in cash to maintain them." He then went on to appease his other family members, leaving his mother $40,000 cash and each of his siblings significant sums, as well. He made a point to acknowledge he owed a large debt of $80,000 to his brother Alexander Hagan. Anticipating problems with the settlement of his estate, Hagan added a clause significant to the fate of Lucy and the children: "In case this will cannot be carried into effect, then I wish my mother to have all I may possess, except the woman Lucy Ann Cheatam [sic], and Dolly (child or children) who I wish set free, as soon as possible, said slave having contributed in ready cash a sufficient sum to pay for her freedom." To carry out his wishes, Hagan appointed his brother Alexander and his longtime friend Edward Barnett, who was a go-to notary for slave traders and a former agent of trader J. M. Wilson. In the event of either of these men's deaths, Hagan selected his lawyer of over a decade and frequent legal representative of slave traders, the prominent attorney Christian Roselius.[40]

Between August 1855 and June 1856, during the course of John Hagan's long illness, Lucy Ann Cheatham's legal status changed, and just in time. Shortly after, in 1857, Louisiana outlawed individual manumissions altogether. Though the documents are missing from the archives, Hagan must have used the court system to free Cheatham and their children, because he no longer emancipated them in his second will. Rather, he left them $10,000 and the lot on Esplanade Street. Hagan specified that the money was due to Cheatham for "services rendered me as a nurse while sick." In a statement evocative of the work of *ménagères* of the French Caribbean, John Hagan justified his bequest to Cheatham and their children while still veiling it under the guise of domestic, and not sexual, labor. Even with this clause, Hagan continued to foresee trouble. He made a point to note "I . . . desire that Christian Roselius be employed as the lawyer if one is needed."[41]

Perhaps because of his attention to detail, John Hagan's will was executed without any legal contest. His estate inventory, taken by Alexander Hagan and Edward Barnett, was a testament to the wealth he attained through the slave trade, and to his continued interest in financial markets. At his death, Hagan owned forty-three drafts totaling $121,235.61 in money due him. To this his executors added ten promissory notes worth $24,645.50, and four due bills valued at $47,720.84. The largest of these was from Alexander Hagan, who by then owed John $26,159.84. The remainder of Hagan's assets were in real estate and household goods. He owned the two lots of ground bequeathed to Lucy and the children, as well as a lot of ground in the Fourth District and five lots of ground in Lafayette.[42]

John Hagan's estate totaled $253,091.93. Considering this sum, Lucy and the Hagan children received a paltry inheritance: the house on Esplanade was worth $4,000 and the furniture a little over $300. The additional $10,000 to the children was helpful but nothing in comparison to the amounts Hagan's white relatives received. Yet, perhaps because she received so little, Cheatham faced no opposition from the Hagan family.[43]

Despite her comparably small inheritance, Lucy Ann Cheatham was by the latter part of 1856 in control of her own money and her own future. Using the finances, skills, and experiences she already had, Cheatham took the path of many former enslaved concubines: she began taking on renters in a house on Customhouse Street. The 1850s were a wise time for Cheatham to enter this business. According to one of her contemporaries, "times were prosperous, business of all kinds flourishing, and in a prosperous condition. Strangers from all parts of the country were flocking to the city giving encouragement particularly to those keeping Hotels & Boarding Houses."[44]

As a provider of furnished rooms, Cheatham entered a particular occupation distinct from running a boardinghouse or hotel. Hotels were primarily, but not exclusively, the province of male proprietors. They were usually larger, requiring more capital and grander amenities. Boardinghouses provided lodging as well as regular meals ("board") at a common table each day. They could be public, which meant they offered meals for a fee to individuals not lodging there, or private. Private boardinghouses were supposedly more respectable, limiting their services to lodgers. Women who advertised "furnished rooms," "rooms to let," or "rented rooms," in contrast, offered only dwelling spaces, usually furnished, for rent. Occasionally, people who rented rooms would offer meals, but only if the renter paid an additional fee.[45]

Unlike hotels, running boardinghouses and renting rooms was primarily the work of women. Even when men owned the property or claimed to be the proprietor, it was usually a woman who interacted with boarders and maintained the business. In New Orleans' Fifth Ward, for example, Cheatham was one of forty-three women who rented out furnished rooms. The census taker considered eleven of these women mulatto, ten black, and twenty-two white. The census also listed one black and five white female boardinghouse keepers in 1860. The female proprietors of rooms and boardinghouses in the Fifth Ward came from a variety of backgrounds; Marie Albert was born in Germany; Jeanne Clemens in France; and Widow Moran in Havana. They also worked with a range of economic assets. Pauline Girard, a white woman born in Louisiana, owned $12,000 in real estate, while Arthemsia Francois, a black woman also from Louisiana, owned no real estate.[46]

The city placed more regulations on boardinghouses than on rented rooms. According to the 1858 City Ordinances, hotel and boardinghouse keepers had to register with the city, obtain a license, and pay a tax. The amount paid depended on the number of people housed; the fewer people one boarded, the less the tax. Overall in the First through Fifth Wards, New Orleans had slightly more keepers of furnished rooms than boardinghouses, with 151 proprietors of rooms and 125 proprietors of boardinghouses. While white women were just as likely to keep rooms as boardinghouses, women of color were far more likely to keep furnished rooms. Only two women of color ran boardinghouses in these wards, compared to seventy-five rooms to let. This was likely due to a combination of fees, taxes, and the requirement for licensing. Women of color may have been less desirous of going to the city government for a license.[47]

Even if they did not provide board, the labor involved in renting out lodgings was substantial. As a keeper of rented rooms, Cheatham had the daily tasks of emptying slop jars, sweeping private rooms and common areas, brushing carpets, and cleaning chamber pots. She also had to regularly launder bed linens (and potentially pick bed bugs from them), take up and beat carpets, wash the walls, restock candles or oil for light, clean windows and other glass, and wash the curtains. Some landladies included laundry in the price of rent or room and board, while some offered the service for an extra fee. Others refused to deal with laundry at all, leaving customers to find washerwomen to hire.[48]

Boarders and renters often also expected, even if they did not receive, emotional labor on their behalf. As they exchanged money for domestic space, many lodgers could not separate this market transaction from assumptions about women's supposed nature. They expected the feminine virtue of selfless nurturing from their landlady and when such nurturing was not forthcoming, they readily impugned a landlady's character. Ignoring the fact that the landlady had to make a living, lodgers turned on the woman they believed owed them emotional labor.[49]

Ideological battles over the limits of domestic and emotional labor often came to the fore over nursing. Caring for sick family members was women's work, and boarders expected a landlady to fulfill a similar role. Take, for instance, the case of Eliza Hammond, a free woman of color who rented out rooms in the Third Ward of New Orleans. Hammond was a seasoned landlady who offered specific domestic tasks for specific fees. Unlike many women who rented rooms, Hammond owned a considerable amount of personal property, which the census taker valued at $4,300 in 1860. Hammond rented a bedroom and adjacent parlor for a relatively steep sum, $60 a month. The rent of this space did not include any additional labor, but Hammond would do laundry and provide meals for an extra charge. Breakfast cost around $15 a month; laundry services required an additional $10.[50]

Hammond's fees became a point of contention when she attempted to recover $328.38 from a boarder who had been ill. Englishman T. B. Blackburn lodged with Hammond from 3 February to 6 April 1855. In addition to the monthly rent, cost of breakfast, and laundry, Hammond charged Blackburn for "services rendered him during illness for 55 days," "extra gas and fire during illness," and "renovating worn spring mattress carpet matting & table cloth spoiled." When Blackburn had hired a professional nurse, Hammond had lodged her for a reduced rate. Blackburn, however, refused to pay all that Hammond asked, calling her fees "illegal, excessive, and exorbitant." He agreed to pay a "reasonable" amount for such services as were rendered but found her request "malicious" and considered it "an attempt to extort money." Though he did not dispute the $60 a month in rent, the laundry charges, or the fees for board, Blackburn discounted the significant work that went into caring for him during his illness, as well as the extra expenses that came with a sick lodger. It was an easy ideological jump for Blackburn to call a woman—particularly one of African descent—malicious if she charged for the full value of the care she provided.[51]

It was equally easy to use the sex and race of a landlady to impugn her morals. Women who exchanged domestic labor in the market appeared suspicious to many nineteenth-century commentators. The very act of making such supposedly altruistic work a commercial exchange was a cause for concern. Landladies performed the work of wives—cleaning, laundering, cooking, nursing—and often in close physical proximity to men. Some men assumed that other wifely duties were also available to them. It didn't help landladies' moral standing that some brothels operated under the guise of boardinghouses, or that houses of assignation placed advertisements for "rooms to let, with board for the lady only."[52]

The risk of sexual abuse was even greater for free women of color who rented lodgings and for enslaved laborers who worked in them. Proslavery ideologues already argued that women of color were promiscuous and sexually available to white men, how much more so for women of color in commercialized domestic spaces? The anonymous author of New Orleans As It Is, though he or she criticized slavery and the sale of enslaved women for sex, assumed that "quadroon girls" who had "lost [their] charms" operated "the lowest grade brothels in New Orleans," where one could find "a large number of men, boarding and lodging, who are seen in the morning, creeping out through some back lane or alley." The author conflated paying for domestic labor in a boardinghouse with paying for sex. While some free woman of color did operate brothels, the author assumed that *every* free woman of color who exchanged domestic spaces for cash was really running a brothel. The association between light-skinned enslaved women and concubinage, and commercialized domestic labor and illicit sexuality, led them to such a conclusion.[53]

Louisa Picquet, while hired out to boardinghouse keeper Mrs. Bachelor, experienced firsthand the vulnerabilities of domestic service. The man who enslaved her at the time, David Cook, was boarding at the same house. She recalled, "One day Mr. Cook told me I must come to his room that night, and take care of him. He said he was sick, and he wanted me and another slave girl to come to his room and take care of him." Again, a slaveholder used nursing as an excuse to get an enslaved woman in close physical proximity to him, and in a private room, so that he could sexually assault her. Picquet knew the real meaning behind Cook's request, as did Mrs. Bachelor. Mrs. Bachelor decided to look after Cook herself with the help of another woman. Cook, however, continued to try to get Picquet alone in his room, eventually offering her money in exchange for visiting him. Picquet took the money and purchased a white floral muslin dress, but then refused to go to Cook's room.[54]

Enslaved women who ran boardinghouses or rented out rooms were also vulnerable to assault. Although this was against New Orleans ordinances, enslaved women did operate as well as work in rented lodgings. Rashauna Johnson, for instance, notes the case of Susan, an enslaved woman who boarded sailors in her home. Susan ran into trouble when her boarders complained that she was not doing their laundry. As in other disputes between boarders and landladies, the price or inclusion with board of specific domestic tasks were points of contention. When enslaved boardinghouse keepers displeased customers, they were at risk of personal violence from the customer as well as from the person who enslaved or hired them out, revealing "the risks that enslaved female services workers experienced inside the global households in which they labored."[55]

Even when free, women of color were still at risk if boarders decided to question their legal status. Whether as means of avoiding payment or exacting revenge, boarders could argue that their landlady was enslaved and thus not able to sue for back rent. Bringing into question one's freedom meant not only derailing a landlady's pursuit of payment, it could also mean enslavement. Mary Powell, a formerly enslaved woman, experienced these risks when she sued her former renter, Joseph McQuiston, for $75 "room rent washing and board." Though Powell had gained her freedom eleven years earlier in 1849, McQuiston asked for the case against him to be dismissed because "the plaintiff is a slave and consequently has no right of action." Powell had to then produce proof of her emancipation before the case could proceed. Based only on the color of her skin, McQuiston could stall the case and call into question his former landlady's freedom.[56]

Lucy Ann Cheatham v. Her Creditors, May 11, 1863
Ordinary Debts . . . Sampson & Keene [Furniture Dealers] due $469.50

As she rented out rooms on Customhouse Street, Cheatham chose in 1861 to move back to Esplanade Street to the slave-trading compound John Hagan had purchased from Hope Slatter but to do so on her own terms. Rather than return to the building she had lived in with Hagan, Cheatham ordered it demolished. On 21 August 1861 Cheatham signed a contract with John R. Hobson to build a new two-story home after tearing the old structure down. Cheatham instructed him to use as much of the old brick as possible in constructing the new, repurposing the material of a difficult past to build a future of her own design. Cheatham wanted the home painted in imitation brick, the front rooms papered with "the best paper," and marble fireplace mantles in the parlors. Cheatham then arranged for Hobson to build a second, identical dwelling on the adjoining lot, presumably after the jail and salerooms were demolished.[57]

Unfortunately, Cheatham chose to finance her renovations using tactics similar to those John Hagan had used to purchase enslaved people, and 1861 was not a fortuitous time to be issuing promissory notes and mortgaging property. Cheatham signed promissory notes to pay for most of the building expenses, as well as more mundane bills, such as those for clothing and medical care. In many cases the recipient required Cheatham to secure payment of the promissory note by mortgaging or hypothecating some of her property. Cheatham paid the builder, Hobson, with fourteen promissory notes totaling $5,000, payable at predetermined intervals at the Bank of Louisiana. She also hypothecated the land on Esplanade to Hobson in the event of nonpayment. Other debts she secured with mortgages on her home and the bank stock she inherited from Hagan, often mortgaging the same property more than once.[58]

Cheatham chose to secure further debts by taking out mortgages on an enslaved boy she owned, George, and an enslaved woman, Martha. After Hagan's death, Cheatham invested not only in land but also in people. She purchased seven enslaved people; she bought four people from Alexander Hagan, suggesting the sale may have actually been part of her inheritance from John Hagan. Interestingly, all of the enslaved people Cheatham purchased were described as "mulatto," "yellow," or "grifonne," and the only two men she enslaved were young. From Alexander Hagan, she purchased Martha, "griffonne," about twenty-eight years old; Lavinia, "griffonne," about twenty years old, Isaac, "griffe," about sixteen years old, and Margaret, "griffonne, an orphan," aged about nine years. A year later Cheatham purchased from Bernard Kendig, an old trading associate of John Hagan's, a "yellow boy," George, who was thirteen. Finally, in 1859, when she purchased land in the second district, she also bought Mary, a thirty-two-year-old "mulatress" and her daughter, Alice Ann, age two.[59]

Given the available evidence on Lucy Cheatham, it seems unlikely she purchased these enslaved women and children for personal profit. She had, after all, named her daughter Frederika Bremer, and kept in close contact with her own enslaved family members in Virginia. Perhaps Cheatham saw circumstances similar to her own in those people she bought. Yet even if Cheatham identified with these women, self-interest eventually took over and she mortgaged George and Martha to secure her debts. She had already mortgaged and hypothecated all of the other property she owned before she did so, however; the mortgages on George and Martha were the final ones she took before filing for bankruptcy. And when her creditors came calling, looking to liquidate her assets by selling George and Martha, she defiantly told them "the slaves . . . are all run away."[60]

In an effort to solve her financial issues without outside interference, Cheatham decided to sell some of her personal property. Before 1863 she sold most of her household furniture, worth "from $1500 to $2000," "as well as a small quantity of jewelry." As a renter of furnished rooms, her household furniture was one of her greatest assets. Even some of the money Cheatham owed was for the purchase of other furniture: $469.50 worth from Sampson & Keene, New Orleans furniture dealers. Cheatham claimed she felt "compelled to sell" these valuable items "for the purpose of supporting herself and children, paying physicians bills, lawyers' fees & court expenses caused by certain of her greedy creditors, etc." She kept only "her linen, two beds, one for herself and one for her two children and her clothes and those of her children which are exempt by law from seizure," putting a temporary end to her renting of furnished rooms.[61]

The sale of her furniture and jewelry was not enough. In March 1863, Cheatham officially filed for bankruptcy. In an attempt to reconstruct an ideal home for herself and her children, Cheatham had overextended her finances. If the country had not been at war, she might have fulfilled this dream. Cheatham said as much to the court, reporting "within the last eighteen months she has been so unfortunate in her business and has become so much involved, owing in a very great degree to the present civil war in the United States, the consequent stagnation of business, the decrease of real estate, slaves, and bank stock." Eliza Hackman, one of the few female hotel proprietors in the city, agreed with Cheatham. She sued her landlords for lower rent, arguing that since 1861 "the protraction of business and the almost entire suspension of all intercourse between the city and country" meant "that not only your petitioner but all others keeping houses of a similar business have been hardly able to meet current expenses without the payment of rent."[62]

Filing for bankruptcy put Cheatham's children at risk. Anticipating trouble, Cheatham had, only weeks before filing, petitioned the court to be appointed the administrator of their estate, or tutrix, while they were underaged. Cheatham asked for Edward Barnett as her under tutor. As under tutor, it was Barnett's job to act in the children's interest if he felt it was contrary to Cheatham's. Shortly after the court confirmed her request, she petitioned again to convene a family meeting. The purpose of the family meeting, which took place before a justice of the peace, was to advise the tutrix, under tutor, and court on how best to handle her financial catastrophe for the sake of her children's inheritance. Normally the judge appointed at least five relatives to attend the meeting, but in the absence of biological relatives who lived nearby, eight "family friends" attended the meeting.[63]

In addition to Edward Barnett as under tutor, the family meeting included an eclectic collection of individuals. It is unclear if Cheatham personally selected each person, or if Barnett influenced her decisions. Two of the "family friends" were J. M. Wilson and H. F. Peterson, both of whom had worked with the Hagan brothers in the slave trade. Though they were an odd choice on the surface, both men also had children with enslaved women, and Cheatham may have hoped they would understand her situation. Cheatham was friends with Mary Wilson, and she likely knew Louisa Peterson as well. Another slave trader, John Buddy, also made the list of "family friends." Two of the other attendees were artisans, one a shoemaker and one a coach maker. Another two, John M. Crawford and Charles Faurie, were likely former business associates of Hagan, as they worked as secretary of the Union Insurance Company and as bookkeeper at the Crescent City Bank, respectively. One, J. M. Levy, was a "broker" who had also served as one of the appraisers of Hagan's estate.[64]

This motley collection of "family friends" decided it was in the best interest of the Hagan children to sell Cheatham's interest in the inherited bank stock. Cheatham's other creditors agreed, but at their meeting in March 1863, they found that the bank stock would not be enough to cover all of her debts. In the court-ordered inventory, her stock was only valued at $1,005, hardly enough to make her creditors happy. Four of the enslaved people whom Cheatham claimed had "run away" had been found; her creditors ordered Lavinia and her child, George, and Martha sold at public auction on 7 November 1863 at the Merchant and Auctioneer's Exchange, undoing Cheatham's attempt to hide them from the courts. All of her assets brought $2,920, which her creditors fought over. The syndic of the bankruptcy case observed that the "property was worth previous to the present war in the U.S. say $20,000.00."[65]

When the Civil War ended, Lucy Ann Cheatham was left with nearly nothing. Her time with John Hagan may have benefited her materially during his lifetime, but these benefits were fleeting. Cheatham had sent her mother and half-sisters money that had likely come from Hagan, but they remained enslaved in Richmond until the Civil War. Cheatham managed to scrape together enough money to send Frederika Bremer Hagan to school at the Mount St. Vincent Academy, a women's school in New York, for a few years, but could not pay the entirety of her daughter's room and board. Clearly, Cheatham wanted a good education for her daughter if she spent such a substantial sum on her schooling and sent her out of the South. This desire landed her in the courts again, when the school sent an agent to New Orleans to collect $592.24 in unpaid tuition. Arguably the greatest debt of all was the psychological effect of being torn from one's family as a young woman, shipped to a strange new city, and forced into concubinage. How can we measure this cost?[66]

Yet Cheatham persevered. She continued to rent out rooms in residences she leased on Bourbon Street and then Common Street in the late 1860s. Her efforts paid off: by the 1880s she had acquired two homes of her own at 38 South Rampart Street and 45 North Rampart Street and even employed two domestic servants. She and her longtime friend Mary E. Wood had sufficient funds to visit Frederika at her school in New York. Cheatham may also have acquired land in Mississippi. Though it did not appear on her estate inventory, several family members and friends referenced Cheatham owning out-of-state property.[67]

Cheatham, who by the mid- to late 1860s was going by the name Mrs. L. A. Hagan, continued to rely on her female friends for emotional and economic support. In 1860 Mary F. Lumpkin had left Richmond for Philadelphia, where she remained for the remainder of the Civil War. After Robert Lumpkin's death in 1866, she again left Richmond and traveled this time to New Orleans, where she often visited with Lucy. Cheatham lodged with various women when she was in between homes or let them stay with her. Her friendships with Mary Wilson and Mary Lumpkin outlasted the emotional toll of concubinage, civil war, economic hardship, and old age.[68]

In fact, it was at the home of Mary Wilson that Lucy Ann Cheatham died on 7 July 1887. Cheatham had stopped at her friend's house at 65 Bourbon Street to visit a few days before she traveled to Bay St. Louis in Mississippi, where she evidently owned land and could visit another friend, an African American woman named Laurette Freeman. Cheatham was only fifty-five when she died; she left behind two living children, many friends, and an estate valued at $10,307.50. While her "agent in regard to land in Mississippi," Howard Wilkinson, testified that Cheatham had dictated her will to him in the presence of Laurette Freeman, neither Wilkinson nor the courts could locate it after her death.[69]

The lack of a will opened Cheatham's estate to dispute, particularly when a man named John Thomas Clark of Manchester, Virginia, appeared on the scene and announced that he was Cheatham's only legitimate heir. Clark, born in 1846 in Chesterfield County, Virginia, petitioned the court of Orleans Parish, claiming to be the son of Lucy Ann Cheatham and Warner Clark, Cheatham's alleged husband before Hagan purchased her. Clark got many facts about Cheatham's life correct: he knew when she had landed in New Orleans, he knew that she had lived with John Hagan, and he knew that she had two children with him. These two children, he argued, were illegitimate and thus he should be the primary heir. None of Cheatham's friends or family, however, had ever heard of John Thomas Clark, and each and every one insisted that Cheatham had only two living children. Clark's claims were why L. M. Dawson approached Mary Lumpkin in 1887. He wanted to hear from Cheatham's closest friends whether or not she had a son before leaving Virginia.[70]

In the end, not even Clark's court-appointed representative could find any evidence that he was truly Cheatham's son. He was likely related in some way to Cheatham's family, but beyond that, how and why he came to New Orleans when he did is unclear. He might have caught word of the estate Cheatham had built up over the years. In any event, his claims against the estate produced a wealth of evidence about Cheatham's life, and prompted Cheatham's daughter to testify about what she knew of her mother's past, resulting in a rare interview with the female child of an enslaved concubine and a slave trader.[71]

When Cheatham died, Frederika Bremer Hagan said that she was living in New York City, where she had remained after attending school at Mount St. Vincent Academy. Yet there is no record of a Frederika Bremer Hagan, a Frederika Hagan, or a Frederika Cheatham living in New York in the second half of the nineteenth century. It is likely that Frederika, perhaps as her mother hoped she would, "passed" and created a new identity for herself in New York City, where she could blend in with thousands of other migrants. Frederika's brother William Alexander Hagan was living with his mother in 1880, working as a clerk, and going by the name W. W. Lowndes. He remained in New Orleans after Cheatham's death.

Frederika testified that she and her brother were the only two living heirs of Lucy Ann Hagan, and that after she left New Orleans in 1867, she "visited her [mother] off & on." Frederika was familiar with Mary Lumpkin, and it was at her request that the parish court commissioned L. M. Dawson to take Lumpkin's testimony. In a statement as delicately worded as Mary Lumpkin's, Frederika informed the court, "My mother told me that she had no other children & that I was her first child . . . My mother told me that she had been living with Mr. Hagan for about a year before I was born. She told me that she had never lived with anyone else or had any other husband but Mr. Hagan. She was born in Virginia. Her maiden name was Lucy Ann Cheatham & she kept the name until she went to live with Mr. Hagan."[72]

"She had never lived with anyone else." Again, buried in a seemingly benign statement was a long history of sexual violence. By presenting this dark past as a familiar, if slightly improper, tale of a young man and woman living together consensually out of wedlock, Frederika attempted to protect herself and her mother from the prying eyes of outsiders. Lucy may have never told Frederika the truth about her relationship with John Hagan, but this is unlikely. Frederika knew a great deal about her mother's life, and she knew her mother's friends. She called her father "Mr. Hagan." Since Frederika was so young when Hagan died, Frederika had never formed a relationship with her father.[73]

Lucy's daughter kept the family secret well. After 1888, when Frederika and William settled out of court with John Thomas Clark and came into possession of their mother's estate, Frederika Bremer Hagan disappeared from written record. Unlike Alice Morton Omohundro, Frederika likely never had children; she was single and thirty-seven when she returned to New Orleans. Thanks to her mother, Frederika had received a good education and had created a new life for herself in New York, far away from the gossip of neighbors and the painful reminders of the past. Frederika never looked back.

Lucy Ann Cheatham did not have that chance, and one wonders if she worked especially hard to carve out opportunities for her daughter so that Frederika could escape the hardships she herself had endured. The past haunted Cheatham throughout her life; racial tension and prejudice still shaped New Orleans and still affected Cheatham after the end of slavery. Critics of the Republican government, for instance, used Cheatham to criticize the alleged intermingling of races that Reconstruction supposedly promoted. The anonymous author of a newspaper editorial employed the trope of the Jezebel, and Cheatham's name and history, to satirize the actions of Republican representatives to a convention in the city in 1875. The author of the anonymous editorial considered Cheatham's name recognizable enough to be used as a point of reference for illicit sexuality. Signing his letter "Guppy," the man wrote sarcastically that Oliver P. Morton, a visiting Republican representative from Indiana, who was "a white man as far as color of the skin goes," "ought to be taken care of while he remains" in the city. Guppy facetiously implored the "dark hued faithful" to "do the right thing by him [Morton]" and show him a good time in the city. Specifically, P. S. Pinchback, a politician and the first African American governor of Louisiana, and T. B. Stamps, an African American state senator, should "trot him around. Take him out to Lucy Hagan's and make him acquainted with the dusky ones, and introduce him to the mysteries of Mahogany Hall."[74]

Twenty years after John Hagan's death, and after twenty years of hard work and freedom, Lucy Ann Cheatham could not avoid the sexual economy of slavery. The persona that men like Guppy assigned to her—the exotic, sexually available Jezebel—did not disappear with the death of John Hagan or of slavery. In the postemancipation South, black women continued to be at constant risk of sexual violence. Cheatham's person was still used a vehicle for men's personal agendas and for maintaining racial hierarchy. To Guppy, Cheatham was not an individual woman but a caricature of sexuality, available to all white men at a moment's notice. By suggesting that a white Republican politician should visit her to experience "the mysteries of Mahogany Hall," this white author disregarded Cheatham's bodily integrity, and that of black women in general, and continued to draw on antebellum tropes of black women's sexuality.

Yet not all things from the past were so painful. As Stephanie Camp argued, "For bondwomen, even more than for enslaved men, intimate entities, such as the body and the home, were instruments of both domination and resistance. . . . The body and the home were key sites of suffering but also a resource in women's survival." Throughout the case over Cheatham's estate, it is clear that she maintained a close network of female friends, almost all of whom had known her for twenty or thirty years. Just as Mary Lumpkin had formed a protective bond with her when they were young, the women Cheatham met throughout her life presumably brought her much-needed support. Many of them had lived through situations very similar to Cheatham's own, showing how common sexual abuse was under slavery. Plenty of

Cheatham's female friends were willing to come forward to testify on behalf of her children in the settling of her estate and to keep their friend's secret. These friendships continued after death, and, in one case at least, in death found an eternal monument. When Lucy Ann Cheatham was buried in 1887, she was laid to rest in Cypress Grove Cemetery with John Hagan, Alexander Hagan, and her youngest son. But she was also laid to rest beside Sarah Ann Conner, who had purchased the plot next to Cheatham's.[75]

Graves of Lucy Ann Cheatham Hagan and Sarah Ann Connor, Cypress Grove Cemetery, New Orleans. Author's photograph.

Conclusion

In 1892 *Boyd's City Directory of the District of Columbia* included a listing for "Conner, Sarah A. wid. Izard" living at 1735 NW 12th Street. Only five years earlier, the same directory included "Davidson, Corinna wid. Nathaniel" at 1813 NW 9th Street, less than a mile away. Had the two women resided in the same neighborhood at the same time? Had they known of one another's existence? Had they crossed paths going to the market or running other errands? While their stories may be shocking to us, had Corinna and Sarah crossed paths and sat down to talk, it is likely that neither of them would have been surprised by the other's story. Both would have known plenty of women whose lives had played out similarly in the domestic slave trade.[1]

Sarah Conner and Corinna Hinton had spent the majority of their lives in their houses, cooking, cleaning, sewing, and caring for the people they lived with, as did the majority of women in the United States in the time period. They could have found common ground for conversation discussing which vendors had the best prices for meat, sharing tips on removing stains from tablecloths, or commiserating over difficult boarders. In this they could have swapped stories with many women of the era who, whether in the home or for a wage, also spent their days performing the unglamorous but critical work of the household.

In more personal matters, Conner and Hinton would have also had plenty to discuss, much as Mary Lumpkin and Lucy Ann Cheatham had. Both women had been born into slavery, sold to slave traders, and lived out a significant portion of their lives as the enslaved concubines of those slave traders. Both women had moved past these ties, fighting for their freedom and prospering off the fruits of their domestic and socially reproductive labor. Both women lived with secrets and the difficult choices they had made to survive. These intimate subjects they likely could not have shared with white women, wealthy or working class, who would not have understood the physical and psychological terror of slavery and the impossible situations it wrought.

We don't know if Sarah Conner and Corinna Hinton ever met, or what they would have spoken about if they did. In many ways their survival depended on their silence about their history in slavery, on skirting difficult issues and prioritizing the quotidian. The cost of their lives in the slave market could not be rendered accurately in words or numbers. To have written down their experiences, if they had the time and resources, would have been to reopen all of the wounds they had worked so hard to move past. If Sarah Conner and Corinna Hinton ever met, perhaps they wouldn't have talked about the past at all. Perhaps they would have talked about the weather.

THE HISTORIES OF Lucy Ann Cheatham, Sarah Conner, Corinna Hinton, Virginia Ann Isham, and the other women drawn into the economy of the slave market show the complexities of domestic work, its connections to sexual abuse, and the value it holds for the broader economy. While that value is often not quantifiable, it becomes clear when we examine those very basic facts of life that often seem too mundane for consideration. Before any other work could be performed, someone had to cook, clean, and sew. Before the slave traders could hang up the red flag and open the door to the slave jail, they had to eat and dress. Before the enslaved people stepped onto the auction block or stood before a potential purchaser, they had to appear clean and healthy in sale outfits. Before a purchaser could come to the jail, or a cotton broker go to the docks, or a bank agent discount a promissory note, they had to have all the necessities of life to perform their work. Women's labor provided most of these necessities, and thus provided the groundwork for the auctions, the cotton purchases, and the bank discounts. Due to their sex and/or the color of their skin, however, very little of the proceeds of these transactions reached their pockets. Nor did they receive much recognition for enabling the men of a nascent capitalist society to do their buying, selling, and trading.

These case studies use the antebellum slave trade as one particularly brutal example of the value of women's labor, but a similar argument could be made for many different times and places, though the specific types of work and meanings assigned to that work would be different. There were the *signares* who ran the households of Atlantic slave traders in Gorée and assisted them in their trade. Think of the women in port cities who facilitated the Atlantic market economy by selling food in markets and offering lodgings to merchants and sailors. Nineteenth-century Marxists such as Mary Inman argued that it was ultimately proletariat women, whose household labor allowed men to go to work for wages in a factory, that sustained capitalism. The allegedly happy housewife of the postwar period in the United States did more than arrange flowers and host parties, she raised the next generation of citizens and readied her husband for work each day. Even today, with robotic vacuums and food delivery services that have changed the nature of household work, women continue to be the ones to perform the majority of socially reproductive and emotional labor. In the home, women still tend to be the ones to prepare food for children and husbands, wash clothes so that family members have something clean to wear, and take time off work to nurse sick relatives.[2]

Paid domestic work today falls predominantly to immigrant women and women of color, who work in some of the lowest paid and most vulnerable positions. As of 2019, many federal labor regulations still did not apply to domestic workers. Prohibitions against sexual harassment under Title VII of the Civil Rights Act of 1964, for example, applied only to employers with over fifteen employees and thus not to domestics who worked in private homes. Some rights for domestic workers have improved, thanks to the activism of African American domestics in the 1970s, but many loopholes remain, even in terms of the federal minimum wage. This is even more the case for immigrants, who fear that speaking out about abuse will endanger their ability to stay in the United States. Cases of human trafficking, rape, and sexual, physical, and emotional abuse are all too common in domestic work.[3]

One activist for domestic workers' rights, Marcia Olivo, attributes some of the movement's challenges to continued disrespect of domestic labor as a form of work. "People don't see domestic work as real work and they don't recognize the things that happen in the industry," Olivo said, "and part of what is going to help win more protections for them is to make more people respectful of the work." To take these workers' claims, and the importance of their labor, seriously is a crucial part of recognizing the human dignity of all people. It would be a first step in acknowledging that socially reproductive labor is the basis of a functional society. It would also be a recognition of women's worth not just to the private family but to society as a whole. Hopefully, it would be a step toward fair treatment of and compensation for domestic workers and toward a more equitable distribution of socially reproductive labor, so that household work would no longer be women's work, but simply work.[4]

Epilogue

On a sweltering summer afternoon in 2016, I boarded a trolley car just outside of the French Quarter on Canal Street in New Orleans. This particular trolley did not have air conditioning; the passengers had opened the windows in a hopeless attempt at catching a breeze. I tried not to mind the heat, focusing on the reason behind my slow crawl down Canal. Around me, tourists fanned themselves with brochures and city maps as they chatted about the famous cemeteries they were about to see. I was not in the market for a cemetery tour or a macabre tale about the alleged origin of the term "dead ringer." I was in search of perhaps the only material evidence, outside of court cases and newspaper accounts, of two women whom I had spent the past six years of my life studying.

With the rest of the passengers I filed out of the trolley, at the end of the line, surrounded by the New Orleans's famous "cities of the dead." As others wandered into the larger cemeteries to our right, I gingerly stepped across the trolley tracks and stood outside the opened iron gates of another burial ground. I referenced the note in my hand, hastily scribbled at the New Orleans Public Library. It read, "Cypress Grove," and it matched the name emblazoned above the cemetery gate. Laptop bag and research notes in tow, I tucked the paper in my pocket and walked inside.

Paved streets spread out before me, each leading into a different section of the cemetery. I had no additional information to go on; I only knew that Sarah Conner and Lucy Cheatham were buried somewhere inside these walls. Expecting to be searching for several hours, I embarked down the path straight in front of me and started reading the inscriptions on the graves. Only ten minutes later I stumbled upon Sarah Conner's grave. I set down my bag in the dirt outside of the broken fence around the monument, which was a testament to Conner's postwar work as a boardinghouse operator, and started taking photographs. I noted that Conner kept her maiden name even as she described herself as Isard's wife. I zoomed in to make sure I had a legible photograph of the words.

I continued my journey, looking now for a grave marked Cheatham or Hagan. I was stunned when, four steps later, I found it. I dropped my bag and looked back at Conner's grave, making sure that the two women were indeed buried side by side. Taking out my camera again, I stepped back so that I could get a photograph of both of them together. I had never guessed that they would be so close, let alone next to one another. Yet when I truly considered it, I was not that surprised.

The trolley car for the return trip down Canal was late. By the time I made it back, the city archives would be near closing. It was not worth hurrying to open up another folder of court cases today. There was one place to wait besides the trolley stop bench, a coffee shop appropriately named Sacred Grinds ("Coffee to Wake the Brain Dead"). Despite the weather, I ordered a plain black coffee and sat as close to a fan as I could, since the café had no air conditioning. As I waited for my coffee to cool, I looked back over my photographs and reflected on this latest discovery.

My research had taken me over the years to an eclectic mix of places: a quaint historical society in Lancaster, Pennsylvania; an active courthouse in Richmond where I took notes next to folks complaining about traffic citations; a museum in Chicago; and too many state libraries to count. I had traveled to each in hopes of finding a new window into the lives of the women I studied. Their experiences, if recorded at all, were not housed in well-funded private libraries and were catalogued, not under their own names, but under the names of the men who enslaved them. They had not been able to share their own stories, at least not outside of courtroom battles over freedom and property. When they shared stories in the courtroom, they wove them in a particular way for a legal setting. I wanted the kinds of stories that they would share with their daughters, their sisters, or their closest friends.

Outside of legal records, I knew of only one source of these women's own writing. In April 1865, soon after the Union army entered Richmond and a decade or so after Silas Omohundro had paid Mr. Cawfield to tutor her, Corinna Hinton took pen to paper to address a brigadier general. Her voice comes through in the letter clear and measured, even forceful. Hinton described in detail how a group of Union soldiers had "forcibly entered" "a house belonging to me on 17th street between Grace and Broad" and "taken possession of three rooms" that Hinton was renting out. She described her renters thus: "One room was occupied by a colored man who had rented it and the others had been engaged by two federal officers. The colored man was compelled to move out and three ladies occupying rooms in the house were told unless they kept still they would be moved out also or all compelled to occupy one room." Hinton made sure to point out that one of the men was "claiming to be a Captain (although wearing no insignia of rank)" and questioned the legitimacy of his orders. She concluded by saying, "I would most respectfully request these persons be ordered to vacate these premises, as this house is my private property and has always been used for private purposes. I am very respectfully &c Mrs. C Omohundro."[1]

Only three days later, apparently having received no response or relief, Hinton tried again. This letter was written in a different handwriting and took a very different tone, though it was also signed Mrs. C Omohundro. The signature did not match the handwriting in the body of the letter. It began, "I am a widow with five small children of my own & two of a deceased sister to support & educate. My only means for this purpose at present are two houses in this city and a market garden near Camp Jackson." This letter also described how soldiers had occupied the house without her consent, but it emphasized that her renters were her "principal means of support to supply myself & my children with even the necessaries of life." There was no mention of the "colored man," the "federal officers," or the "three ladies." There was no questioning of the soldier's rank or authority. The tone had shifted to one of pleading and supplication.[2]

Who wrote the second letter, and why? Given that Hinton's signature on both letters match the handwriting of the first letter, it was likely someone else was the author. Had this person written it at Hinton's direction? Had they suggested that Hinton try a different tactic, appealing to the recipient's duty to protect suffering women and children? In the first letter she stressed her rights to her private property; in the second the author stressed the needs of a widow with young children. The questions only continued from there. Was Hinton's deceased sister Eliza Cheatham (and was Eliza related to Lucy Ann Cheatham)? Who was the "colored man," and why did she describe him as such? Did she see herself as something other than "colored"? Who were the three women? Were they white women? How had she acquired her market garden?

These were the scraps of Hinton's life with which I had to work. They were not scraps that, neatly sewn together, would do the woman justice. There would always be too much left unsaid, too many questions hanging in the air. Her life had not been simple and linear, and so her history could not be, either. No matter how many archives I searched, newspapers I scanned for her name, or court cases I transcribed, I couldn't tell her story with the details I wanted to. Even the identity of the woman in the stunning photograph from the Omohundro family was a question. Was she Corinna? Was she Louisa Tandy? Was she someone else entirely?

The answers to these questions continue to elude me. Out of respect for the lives of the women I've written about, I have chosen to embrace the questions rather than make statements when the archive provides no clear answer. I have done what I can to interpret their lives, but in the end I cannot definitively say, as I am often asked to, how Corinna Hinton really felt about Silas Omohundro. I can make comparisons, use theory, and employ what evidence is available, such as Lucy Cheatham naming her daughter after an abolitionist, or the language of Corinna's letter to the Union general, but some questions remain unanswerable.

Even without definitive statements and big, bold claims, these women's stories have value. They have value as windows into women's experiences under slavery. They have value as examples of how women's labor undergirds market economies. They have value as microhistories of the sexual economy of slavery. They have value because they are the remnants of people's lives. Corinna Hinton didn't alter the course of American history or fundamentally influence cultural or political discourse, but she lived a life that reveals a great deal about American culture and politics. She lived a life that is worthy of recognition not because it was extraordinary but because it was not. Her life was the life of the majority, the daily struggles of slavery, of motherhood, of the mundanity of washing, cooking, and cleaning. That mundanity is rarely recognized, let alone celebrated, and so the voices of women, of people of color, of domestic workers, continue to be undervalued today.

This was why finding Lucy Cheatham and Sarah Conner's graves side by side really struck me. It was a window into the private, daily lives of two formerly enslaved women caught in the sexual economy of slavery. I had suspected throughout my research that many of the enslaved concubines I studied knew one another. How could they not, living side by side in Richmond, or living with men who were business partners? But concrete confirmation of this had eluded me, at least until I found Lucy Cheatham's estate case and, now, until I saw her grave. It was possible, of course, that it was all a coincidence, that the two women had never known one another and had purchased burial plots with no knowledge of what the other one was doing. This seemed unlikely given the circumstantial evidence, but this, like so much else, was a question I couldn't definitively answer.

I had barely touched my coffee, given the unrelenting heat and humidity, but I saw the street car approaching in the distance and hurried to meet it outside. I had plans to walk down Gravier Street between Carondolet and Baronne, and to explore Esplanade between Victory and Moreau. I knew that

163 Gravier would not be standing, but I suspected that a certain house on Esplanade, built on the site of a former slave jail, might be. Whether I found nineteenth-century structures, empty lots, or parking garages, I could imagine what the neighborhoods might have looked like in Conner and Cheatham's time. And I could ask questions.

Notes

Introduction

1. The specifics of this vignette will appear in more detail in later chapters, but Omohundro's financial transactions are based on entries in the account books of Silas Omohundro and R. H. Dickinson. On 15 November, Dickinson, on behalf of Robinson & Smith, exchanged $415 in banknotes from Virginia for $415 in South Carolina notes from Omohundro. The same day, Omohundro made a deposit of $300 in his account at the Farmer's Bank. While Omohundro did not give Hinton $5 on 15 November, he paid her in cash for various household purchases with frequency, including on 25 November. "Robinson & Smith in Account with Dickinson, Hill & Co.," Dickinson, Hill & Co. Account Books, 1846–49, 1855–58, Library of Virginia, Richmond (hereafter cited as LVA); Farmer's Bank in Account with Silas Omohundro, Silas Omohundro Business and Estate Records, LVA; Silas Omohundro General Market and Account Book, Silas Omohundro Business and Estate Records, LVA.

2. Important works on the antebellum slave trade include Bancroft, *Slave-Trading in the Old South*; Baptist, "'Cuffy,' 'Fancy Maids,' and 'One-Eyed Men'"; Baptist, *Half Has Never Been Told*; Deyle, *Carry Me Back*; Gudmestad, *A Troublesome Commerce*; Johnson, *River of Dark Dreams*; Johnson, *Soul by Soul*; Jones-Rogers, *They Were Her Property*; McInnis, *Slaves Waiting for Sale*; Schermerhorn, *The Business of Slavery*; Tadman, *Speculators and Slaves*; Winter, *American Dreams of John B. Prentis, Slave Trader*.

3. Nelson, "Feminism and Economics," 136. Theoretical works on the role of socially reproductive labor in capitalism as well as other economic systems include Mariarosa Dalla Costa and Selma James, *The Power of Women and the Subversion of the Community*; Delphy, *Close to Home*; Ferber and Nelson, eds., *Beyond Economic Man*; Folbre, "A Patriarchal Mode of Production," in *Alternatives to Economic Orthodoxy*, eds. Albeda, Gunn, and Waller ; Folbre, "Exploitation Comes Home"; Fox, ed., *Hidden in the Household*; Hartmann, "The Family as the Locus of Gender, Class and Political Struggle"; Hewitson, *Feminist Economics*; Inman, *In Woman's Defense*; Kuhn, "Structures of Patriarchy and Capital in the Family," in *Feminism and Materialism*, ed. Kuhn and Wolpe; Laslett and Brenner, "Gender and Social Reproduction"; Leghorn and Parker, *Woman's Worth*; May, "The Feminist Challenge to Economics"; Mies, *Patriarchy and Accumulation on a World Scale*; Waring, *If Women Counted*.

4. Hochschild, *The Managed Heart*, 7.

5. Beecher, *Treatise on Domestic Economy*, 156.

6. Boydston, *Home and Work*, 44. The historiography of domestic ideology and its rise in the nineteenth century is extensive. Major works on the subject include Boydston, *Home and Work*; Cott, *Bonds of Womanhood*; Stansell, *City of Women*; Romero, *Home Fronts*; Welter, "Cult of True Womanhood." For broader consideration

of domesticity in national politics and colonialism, see Kaplan, "Manifest Domesticity"; Shire, *The Threshold of Manifest Destiny*.

7. See Miller, *The Needle's Eye*. See also Cowan, *More Work for Mother*.

8. Glymph, *Out of the House of Bondage*, 64–65. See also Deetz, *Bound to the Fire*; Fox-Genovese, *Within the Plantation Household*. For the position of domestic labor in southern society, see Hunter, *To 'Joy My Freedom*; Jones, *Labor of Love, Labor of Sorrow*; McCurry, *Masters of Small Worlds*; Sharpless, *Cooking in Other Women's Kitchens*; White, *Ar'n't I a Woman?*

9. Block, *Rape and Sexual Power in Early America*, 66–70; Katzman, *Seven Days a Week*.

10. Morgan, *Laboring Women*. See also Berry, *Price for Their Pound of Flesh*; Jones, *Labor of Love*; Owens, *Medical Bondage*; Turner, *Contested Bodies*; White, *Ar'n't I a Woman?*

11. Laslett and Brenner, "Gender and Social Reproduction."

12. Engels, *Origin of the Family, Private Property and the State*, 71; Folbre, "Unproductive Housewife." For more on Marx, Engels, and essentialist explanations of the sexual division of labor, see Mies, *Patriarchy and Accumulation*.

13. Inman, *In Woman's Defense*, 17–18, 143; Kuhn, "Structures of Patriarchy," 46–47. See also Delphy, *Close to Home*; Fox, ed., *Hidden in the Household*; Folbre, "A Patriarchal Mode of Production"; Hartmann, "Family as the Locus"; Mies, *Patriarchy and Accumulation*.

14. May, "Feminist Challenge to Economics,"45–69. See also Benston, "The Political Economy of Women's Liberation," in *The Politics of Housework*, ed. Ellen Malos, 119–29; Dalla Costa and James, *Power of Women*; Ferber and Nelson, eds., *Beyond Economic Man*; Hewitson, *Feminist Economics*; Leghorn and Parker, *Woman's Worth*; Rubin, "The Traffic in Women," in *Toward an Anthropology of Women*, ed. Rayna Reiter; Waring, *If Women Counted*.

15. Owens, "Fantasies of Consent," 13. For more on the fancy trade, see Baptist, "'Cuffy,' 'Fancy Maids,' and 'One-Eyed Men'"; Davis, "'Don't Let Nobody Bother Yo' Principle'"; Green, *Remember Me to Miss Louisa*; Green, "'Mr Ballard, I Am Compelled to Write Again'"; Johnson, "The Slave Trader, the White Slave, and the Politics of Racial Determination in the 1850s"; Stevenson, "What's Love Got to Do with It?" For considerations of enslaved men and sexual economy, see Jim Downs, "With Only a Trace," in *Connexions: Histories of Race and Sex in North America*, ed. Brier, Downs, and Morgan; Friend, "Sex, Self, and the Performance of Patriarchal Manhood in the Old South," in *Old South's Modern Worlds*, ed. Barnes, Schoen, and Towers; Foster, *Rethinking Rufus*.

16. Bremer, *Homes of the New World*, 535.

17. Davis, "Slavery and the Roots of Sexual Harassment," in *Directions in Sexual Harassment*, ed. MacKinnon and Siegel, 459; Owens, "Fantasies of Consent," 13.

18. Roper, *Narrative of the Adventures and Escape of Moses*, 61. See Baptist, "'Cuffy'"; Schermerhorn, *Business of Slavery*.

19. Owens, "Fantasies of Consent," 54; Stevenson, "What's Love Got to Do with It?," 115. See also Fuentes, *Dispossessed Lives*, 10; Hartman, *Scenes of Subjection*, 85; Block, *Rape and Sexual Power*, 69.

20. Stevenson, "What's Love Got to Do with It?," 102. For considerations of concubines, household and sexual economies, and racial discourse, see Burnard, *Mastery, Tyranny, and Desire*; Ghosh, *Sex and the Family in Colonial India*; Hoefte and Vrij, "Free Black and Colored Women in Early-Nineteenth-Century Paramaribo, Suriname," in *Beyond Bondage*, ed. Gaspar and Hine; Ipsen, *Daughters of the Trade*, 9; Jones, "From Marriage à la Mode to Weddings at Town Hall"; Jones, *The Metis of Senegal*; Searing, *West African Slavery and Atlantic Commerce*; Livesay, "Children of Uncertain Fortune"; Morrison, "Slave Mothers and White Fathers"; Stoler, "Making Empire Respectable."

21. Ze Winters, *The Mulatta Concubine*, 14.

22. Olmsted, *The Cotton Kingdom*, 306.

23. Beckert and Rockman, eds., *Slavery's Capitalism*, 10. Literature on the "new history of capitalism" and the economy of the antebellum South is extensive; some major works include Baptist, *Half Has Never Been Told*; Barnes, Schoen, and Towers, eds., *Old South's Modern Worlds*; Beckert and Desan, eds., *American Capitalism*; Beckert, *Empire of Cotton*; Berry, *Price for Their Pound of Flesh*; Deyle, *Carry Me Back*; Heier, "Accounting for the Business of Suffering"; Johnson, "Pedestal and the Veil"; Johnson, *Soul by Soul*; Kilbourne, *Debt, Investment, Slaves*; Kilbourne, *Slave Agriculture and Financial Markets*; Luskey and Woloson, eds., *Capitalism by Gaslight*; Martin, "Slavery's Invisible Engine"; Nelson, *A Nation of Deadbeats*; Nelson, "Who Put Their Capitalism in My Slavery?"; Rockman, *Scraping By*; Rockman, "Slavery and Capitalism"; Rosenthal, *Accounting for Slavery*; Rothman, *Flush Times and Fever Dreams*; Schermerhorn, *Business of Slavery*; Wright, *Slavery and American Economic Development*.

24. Gamber, *The Boardinghouse in Nineteenth-Century America*.

25. Rockman, *Scraping By*, 8.

26. Hartman, "Venus in Two Acts," 3. See Hartman, *Scenes of Subjection*; Fuentes, *Dispossessed Lives*; Ze Winters, *Mulatta Concubine*.

27. Schermerhorn, *Business of Slavery*, 234–35.

28. McInnis, *Slaves Waiting for Sale*, 157.

29. Enslaved concubines' urban mobility, and in particular their mobility throughout the South and even the North, highlights Rashauna Johnson's "geographies of containment" and "how, under particular conditions, the entire world could become a slave space." Johnson, *Slavery's Metropolis*, 7.

30. Lerner, *The Creation of Patriarchy*, 216.

Chapter One

1. Silas Omohundro General Market & Account Book, Silas Omohundro Business Records (LVA). See entries for 31 July 1855 (clothes); 20 Oct. 1855 (dresses); 31 Mar. 1856 (likeness); 10 Apr., 24 May, 24 Oct. 1856 (additional dresses); 15 June 1857 (teeth); 3 Dec. 1857 (watch); 22 Aug. 1859 (corsets); 20 July 1861 (slippers); 4 Jan. 1862 (bonnet); 7 Sept. 1858 (stockings); 17 July 1862 (garters); 1 Oct. 1862 (tea set); 19 May 1857 (one set of jewelry).

2. Silas Omohundro General Market & Account Book. See, for example, 10 July 1857 ("negroes cloths"); 30 July 1857 (market); 29 Aug. 1855 (fruit); 11 Apr. 1856 (children's

clothes); 30 Jan. and 2 Mar. 1858 (Mrs. Brown); 5 and 11 Sept. and 10 Oct. 1862 (kitchen supplies); 1 and 24 Jan. 1863 (Caroline);18 and 30 Jan. and 1 Feb. 1864 (Mrs. Murphy).

3. Genovese, *Roll Jordan Roll*, 417. The idea that "love" is an ahistorical category that can be identified across time and situation is in itself problematic. For more on changing understandings of "love" within slaveholding societies, see Gordon-Reed, *The Hemingses of Monticello*, and Owens, "Fantasies of Consent."

4. I use the term "soul value" as defined by Daina Ramey Berry; Berry, *Price for Their Pound of Flesh*. On the body as a site of resistance, see Camp, *Closer to Freedom*. For the violence of "becoming a 'type,'" see Baucom, *Specters of the Atlantic*, 11.

5. Hotten, *The Slang Dictionary*, 130; Grose, *Classical Dictionary of the Vulgar Tongue* (nonpaginated). The term "fancy man" had essentially the same definition from the late eighteenth century to the second half of the nineteenth.

6. *Webster's Dictionary*, 2nd ed. (1828), s.v. "fancy." For the terms "fancy" and "fancy stocks," see Baptist, "'Cuffy,' 'Fancy Maids,' and 'One-Eyed Men'"; Green, *Remember Me to Miss Louisa*, 17.

7. John J. Toler to unknown, undated, Elias Ferguson Papers, North Carolina State Archives, Raleigh (hereafter cited as NCSA); John J Toler to E. W. Ferguson, 26 Feb. 1859, Elias Ferguson Papers; John J. Toler to Elias Ferguson, 15 Feb. 1859, Elias Ferguson Papers; Phillip Thomas to William A. J. Finney, 26 July 1859, William A. J. Finney Collection, David M. Rubenstein Rare Book & Manuscript Library, Duke University.

8. Philip Thomas to William A. J. Finney, 20 Jan. 1859, William A. J. Finney Collection; D. M. Pulliam & Co. to Elias Ferguson, 3 Apr. 1858, Elias Ferguson Papers.

9. *White v. Slatter*, Docket 943 Supreme Court of Louisiana, Mar. 1849/Jan. 1850, 5 La. Ann 29. Blakeley was occasionally spelled Blakeney.

10. *White v. Slatter*, 943.

11. *White v. Slatter*, 943; Saidiya Hartman, "Venus in Two Acts," 2.

12. Brown, *Slave Life in Georgia*, 96–98.

13. Isaac Franklin to Rice C. Ballard, 11 Jan. 1834, Rice Ballard Papers, Southern Historical Collection, Wilson Library Special Collections, University of North Carolina, Chapel Hill. Quoted in Baptist, "'Cuffy,'" 1619.

14. Coleman, *Slavery Times in Kentucky*, 157–59.

15. Johnson, *Soul by Soul*, 79.

16. Fairbank, *Rev. Calvin Fairbank during Slavery Times*, 26–32.

17. Stanley, *From Bondage to Contract*, 22.

18. Hine, "Rape and the Inner Lives of Black Women in the Middle West," 912–13; Keckley, *Behind the Scenes*, 16.

19. Johnson, *Soul by Soul*, 121.

20. For examples of Omohundro listing enslaved women as "fancy," see Maria Johnson sold 18 Feb. 1859 and Columbia sold 12 Mar. 1859, Omohundro Slave Trade and Farm Accounts, 1857–64, Alderman Library, University of Virginia, Charlottesville; Silas Omohundro General Market and Account Book, 20 June 1856 (Liza), 8 Jan. 1858 (Jane), and 12 Nov. 1858 (Charlotte).

21. For example, see E. W. Ferguson to John J. Toler, 1859, Elias W. Ferguson Collection; Owens, "Fantasies of Consent," 147.

22. Brown, *Slave Life in Georgia*, 98.

23. Former Franklin & Armfield agents who later entered the slave trade in their own right included George Kephart, T. M. Jones, Silas Omohundro, J. M. Saunders, and Bacon Tait; Schermerhorn, *Business of Slavery*, 144. For Franklin & Armfield, see Baptist, "'Cuffy'"; Rothman, *The Ledger and the Chain*.

24. *Littleton J. Omohundro v. Omohundro's Executor*, Records of the U.S. District Court for the Eastern District of Virginia, U.S. Circuit Court, Richmond Division, Law Records 1866–1911, PH-1049: Case Files, Box 5 (RG 21, Stack D, Row 16); Bureau of the Census, *Sixth Census, 1840*, Sixth Ward, Cincinnati, Hamilton County, Ohio, s.v. "Louisa Tandy"; Bureau of the Census, *Seventh Census, 1850*, Sixth Ward, Cincinnati, Hamilton County, Ohio, s.v. "Louisa Tandy"; Bureau of the Census, *Ninth Census, 1870*, Eighteenth Ward Cincinnati, Hamilton County, Ohio s.v. "Littleton Omohundro."

25. *Littleton J. Omohundro v. Omohundro's Executors*. Tandy and Omohundro's children were Littleton J. (born 1838 in Virginia), Martha (born 1840 in Ohio), Sidney (born 1842 in Ohio), Cinderella (born 1844 in Ohio), and Florence "Flora" (born 1853 in Ohio). M. H. Omohundro's *Omohundro Genealogical Record* makes no mention of Louisa Tandy's background, portraying her as a white woman named Martha who died well before Silas met Corinna. Louisa Tandy may in fact have had a sister named Martha whom Silas also enslaved; one or more of the Omohundro children in Cincinnati may have been hers. Sons Sydney and Littleton appeared occasionally in Silas's general account book. Sydney Omohundro lived as an adult in Ohio and Pennsylvania and served in the Union Army during the Civil War. Littleton John also served as a Union soldier and received semiregular payments from his father in the 1850s. After his father's death, Littleton filed suit against Richard Cooper, Silas's executor, for nonpayment of money Silas had promised him for the construction of a house in Cincinnati. Cooper attempted to contest Littleton's claims, bringing into the testimony irrelevant issues, such as race and Louisa's enslaved legal status, in an attempt to discredit the family. Malvern Hill Omohundro, *Omohundro Genealogical Record*; Omohundro General Market and Account Book.

26. Richmond City Hustings Court Order Book, no. 16 (1844–46), 540, 10 Aug. 1846. Traders Robert Lumpkin and Betts & Edmundson received licenses at the same time.

27. "A List of Real and Personal Estate of Silas Omohundro, dec'd . . . ," Estate of Silas Omohundro in the Lancaster County Orphan's Court, Lancaster County Historical Society, Lancaster, PA.

28. Fuentes, *Dispossessed Lives*, 69. In Sharon Block's comprehensive study of rape in early America, she found that "no rape conviction against a white man, let alone a victim's owner, for raping an enslaved woman has been found between at least 1700 and the Civil War." Block, *Rape and Sexual Power in Early America*, 65.

29. Gordon-Reed, *Hemingses of Monticello*, 308–25; Hartman, *Scenes of Subjection*, 85.

30. Gordon-Reed, *Hemingses of Monticello*; Johnson, "On Agency," 115.

31. For the economic obligations of men in legal marriage, see Cott, *Public Vows*, 12.

32. Beecher, *Treatise on Domestic Economy*, 37–38. Omohundro spelled his son's name Colon rather than Colin.

33. Jones, *Labor of Love, Labor of Sorrow*, 12.

34. Silas Omohundro Market and General Account Book. Though not legally free, Clark was included in the 1860 Census within a household that included Hinton and her children, living next door to Omohundro. When Clark died, Omohundro spent over a hundred dollars on her burial, much more than any of the other people he enslaved. The women's apparently close relationship, and the fact that M. H. Omohundro reported Corinna's mother's name as Martha Clark, suggests that Patsy Clark may have been Corinna's mother. U.S. Census Bureau, *Eighth Census, 1860*, Ward 1, Richmond City, Virginia, s.v. "Corinna Hinton"; Silas Omohundro General Account Book. In 1860, though also enslaved, Hinton appeared on the census, as well, with no race indicated. In 1870 and 1880 she was listed as white. *U.S. Census Bureau, Ninth Census, 1870*, Jefferson Ward, Richmond City, Virginia, s.v. "Corinna Davidson"; U.S. Census Bureau, *Tenth Cenus, 1880*, Washington, District of Columbia, s.v. "Nathaniel Davidson."

35. "C. F. Hatcher," *New Orleans Daily Crescent*, 23 Apr. 1860; "James White," *New Orleans Daily Crescent*, 27 Jan. 1852.

36. Omohundro Jail and Board Book; figures based on author's database of the Omohundro General Market and Account Book.

37. Figures based on author's database of the Omohundro General Market and Account Book.

38. "C. F. Hatcher," *New Orleans Daily Crescent*, 23 Apr. 1860; Bancroft, *Slave-Trading in the Old South*, 103, 325.

39. Omohundro General Market and Account Book. See, for example, entries for 11 Nov. 1857 and 19 Dec. 1863.

40. Census information comes from author's compilation, in a database, of all the female domestic workers in Richmond City (Wards 1, 2, and 3) in 1860. In this instance, the census taker assumed that Corinna Hinton was a free woman.

41. Omohundro General Market and Account Book. For more on the valuation of specific domestic tasks in boardinghouses, see Hartigan-O'Connor, *The Ties That Buy*, and Wood, "Making a Home in Public."

42. "Paid Out and Received, No. 1, 1851–1877," Silas Omohundro Business Records, LVA.

43. Diary of Julia Wilbur, 18 May 1865, Haverford College, Quaker and Special Collections, emphasis in original. My thanks to Robert Colby for informing me of this extraordinary source. Schermerhorn, *Money Over Mastery, Family Over Freedom*; Robert Lumpkin Will, Richmond City Hustings Wills, 1866, vol. 24, 419–22, LVA; Charles H. Corey, *A History of the Richmond Theological Seminary*, 74–75. For more on the Lumpkins, see Rothman, *Notorious in the Neighborhood*, and Schermerhorn, *Money Over Mastery*.

44. I describe the Omohundro and Davis families as friends due to the intimacy implied by Omohundro's accounts as well as the way each man treated his enslaved family. Omohundro recorded several gifts given to Ann Davis and her children with Hector, including expensive items such as silver teaspoons. Omohundro and Davis occasionally did business together, and both men sent their children to Pennsylvania to be educated. See, for example, Omohundro General Market and Account Book, Oct. and Dec. 1859.

45. Like Davis, Tait was a respected man in Richmond, as voters elected him to serve as city councilman and commissioner of the streets for Jefferson Ward. Bacon Tait to Rice Ballard, 13 Aug. 1839, Rice Ballard Papers, Southern Historical Collection, quoted in Baptist, *Half Has Never Been Told*, 241; William L. Montague, *Montague's Richmond Directory and Business Advertiser for 1850-1851*, 31, 104; 1860 United States Census, Essex County, Massachusetts, digital image, s.v. "Bacon Tait," available at *Ancestry.com*; 1850 United States Census, Richmond, Virginia, digital image, s.v. "Bacon Tait"; Will of Bacon Tait, executed 20 June 1871, Richmond City Chancery Court Wills, microfilm: Reel 846 no. 1, LVA; see Hank Trent, *The Secret Life of Bacon Tait*.

46. Will of William Goodwin, executed 4 May 1864, Richmond City Circuit Court Will Book, Reel 76, no. 2, LVA; Diary of Julia Wilbur, 10 June 1865.

47. *Michael Hughs's Admin. v. Salem Downing*, Fayette County Kentucky Circuit Court, 1854; Tyre Glen Account Book, 1838-40, Tyre Glen Papers, David M. Rubenstein Rare Book & Manuscript Library, Duke University.

48. G. W. Eustler to Elias Ferguson, 16 Aug. 1856; E. W. Ferguson to unknown, 13 Aug. 1856, Elias W. Ferguson Papers.

49. Calling attention to Corinna's material wealth is not meant to detract from the violence of her ties to Omohundro. As Marisa Fuentes writes, "when concentrated on the economic possibilities for enslaved and free(d) women of color, it is easy to equate black female agency with sexuality without critically examining some of the violating attributes of this labor." Fuentes, *Dispossessed Lives*, 50.

50. Camp, "The Pleasures of Resistance," in *New Studies in the History of American Slavery*, ed. Baptist and Camp, 107-9; Kimball, *American City, Southern Place*, 108; Omohundro General Market and Account Book. For an example of Corinna's dress, see 5 Apr. 1856 and 3 July 1858.

51. Hartigan-O'Connor, *The Ties That Buy*, 101; Omohundro General Market and Account Book.

52. For cash payments to Corinna, see Silas Omohundro General Market and Account Book, 22 Sept. 1855, 2 Mar. 1856, and 24 Apr. 1857, among others. For an example of payment in gold, see 6 Jan. 1855.

53. Silas Omohundro, will executed 8 July 1864, Richmond City Circuit Court Will Books, vol. 2, 228-30, LVA.

54. Silas Omohundro will; *Cooper, Executor, v. Omohundro*, Supreme Court of the United States, 86 U.S. 65; 22 L. Ed. 47; 1873 U.S. LEXIS 1426; 19 Wall. 65; *Omohundro's Ex'or v. Crump*, Supreme Court of Virginia, 59 Va. 703; 1868 Va. LEXIS 30; 18 Gratt. 703; *Omohundro's Estate*, Supreme Court of Pennsylvania, 66 Pa. 113; 1870 Pa. LEXIS 285.

55. *Cooper, Executor v. Omohundro*; *Omohundro's Ex'or v. Crump*; *Omohundro's Estate*.

56. Estate of Silas Omohundro in Lancaster County, Pennsylvania, Orphan's Court. Multiple parties in the cited orphan's court case refer to Eliza Cheatham as Corinna's sister or Silas's sister in law. In the 1860 census, Cheatham was living in Richmond with two adult women and one young boy. The census taker considered all of them "mulatto." One of the women worked in a hotel, but Cheatham had no employment listed. She owned, however, personal property worth $4,000 and real estate worth

$1,000. Omohundro may have paid her some of this money in exchange for caring for his children. It is unclear how she became free. For examples of Omohundro purchasing school supplies and paying tuition, see Silas Omohundro General Market & Account Book, 29 Mar. 1856 and 28 Dec. 1859.

57. Estate of Silas Omohundro in Lancaster County, Pennsylvania, Orphan's Court. For "passing," see Hobbs, *A Chosen Exile*; Jordan, *White Over Black*, 176–78; Rothman, *Notorious in the Neighborhood*.

58. Estate of Silas Omohundro in the Lancaster County Orphan's Court; *Omohundro's Estate*.

59. It is unclear whether Nathaniel and Corinna were legally married. "Death of Nathaniel Davidson," *Washington Critic*, 29 Apr. 1886; U.S. Census Bureau, *Ninth Census, 1870*, Richmond City, Virginia, s.v. "Nathaniel Davidson"; Richmond City Directory, 1870, 93, Microfilm 229, Reel 1A, LVA; Richmond City Directory, 1871–72, 69, Microfilm 229, Reel 1A, LVA; Richmond City Directory, 1873–74, 56, LVA; *Omohundro's Executor v. Omohundro*.

60. *Omohundro's Executor v. Omohundro*; Nathaniel Davidson, "Virginia Duplicity," *National Republican*, 31 Aug. 1876; "War Department Changes," *Evening Star*, 2 Feb. 1883; Estate of Silas Omohundro in the Lancaster County Orphan's Court (1866); United States Census Bureau, *Tenth Census, 1880*, Philadelphia, Philadelphia County, Pennsylvania, s.v. "Edward C. Street"; and Washington, District of Columbia, s.v. "Colon Omohundro"; U.S Census Bureau, *Twelfth U.S. Census, 1900*, 1900 Hyde Park, Chicago, Illinois, s.v. "William R. Omohundro."

61. "District of Columbia, Deaths and Burials, 1840–1964," Genealogical Society of Utah (Salt Lake City, 2008), digital image, s.v. "Corinna Davidson," available at *FamilySearch.org*.

62. Engels, *Origin of the Family, Private Property, and the State*, 57–58.

63. Fitzhugh, *Sociology for the South*, 86, 206, 213, 215.

64. Fitzhugh, *Sociology for the South*, 86, 206, 213, 215.

65. Engels, *Origin of the Family*, 57–58; For more on the metaphor of slavery and marriage in the arguments of proslavery Southerners, see McCurry, *Masters of Small Worlds*, 208–38.

66. Engels, *Origin of the Family*, 57–58; "Jezebel" and "Mammy" are references to White, *Ar'n't I a Woman?*

67. Engels, *Origin of the Family*, 57–58; Johnson, "Making a World Out of Slaves," in *Soul by Soul*, 78–116.

Chapter Two

1. Hector Davis was one of Richmond's most prominent slave traders and auctioneers. His signature appeared on promissory notes, bills of sale, and bills of exchange throughout the slave states. He worked with a variety of other successful slave traders in various partnerships such as Davis, Lee, & Co., Templeman & Co., and Hector Davis & Co. In the few months of its existence before Davis's death, Hector Davis & Co. made nearly $40,000 in profit; in 1859 the market value of sales made at Davis's auction house exceeded that of all of the flour exported from Virginia the same year.

Davis owned more than $75,000 in stocks and bonds of Virginia's banks and other corporations; he sat on the board of directors of the Bank of the Commonwealth; he even founded and presided over a bank by and for slave traders, the aptly named Traders Bank of Virginia.

2. Examples come from Account, Nov. 12, 1830, Box 1, Tyre Glen Papers, David M. Rubenstein Rare Book & Manuscript Library, Duke University; E. W. Ferguson to John J. Toler, 1859, Elias W. Ferguson Collection, NCSA; *White v. Slatter*, Docket 943, Supreme Court of Louisiana, Mar. 1849/Jan. 1850, 5 La. Ann 29; 1843 Accounts, Matthew Bates Nowlin Papers, Virginia Historical Society, Richmond (hereafter cited as VHS). For more on white women as customers and traders, see Jones-Rogers, *They Were Her Property*.

3. Boydston, *Home and Work*, 147; Account, 1831, Box 1, Tyre Glen Papers. For more on the difficulties of locating women's labor in the census, particularly when it was part-time or occasional, see Dudden, *Serving Women*, 73–74.

4. Hartman, *Scenes of Subjection*, 37.

5. Jones-Rogers, *They Were Her Property*, 133 (Susan Boggs); Roper, *A Narrative of the Adventures and Escape of Moses Roper from American Slavery*, 61–63; Johnson, *Soul by Soul*, 119.

6. Brown, *From Fugitive Slave to Free Man*, 191; Northup, Logsdon, and Eakin, *Twelve Years a Slave*, 52.

7. "Deposition of C. F. Hatcher," *Mark Davis v. Obediah D. Hammett*, Docket 6094 (1846), Supreme Court of Louisiana.

8. *Mark Davis v. Obediah D. Hammett*. For enslaved women, reproductive health, and medicine, see Fett, *Working Cures*; Owens, *Medical Bondage*; Schwartz, *Birthing a Slave*; Turner, *Contested Bodies*.

9. *Mark Davis v. Obediah D. Hammett*.

10. Andrews, *Slavery and the Domestic Slave Trade in the United States*, 139–40; Northup, Logsdon, and Eakin, *Twelve Years a Slave*, 51.

11. Betty Wass, "Yoruba Dress in Five Generations of a Lagos Family," in *The Fabrics of Culture*, ed. Cordwell and Schwarz, 331; Johnson, *Soul by Soul*, 121. See also Buckridge, *The Language of Dress*, 18.

12. Johnson, *Soul by Soul*, 121. For more on visual representations of slave auctions, see McInnis, *Slaves Waiting for Sale*.

13. Bancroft, *Slave-Trading in the Old South*, 320; L. F. Tasistro *Random Shots and Southern Breezes*, 88, quoted in Bancroft, 330; Chesnut, *A Diary from Dixie*, 13.

14. Weekly figures from author's database; total expenses from McInnis, *Slaves Waiting for Sale*, 137. *J. W. Boazman v. Elisha Cannon*, Docket 2466 (Nov. 1853), Supreme Court of Louisiana (unreported); *White v. Slatter*. See also *Thomas Davis v. Boazman and Kendig*, Docket 6524, Third District Court, Orleans Parish, City Archives, Louisiana Division, New Orleans Public Library (hereafter cited as NOPL).

15. *J. J. Poindexter v. Mrs. Giles & Mr. Harmon*, Docket 13,001 Third District Court, Orleans Parish, NOPL.

16. Martha E. Twyman to Jonathan Austin, 14 Oct. 1848, Folder 51, Austin-Twyman Papers, Swem Library, College of William & Mary; Martha E. Twyman to Frances Austin, 30 July 1838, Folder 51, Austin-Twyman Papers; Martha E. Twyman to

Iverson Twyman, 27 Feb. 1855, Folder 53, Austin-Twyman Papers. Thanks to Robert Colby and Sarah E. Thomas for helping me locate these letters.

17. For the evolution of ready-made apparel, see Miller, *The Needle's Eye*, 193–200; Gamber, *The Female Economy*; Zakim, *Ready Made Democracy*.

18. Foster, *New Raiments of Self*, 77–80. See also Shaw, "Slave Cloth and Clothing Slaves."

19. For more on "Negro cloth" and the clothing of enslaved people, see Buckridge, *Language of Dress*; Camp, *Closer to Freedom*; Foster, *New Raiments of Self*; Clark-Pujara, *Dark Work*; Rockman, "Negro Cloth: Mastering the Market for Slave Clothing in Antebellum America," in *American Capitalism*, ed. Beckert and Desan, 170–94; Shaw, "Slave Cloth and Clothing Slaves"; Weaver, "Fashioning Freedom," 44–59. For references to "Negro cloth" in Richmond advertisements, see "Second Supply of Goods," *Daily Dispatch*, 11 Oct. 1853; "Splendid Stock of Dry Goods," *Daily Dispatch*, 18 Oct. 1858. For examples of "negro cloth" in New Orleans advertisements, see "Removal," *Planter's Banner*, 10 Mar. 1853; "Bargains," *Daily Crescent*, 6 Mar. 1852; "Louisiana Plantation Clothing Manufactory," *Opelousas Patriot*, 21 Feb. 1857.

20. My thanks to Seth Rockman for his assistance and for sharing price lists from Peacedeale Manufactory. Rockman, "Negro Cloth."

21. "Bed Blankets," *Daily Dispatch*, 21 Nov. 1860; "Negroes' Clothing, Negroes' Clothing," *Daily Dispatch*, 9 Nov. 1859; "Negro Clothing," *Southern Sentinel*, 19 Mar. 1853.

22. "In Store and for Sale," *Daily Dispatch*, 1 Dec. 1855; "Fresh Arrival of Winter Goods," *Daily Dispatch*, 12 Nov. 1856; "Second Supply Goods," *Daily Dispatch*, 11 Oct. 1853. For more on textile mills in the antebellum southern states, see Billings, *Planters and the Making of a New South*; Rockman, *Scraping By*; "Louisiana Plantation Clothing Manufacture," *Opelousas Patriot*, 21 Feb. 1857; "Louisiana Plantation Clothing Manufactory," *New Orleans Daily Crescent*, 1 May 1856; "New Goods," *New Orleans Daily Crescent* 10 Nov. 1854; Seth Rockman, email communication to author, Aug. 15, 2018.

23. "Negroes' Clothing, Negroes' Clothing," *Daily Dispatch*, 9 Nov. 1859; "Ready Made Clothing," *Staunton Spectator*, 28 Aug. 1860; "Kent, Paine, and Co., Importers," *Daily Dispatch*, 20 Oct. 1853; "Richmond Made Clothing," *Daily Dispatch*, 2 Mar. 1860, emphasis in original.

24. Rockman, *Scraping By*, 132. The history of women's work in New England textile mills is extensive. Some of the foundational works on the subject include Cott, *Bonds of Womanhood*; Dublin, *Women at Work*; Kessler-Harris, *Out to Work*; Lerner, "The Lady and the Mill Girl."

25. Calculation of sums made from Hector Davis Account Books, vols. 1 and 2; Silas Omohundro General Market and Account Book.

26. "Goods for Negroes Clothing," *Daily Dispatch*, 25 Nov. 1853; "Servants' Clothing," *Daily Dispatch*, 10 Nov. 1859; Moses Jacob Ezekiel, *Memoirs from the Bath of Diocletian*, ed. Joseph Gutmann (Detroit: Wayne State University Press, 1975), 98–99, quoted in McInnis, *Slaves Waiting for Sale*, 137–38.

27. "Plantation Clothing," *Daily Crescent*, 14. Nov. 1848; "Wholesale and Retail Clothing Warerooms," *Daily Crescent*, 1 Oct. 1857; "Clothing! Clothing," *Daily Crescent*, 28 Dec. 1859; *N.C. Folger v. J. M. E. Sharp*, Docket 8852, Second District Court,

Orleans Parish, NOPL; *N.C. Folger v. Charles Lamarque, Jr.*, Docket 7374, Third District Court, Orleans Parish, NOPL; *L. M. Foster v. His Creditors*, Docket 13,622, Fourth District Court, Orleans Parish, NOPL.

28. Gamber, *Female Economy*, 1.

29. Miller, *Needle's Eye*, 60–61; Gamber, *Female Economy*, 29.

30. Miller, *Needle's Eye*, 212. For more on the feminization of sewing, see Gamber, *Female Economy*, and Kessler-Harris, *Out to Work*.

31. 1860 New Orleans Census, Wards 1–5, author's database. Of the twenty-five women, the census taker identified twenty-four as white.

32. Other merchants also advertised ready-made clothes while simultaneously advertising their need for seamstresses and tailors. See, for example, "E. Morris," *Daily Dispatch*, 27 Nov. 1856; "Wanted Immediately," *Daily Dispatch*, 4 Dec. 1855; "Richmond Made Clothing," *Daily Dispatch*, 2 Mar. 1860; "New Goods," *New Orleans Daily Crescent*, 10 Nov. 1854. On the trope of the impoverished seamstress, see Miller, *Needle's Eye*, 212; Gamber, *Female Economy*. Spence's rhetoric about seamstresses is similar to that of the Baltimore manufacturers discussed by Rockman in *Scraping By*. For more on sewing in prisons and asylums, see Manion, *Liberty's Prisoners*.

33. For examples of payments to Miss Patterson, see entries for 11 July 1857 and 15 May 1858, Hector Davis Account Book, vol. 1.

34. For examples of payments to Mrs. S. N. Davis, see entries for 14 May 1859 and 21 Dec. 1859, Hector Davis Account Books. Solomon N. Davis became a successful slave trader; by 1860 he had accumulated enough money to build a three-story brick home in Richmond's fashionable and wealthy Court End neighborhood. At the time she sewed for Hector Davis, Anna Davis had five children. After the Civil War, Solomon transferred his financial knowledge and investments in manufacturing to a position as a banker in New York City. McInnis, *Slaves Waiting for Sale*, 98; U.S. Census Bureau, *Ninth Census*, 1870, New York City, New York, s.v. "Solomon Davis."

35. "50,000 Dollars Worth of Ready Made Clothing," *Daily Dispatch*, 5 Jan. 1854; "E. Morris," *Daily Dispatch*, 27 Nov. 1856; *N.C. Folger v. J. M. E. Sharp*.

36. Account, July 1830, Box 1, Tyre Glen Papers; Account, 16 Apr. 1834, Box 2, Tyre Glen Papers.

37. Account, 12 Nov. 1830, Box 1, Tyre Glen Papers; Carrie Charles to "sister," 13 Oct. 1858, McGee & Charles Family Papers, South Caroliniana Library, University of South Carolina.

38. John H. Charles to Mary A. Charles, 22 Apr. 1857, McGee & Charles Family Papers; Carrie Charles to "sister," 13 Oct. 1858; Carrie Charles to John H. Charles, 16 Oct. 1855, McGee & Charles Family Papers; Winter, *American Dreams of John B. Prentis*, 107.

39. Winter, *American Dreams*, 107.

40. Hector Davis Account Books, vols. 1 and 2; *Crouch et al. v. Davis's Ex'or*, Richmond City Chancery Court, John Marshall Court House; U.S. Census Bureau, *Ninth Census*, Jefferson Ward, Richmond City, Virginia, s.v. "William Isham"; U.S. Census Bureau, *Tenth Census*, 1880, Richmond City, Virginia, s.v. "William Isham"; U.S. Census Bureau, *Twelfth Census*, 1900, Richmond City, Virginia, s.v. "William H. Isham." William Isham Sr. worked as a barber.

41. For examples of Isham purchasing sewing supplies, see entries for 7 Apr. 1858 and 6 Aug. 1859, Hector Davis Account Book, vol. 1. For Isham buying ready-made clothing, see entries for 15 Feb. and 29 Mar. 1862, Hector Davis Account Book, vol. 2.

42. For examples of William Isham buying medicine, see entry for 21 Apr. 1858, Hector Davis Account Book, vol. 1. For William Isham running errands and buying shoes, see entries for 31 Aug. and 31 Dec. 1859, Hector Davis Account Book, vol. 1. For Virginia Isham acting as midwife, see entry for 3 Dec. 1862, Hector Davis Account Book, vol. 2.

43. 30 Aug. 1862 and 8 Nov. 1862, Hector Davis Account Book, vol. 2.

44. Davis specified he paid Isham one-fourth of his profits; 3 June 1859, Hector Davis Account Book, vol. 1.

45. Winter, *American Dreams*, 107; Elias Ferguson to John J. Toler, 1859, Elias Ferguson Papers, NCSA; Lisa Kraus, "Archaeology of the Bruin Slave Jail," 65, 113. The Edmondson sisters were part of the attempted escape on the *Pearl*, and their story drew the attention of many abolitionists.

46. Due to Omohundro's irregular spelling and the multiple meanings of "cloth" and "clothe," the phrase "to get Negroes cloths" could still signify a number of different activities. For two examples of yearly payments to Corinna, see entries for 1 Jan. 1859, 22 Dec. 1860, 10 July 1857, and 8 Apr. 1862, Silas Omohundro General Market & Account Book.

47. 4 Dec. 1861, Silas Omohundro General Market & Account Book.

48. Kennedy, "A Slave to Fashion." See also Buckridge, *Language of Dress*, and Weaver, "Fashioning Freedom," 44–59.

49. "For Sale," *Daily Dispatch*, 5 Feb. 1858; "For Sale," *Daily Dispatch*, 16 Aug. 1853.

50. "Wanted to Purchase," *Daily Dispatch*, 29 Nov. 1864; "Nurse and Seamstress Wanted," *Daily Dispatch*, 19 Aug. 1854; "For Hire," *Daily Dispatch*, 13 Aug. 1855.

51. *White v. Slatter*.

52. Browning, *Diary of Orville Hickman Browning*, 138–39, quoted in Bancroft, *Slave-Trading in the Old South*, 130–31; John J. Toler to Elias Ferguson, 22 June 1858, Elias W. Ferguson Papers.

53. "Slaves for Sale," *Daily Dispatch*, 20 Jan. 1858; "Valuable Seamstress for Sale," *Daily Dispatch*, 20 Mar. 1852; "First Rate Seamstress and Ladies Made for Hire," *Daily Dispatch*, 7 Jan. 1853; "A Good Seamstress for Sale," *Daily Dispatch*, 13 Feb. 1865; "Wanted," *Daily Dispatch*, 16 May 1856.

54. Thanks to Neil Heinig, Maurie D. McInnis, and Calvin Schermerhorn for information on the printing and circulation of the Trader's Bank notes.

55. Stephen Mihm notes, "Banks generally opted for designs that reflected the particular sensibilities of the board of directors, the state, or the larger region in which the bank operated. In the antebellum era, banks in the South adorned their currency with images of slaves and slavery." Engraving firms, such as the American Bank Note Company, "accumulated extensive inventories of vignettes and other bits and pieces of banknotes that could be used and reused. In this way, when the time came for a bank to commission a new note, it could pick out the various elements it wanted and craft a 'custom' look from what was already in the inventory (and if desired, have new elements engraved from scratch)." Fiege and Mihm, "On Bank Notes," 350–59. For

more on antebellum Southern ideas of progress and modernity, see Barnes, Schoen, and Towers, eds., *Old South's Modern Worlds*.

56. Michel, "Christian Schussele," 249–67. My thanks to Elizabeth Eager for her help in interpreting the significance of the banknote's artwork.

Chapter Three

1. New Orleans in the 1850s was the third-largest city in the United States and globally the fourth-largest port in the value of its exports. Johnson, *River of Dark Dreams*, 84.

2. Totals derived from U.S. Census Bureau, *Eighth Census, 1860*, Wards 1–5, Orleans Parish, Louisiana. Author's database.

3. Deed Book 23, 343, New Orleans Notarial Archives; Louisiana Register of Free Colored Persons Entitled to Remain in the State, vol. 1, 1840–56, 51, NOPL. James G. Blakeley was from Orange, Virginia, and had worked in the buying and selling of bondspeople since at least the early 1830s. Born around 1795, Blakeley worked as an agent of Rice Ballard of the firm of Franklin & Armfield. As such, he worked alongside Silas Omohundro. Blakeley retired a decade after he bought and sold Sarah Conner. He took his profits from the slave trade and purchased a hotel on Wall Street, the heart of the slave-trading district in Richmond, Virginia; he managed the hotel until his death in 1854. Schermerhorn, *Business of Slavery*, 144, 166.

4. The frequency with which female "quadroons" or "octoroons" appeared in writings about antebellum New Orleans overshadowed the existence of mixed-race women elsewhere, as well as men of mixed ancestry in the Crescent City. For more on the trope of the "tragic mulatto" and the "quadroon," see Clark, *Strange History of the American Quadroon*; Guillory, "Under One Roof," in *Race Consciousness*, ed. Fossett and Tucker, 67–92; Landau, *Spectacular Wickedness*; Long, *The Great Southern Babylon*; Manganelli, *Transatlantic Spectacles of Race*; Owens, "Fantasies of Consent"; Roach, "Slave Spectacles and Tragic Octoroons," 167–87.

5. Owens, "Fantasies of Consent," 7.

6. *A. F. Dunbar v. Sarah Conner*, Docket 2496, Fifth District Court, Orleans Parish, NOPL; Succession of Sarah Jane Bennett, Docket 4983, Fourth District Court, Orleans Parish, NOPL. When she purchased Conner, Jane Shelton, also known as Jane Bennett, was in her early fifties and had outlived three husbands. Bennett was born in Virginia and moved to New Orleans as a young woman. She was an active participant in financial exchange, employing a "money broker," J. E. Faures, with whom she purchased and sold promissory notes, mortgages, and other debt instruments. At the time of her death, Bennett was linked in business, through financial paper, to G. W. Montgomery, the president of the Bank of Louisiana, to "Mr. Dupon, a colored man," to a single woman in New York City, and to "a capitalist in Europe" who ended up being the holder of one of her large promissory notes.

Bennett also engaged in the purchase and sale of enslaved people, most of them young women. When she died, she was the owner of Julia, "a griffe girl of 16 years," Minty or Moiety, and Matilda, "a mulatto woman of 18 years." Bennett emancipated these three women in her will. However, the executor of the estate claimed that her debts were too large to follow through on this promise. Specifically, a Miss Sarah Cohn of New York City petitioned the court to sell Julia, Minty, and Matilda, because Cohn held a mortgage on the women for a promissory note Bennett's estate otherwise could not pay. The three women protested that the estate had plenty of resources, including almost $1,000 worth of property and three pieces of real estate. Nonetheless, the court ordered the women sold at public auction, denying them the freedom that Bennett intended for them. Quotation from "A Resident," *New Orleans As It Is*, 42–43.

7. Williams, "Can Quadroon Balls Represent Acquiescence or Resistance?," in *Gendered Resistance*, ed. Frederickson and Walters, 122–25; de Tocqueville, *Journey to America*, 164, quoted in Williams, 124. See also Jones-Rogers, *They Were Her Property*, 147–49; Schafer, *Brothels, Depravity, and Abandoned Women*, 11, 40; Owens, "Fantasies of Consent."

8. *A. F. Dunbar v. Sarah Conner*, 2496; Spear, *Race, Sex, and Social Order in Early New Orleans*, 109–10, 193; Jones-Rogers, *They Were Her Property*, 97–98. The legislature also imposed age requirements on manumission; in 1827 the state waived the stipulation that the person in question had to be thirty years of age, but only if they were born in Louisiana and received official permission. In the 1850s the state further restricted manumissions. Schafer, "'Open and Notorious Concubinage,'" 165–82.

9. *A. F. Dunbar v. Sarah Conner*, 2496.

10. Jones-Rogers, *They Were Her Property*, 132; U.S. Census Bureau, *Seventh Census, 1850*, Third District, Orleans Parish, New Orleans, s.v. "Sarah Conner"; *James Whitefield Boazman v. His Wife C. Emeline Robinson*, Docket 5930, Fourth District Court, Orleans Parish, NOPL; advertisement, *Daily Crescent*, 25 Mar. 1851; *Willis J. Bishop v. Celeste Powell*, Docket 8143, Fourth District Court, Orleans Parish, NOPL. For other accounts of enslaved women renting out rooms and living on their own, see Johnson, *Slavery's Metropolis*.

11. Single at the time she met Conner, Melissa Tarrington later married a man named William Garrison in Hamilton County, Ohio. Though married in Ohio, the Garrisons continued to live in New Orleans in the later 1840s, moving into "Mrs. Hickey's on Gravier Street" on the same block as Conner. That they married in Ohio suggests that the Garrisons may have been a mixed-race couple and that Tarrington was able to pass as white, and thus legally marry Garrison, in the North. *Bank of Kentucky v. Theophilus Freeman*, Docket 150, Fourth District Court, Orleans Parish, NOPL.

12. *Bank of Kentucky v. Freeman*, 150.

13. *Sarah Conner v. Bank of Kentucky*, Docket 1704, Fourth District Court, Orleans Parish, NOPL.

14. *Bank of Kentucky v. Conner, f.w.c. et al.*, Docket 1315, Supreme Court of Louisiana, 4 La. Ann. 365; *A. F. Dunbar v. Sarah Conner*, 2496.

15. Deed Book 30, 446, New Orleans Notarial Archives; *Bank of Kentucky v. Conner, f.w.c. et al.*, 1315; *A. F. Dunbar v. Sarah Conner*, 2496.

16. *Sarah Conner v. Theophilus Freeman, Bank of Kentucky*, Docket 1883, Fifth District Court, Orleans Parish, NOPL

17. Northup, Logsdon, and Eakin, *Twelve Years a Slave*, 50–58.

18. *Sarah Conner v. A. F. Dunbar*, 2496.

19. The Globe was a "large house in Broadway" that had formerly been "kept by Mrs. Mann." "Globe Hotel," *Mercury*, 19 May 1836; *Sarah Conner v. A. F. Dunbar*, 2496.

20. Melissa Tarrington Garrison said she was married in Hamilton County. U.S. Census Bureau, *Seventh Census, 1850*, Ward 1, Cincinnati, Hamilton County, Ohio, s.v. "Fanny Preston"; U.S. Census Bureau, *Eighth Census, 1860*, Ward 1, Cincinnati, Hamilton County, Ohio, s.v. "Fanny Preston"; *Sarah Conner v. Bank of Kentucky*, 1704.

21. Coffin, *Reminiscences of Levi Coffin*, 287–88. For more on people of African descent in Cincinnati, see Taylor, *Frontiers of Freedom*; for enslaved women who had children with slave traders in particular, see Green, *Remember Me to Miss Louisa*.

22. See Fuentes, *Dispossessed Lives*; Hartman, *Scenes of Subjection*; Owens, "Fantasies of Consent"; Williams, "Quadroon Balls."

23. *A. F. Dunbar v. Sarah Conner*, 2496.

24. *Bank of Kentucky v. Theophilus Freeman*, 150. For Williams, see Forret, *Williams' Gang*.

25. *Sarah Conner v. A. F. Dunbar*, Docket 1193, Fifth District Court, Orleans Parish, NOPL.

26. *Sarah Conner v. A. F. Dunbar*, 1193.

27. *Sarah Conner v. A. F. Dunbar*, 1193.

28. *Theophilus Freeman v. His Creditors & the Creditors of John Goodin & Co.*, Docket 23783, Fifth District Court, Orleans Parish, NOPL.

29. *Theophilus Freeman v. His Creditors & the Creditors of John Goodin & Co.*, 23783. Debts owed to Freeman included notes from slave traders Overby & Saunders in Maryland, Richmond slave trader Lewis A. Collier, and former partner William H. Finnall.

30. *Sarah Conner v. Theophilus Freeman, Bank of Kentucky*, 1883.

31. *Sarah Conner v. Theophilus Freeman, Bank of Kentucky*, 1883, emphasis in original.

32. *Sarah Conner v. Theophilus Freeman, Bank of Kentucky*, 1883.

33. "About Marrying," *Daily Picayune*, 14 May 1871.

34. "About Marrying," *Daily Picayune*, 14 May 1871.

35. "Legislative Proceedings," *Times Picayune*, 4 Feb. 1847; "Legislative Proceedings," *Daily Picayune*, 18 Apr. 1847.

36. Schafer, "'Open and Notorious Concubinage,'" 168–69.

37. *Sarah Conner v. A. F. Dunbar*, 2496.

38. *Succession of Pierre Pereuilhet, Opposition of Doria Hauthe*, Docket 2031, Supreme Court of Louisiana (unreported).

39. *Sarah Conner v. A. F. Dunbar*, 2496; *Junius Amis v. Bank of Kentucky*, Docket 1794, Fourth District Court, Orleans Parish, NOPL; *Sarah Conner v. James White*, Docket 3868, Third District Court, Orleans Parish, NOPL.

40. U.S. Census Bureau, *Seventh Census, 1850*, District 3, New Orleans, Orleans Parish, s.v. "C. S. Fenner"; *Sarah Conner v. J. T. Hatcher*, Docket 5839, Fourth District Court, Orleans Parish, NOPL; *Sarah Conner v. James White*, 3868; *Sarah Conner v. Caroline Stewart*, Docket 3141, Third District Court Orleans Parish, NOPL. Descriptions of Conner's furnishings come from *Sarah Conner v. A. F. Dunbar & J. L. Lewis*, Docket

2568, Fifth District Court, Orleans Parish, NOPL. Conner refused to pay court costs, and the sheriff seized her furniture for auction. She paid the debt the day before the auction was to take place.

41. *A. F. Dunbar v. Sarah Conner*, 2496. Conner also maneuvered to take advantage of the money to be made from renting out space to be used as a slave jail. By 1851 Conner had a part in renting the shed in the back of the property to slave trader James White, charging him $50 a month and suing him when he failed to pay. She allowed another trader, L. H. Huddleston, to rent the top level of the house and imprison enslaved people there, using Freeman as his jailer. *Sarah Conner v. James White*, 3868.

42. Conner may have purchased an enslaved woman in 1846, prior to her purchase of Mary Ann and Ellen. Freeman was involved in this purchase, and it may have been completed with his money. Freeman certainly acted as her agent in other instances. For example, Conner purchased an enslaved woman, Mariah, from Freeman, who was acting as the agent of Edward Baxter, only to sell Mariah—with Freeman acting as Conner's agent this time—to W. M. Myers of South Carolina. Mariah happened to be the former slave of W. D. Amis, a relative of Junius. The U.S. marshal had seized Mariah in relation to Amis's financial and legal troubles, and Baxter had purchased her—allegedly. A slave trader, Archibald Lilly, claimed that Conner had told him, "After the death of Mr. Amis they (I inferred she meant the sheriff) were trying to get possession of this slave and she (Sarah) had secreted the girl in the back of the 2nd municipality." Had Conner worked with Freeman to remove Mariah from seizure for their economic gain, or had she hoped to help Mariah by saving her from public auction? *Sarah Conner v. Bank of Kentucky*, 1704.

43. Hartman, "Venus in Two Acts," 3. As Marisa Fuentes writes, "A legible and linear narrative cannot sufficiently account for the palimpsest of material and meaning embedded in the lives of people shaped by the intimacies and ubiquities of violence." Fuentes, *Dispossessed Lives*, 6.

44. *Freeman v. His Creditors & the Creditors of John Goodin*, 23783.

45. *Bank of Kentucky v. Theophilus Freeman*, 150.

46. *Bank of Kentucky v. Theophilus Freeman*, 150; *Freeman v. His Creditors & the Creditors of John Goodin*, 23783. Robert Mott also represented the Union Bank of Maryland in an 1842 case against Freeman over a protested bill of exchange drawn by R. & I. Smith and accepted by Freeman. The next year he faced Freeman in court yet again, this time representing the Merchants' Insurance Company against Freeman over a protested note signed by Freeman and Lewis A. Collier of Richmond. *Union Bank of Maryland v. Freeman*, Docket 4938, Supreme Court of Louisiana; *Merchants' Insurance Company of New Orleans v. Theophilus Freeman*, Docket 5292, Supreme Court of Louisiana.

47. *Sarah Conner v. Bank of Kentucky*, 1704. Freeman's associate Julius Amis similarly petitioned the court, claiming that the two enslaved men, Emmanuel and Isham, actually belonged to him. For another consideration of Sarah Conner's experiences in the courtroom, and Mott's ability to discredit her via the language of race and concubinage, see Montalvo, "Slavers' Archive."

48. *Jean Pierre Michael Dupré administrator v. Frosine Uzée, tutrix*, Docket 2101 (Mar. 1851), Louisiana Supreme Court, 6 La. Ann 280. For other cases of concubinage

being used as grounds for disinheritance, see Schafer, "'Open and Notorious Concubinage.'"

49. *Jean Pierre Michael Dupré administrator v. Frosine Uzée, tutrix*, 2101.

50. *Jean Pierre Michael Dupré administrator v. Frosine Uzée, tutrix*, 2101.

51. *A. F. Dunbar v. Sarah Conner*, 2496; *Bank of Kentucky v. Sarah Conner*, 1315. They also argued that her emancipation was null and void because she was not of the required age in 1841.

52. *Sarah Conner v. Bank of Kentucky*, 1704; *A. F. Dunbar v. Sarah Conner*, 2496. By the summer of 1848, Conner was involved in five suits pending in the parish courts, while Freeman was and had been party to many more. Conner's suits and counter-suits included: *Bank of Kentucky v. Sarah Conner*, 1315; *Sarah Conner v. Bank of Kentucky*, 1704; *Sarah Conner v. A. F. Dunbar*, 1193; *Sarah Conner v. A. F. Dunbar & J. L. Lewis*, 2568; *A. F. Dunbar v. Sarah Conner*, 2496. For a sampling of Freeman's cases, see *Bank of Kentucky v. Theophilus Freeman*, 150; *Freeman v. His Creditors and the Creditors of John Goodin & Co.*, 23783; *Lambeth et al. v. Freeman*, Docket 5588 (June 1846), Supreme Court of Louisiana (unreported); *Edward C. Mielke v. Freeman and others*, Docket 5874, Commercial Court of New Orleans, NOPL; *Union Bank of Maryland v. Freeman*, Docket 4938 (Jan. 1843), Supreme Court of Louisiana, 3 Rob. 485.

53. *Bank of Kentucky v. Conner, f.w.c. et al.*, 1315.

54. *A. F. Dunbar v. Sarah Conner*, 2496.

55. *A. F. Dunbar v. Sarah Conner*, 2496. Though the sheriff sold Ellen, Emmanuel, Isham, and Mary Ann, litigation over their sale, and over who should receive the proceeds from it, continued into the 1850s. A Mr. Castance purchased Mary Ann, but the deputy sheriff complicated the final sale, as he wanted to buy Mary Ann from Castance. A year later, as the two men wrestled for legal ownership of Mary Ann's body, she was temporarily in the custody of "Mrs. Morse" of the St. Charles Hotel, again performing domestic labor for people renting rooms.

56. Schafer, *Becoming Free, Remaining Free*, 130–37; "The Case of Sarah Conner," *Times Picayune*, 8 Aug. 1851. Though Conner had not received permission to stay, she was still registered in the city's record of "free colored persons entitled to remain in the state" in 1846.

57. "The Case of Sarah Conner," *Times Picayune*, 8 Aug. 1851; "Bound to Leave the State," *Times Picayune*, 7 Aug. 1851; Schafer, *Remaining Free*, 133–37.

58. Peter was also called Pierre. *State v. Sarah Conner*, Docket 7158, First District Court, Orleans Parish, NOPL; *State v. Sarah Conner f.w.c.*, Docket 2759 (June 1852), Supreme Court of Louisiana, 7 La. Ann. 379.

59. *State v. Theophilus Freeman*, First District Court, Docket 7158, Orleans Parish, NOPL.

60. *State v. Theophilus Freeman*, 7158; *State v. Sarah Conner*, 7158.

61. *State v. Theophilus Freeman*, 7158; *State v. Sarah Conner*, 7158.

62. "Suit to Annul Free Papers," *Anti-Slavery Bugle*, 9 Feb. 1850; "Trial for Perjury," *Times Picayune*, 31 Mar. 1852; "The Case of Sarah Conner," *Times Picayune*, 29 June 1852; "Trial of Theophilus Freeman," *Times Picayune*, 3 June 1852; "The Perjury Case," *Daily Crescent*, 21 Aug. 1851.

63. "The Perjury Case," *Times Picayune*, 15 Aug. 1851.

64. My thanks to Maria Montalvo for her research into the penitentiary and the lack of evidence for Conner being jailed there.

65. Northup, Logsdon, and Eakin, *Twelve Years a Slave*, 243. Freeman had for some time rented rooms to prostitutes, and on several occasions, when they tired of their landlord's harassment, these women confronted him. In 1858, Belle Thompson, Kate Brunell, and Mary Doane broke into Freeman's house, destroying "two chairs, a number of window panes & a quantity of glassware and crockery valued at about $15 or $20, and that at the same time and place said Kate Bruenell drew a knife on deponent and cut at him with it; that said Belle Thompson also drew a knife on deponent, and said Mary Doane . . . aided and abetted and assisted said Belle Thompson and Kate Brunell in said assault." *State v. Belle Thompson, Kate Burnell & Mary Doane*, Docket 13612, First District Court of New Orleans, NOPL; "Recorder Summers' Court," *Daily Crescent*, 11 Dec. 1858.

66. Intriguingly, Isard was one of the purchasers at the court auction of the people Freeman enslaved. Conner's association with Isard may have predated her trial for perjury. Isard was also actively involved in the city's Phoenix Fire Brigade and several fraternal organizations. U.S. Census Bureau, *Eighth Census, 1860*, Fourth Ward, New Orleans, Orleans Parish, s.v. "Smith Izard"; Smith L. Isard, *Proofs of Citizenship Used to Apply for Seamen's Certificates for the Port of Philadelphia, Pennsylvania, 1792–1861*, NARA Microfilm publication M1880, 61 rolls, Records of the U.S. Customs Service, Record Group 36. National Archives, Washington, D.C., Roll 34; "Phoenix Fire Co. No. 8," *Times Picayune*, 15 Jan. 1846; "Police Appointments," *Times Picayune*, 22 June 1860; "The Robbery of the Steamship Lizzie," *Times Picayune*, 11 Oct. 1866.

67. "Died," *Times Picayune*, 24 Nov. 1872; U.S. Census Bureau, *Ninth Census, 1870*, Third Ward, New Orleans, Orleans Parish, Louisiana, s.v. "Smith Isard."

68. Succession of Smith L. Isard, Docket 35,917, Second District Court, Orleans Parish, NOPL.

69. *Sarah Conner v. William Schneider*, Docket 5862, Fifth District Court, Orleans Parish, NOPL; U.S. Census Bureau, *Tenth Census, 1880*, New Orleans, Orleans Parish, Louisiana, s.v. "Sarah Conner."

70. Will of Sarah Ann Conner, District of Columbia, filed May 9, 1892. My thanks to Maria Montalvo for sharing this will with me. Conner's bequests included "my pair of diamond earrings containing eight diamonds in each ring," Smith Isard's watch and chain, $700 in the Safe Deposit Bank of Washington, both her "best" and "domestic" bedding and wearing apparel, hair mattresses, a feather bed, pillows, carpets and carpeting, a camphor chest, and furniture. She also made a special provision of bedding and clothing to "such person as shall stay with me and care for me with the attention of a daughter until my death."

71. Will of Sarah Ann Conner; Death Record of Sarah Ann Connor, Louisiana State Archives.

Chapter Four

1. Succession of Lucy Ann Hagan, 21696 Civil District Court, Orleans Parish, Louisiana, NOPL.

2. Succession of Lucy Ann Hagan, 21696.

3. Succession of Lucy Ann Hagan, 21696.

4. Succession of Lucy Ann Hagan, 21696.

5. Succession of Lucy Ann Hagan, 21696.

6. For more on the changing definition of home and domestic life in the antebellum period, see Boydston, *Home and Work*; Gamber, *The Boardinghouse in Nineteenth-Century America*; Matthews, *Just a Housewife*; McCurry, *Masters of Small Worlds*.

7. Gamber, *Boardinghouse*, 7.

8. Glymph, *Out of the House of Bondage*, 76. See also Fox-Genovese, *Within the Plantation Household*; White, *Ar'n't I a Woman?*

9. For the "houseful," see Hartigan-O'Connor, *Ties That Buy*, 14. For the household, see Fox-Genovese, *Within the Plantation Household*, and McCurry, *Masters of Small Worlds*.

10. Here I am drawing on Arlie Russell Hochschild's concept of emotional labor. Hochschild, *The Managed Heart*.

11. *Jean Pierre Michael Dupré administrator v. Frosine Uzée, tutrix*, Docket 2101 (Mar. 1851), Supreme Court of Louisiana, 6 La. Ann 280; "The Reed Case," *Daily Crescent*, 27 Sept. 1848; Clark, *Strange History of the American Quadroon*, 59–61, 148–49, 156–57. For the *ménagère*, see Rogers, "Les libres de couleur dans les capitals de Saint-Domingue"; Garrigus, *Before Haiti*; King, *Blue Coat or Powdered Wig*.

12. Brown, *From Fugitive Slave to Free Man*, 41–45.

13. *Sarah Conner v. A. F. Dunbar*, Docket 2496, Fifth District Court, Orleans Parish, NOPL.

14. *Andrew Quirk v. F. E. Jump and O. B. Chapin*, Docket 7922, Third District Court, Orleans Parish, NOPL.

15. Succession of Lucy Ann Hagan, 21696.

16. *Montague's 1850/51 Richmond City Directory*, 61; *Ferslew's 1859 Richmond City Directory*, 213; advertisement, *Raleigh Register*, 31 Mar. 1860.

17. Succession of Lucy Ann Hagan, 21696.

18. Hendrick and Hendrick, *The Creole Mutiny*, 82–83. At least four of the women kept as "maids" chose to journey on to New Orleans with the *Creole* despite the opportunity of freedom in Nassau. Two of them allegedly attempted to assist the captain in hiding during the mutiny. This information, however, was based on the testimony of the Americans on board the ship, who had an interest in portraying the majority of the enslaved people as complacent and happy with their lot. See also Block, *Rape and Sexual Power in Early America*, 67.

19. Alexander was the oldest brother, born in Charlotte, North Carolina, around 1806. John, the middle brother, was born in 1812 in Lancasterville, South Carolina. The youngest brother, Hugh, was also born in South Carolina. Their parents, John Hagan and Rosanna McDonald, were immigrants from Ireland. "Hugh McDonald" and "Alexander McDonald," U.S. Naturalization Records (NARA), Washington D.C.; Record of Admissions to Citizenship, District of South Carolina, 1790–1906 Series: M1183 (NARA); *Colclough v. Colclough*, Bill 347 (1849), Sumter District Equity Court; *Colclough v. Colclough*, Bill 348 (1852), Sumter District Equity Court, South Carolina Department of Archives and History (hereafter cited as SCA); *Green et al. v. McDonald*

et al., Bill 415 (1866), Sumter District Equity Court, SCA. Thank you to Jill Found for helping me locate these cases.

20. For more on the Hagans, their finances, and their social standing, see Alexandra J. Finley, "A Gentleman and a Scoundrel? Alexander McDonald, Financial Reputation, and Slavery's Capitalism," in *Scoundrels, Shysters, and Confidence Men*, ed. Bruce Baker and Jeff Forret; *John Rist v. John Hagan*, Docket 4503 (June 1844), Supreme Court of Louisiana Eastern District, 8 Rob. 106; *Bank of the State of South Carolina v. John Hagan*, Docket 134, Fourth District Court, Orleans Parish, NOPL.

21. Succession of Lucy Ann Hagan, 21696; for more on African American women and self-representation of sexuality, see Hine, "Rape and the Inner Lives of Black Women in the Middle West," 912–20.

22. Picquet and Mattison, *The Octoroon*, 18–19.

23. Picquet and Mattison, *The Octoroon*, 18–19.

24. Owens, "Fantasies of Consent," 4; Block, "Lines of Color, Sex, and Service: Comparative Sexual Coercion in Early America," in *Sex, Love, Race*, ed. Hodes, 141–63.

25. S. H. Christian to R. H. Dickinson, 24 Jan. 1855, Miscellaneous Files, Robert Alonzo Brock Collection, LVA. My thanks to Robert Colby for sharing this letter with me.

26. S. H. Christian to R. H. Dickinson, 24 Jan. 1855.

27. S. H. Christian to R. H. Dickinson, 24 Jan. 1855.

28. S. H. Christian to R. H. Dickinson, 24 Jan. 1855.

29. S. H. Christian to R. H. Dickinson, 24 Jan. 1855.

30. Although Cheatham's daughter's name appeared in a variety of spellings, I have chosen to spell her name here as Frederika, it being the spelling she used when signing her name in her mother's estate documents. Succession of Lucy Ann Hagan, 21696.

31. Succession of Lucy Ann Hagan, 21696. See, for example, "A String of Items," *Daily Crescent*, 27 Sept. 1850; advertisement, *Daily Crescent*, 18 June 1850; Bremer, *Homes of the New World*, 194–209.

32. Succession of Lucy Ann Hagan, 21696.

33. Mary Nelson Wilson also "knew Mrs. Mary Lumpkin," though she did not mention how. Succession of Lucy Ann Hagan, 21696; Petition of Jonathan M. Wilson, Docket 10417, Second District Court, Orleans Parish, NOPL; U.S. Census Bureau, *Eighth Census, 1860*, New Orleans, Orleans Parish, Louisiana, s.v. "J. M. Wilson." In 1855, after several years of debate and the failure of various emancipation policies, Louisiana turned the question of manumission over to the district courts. Schafer, *Becoming Free, Remaining Free*, 12–14.

34. Succession of Lucy Ann Hagan, 21696; *Sarah Conner v. Bank of Kentucky*, Docket 1704, Fourth District Court, Orleans Parish, NOPL; *Louisa Peterson f.w.c. v. John Stewart and John Lewis, sheriff*, Docket 4798, Fourth District Court, Orleans Parish; *Ann Maria Barclay, f.w.c. v. Sewell, curator*, Docket 4622, Louisiana Supreme Court, 12 La. Ann. 262 (1857). For more on Barclay, see Owens, "Fantasies of Consent."

35. Succession of Lucy Ann Hagan, 21696.

36. Camp, *Closer to Freedom*, 3.

37. Succession of Lucy Ann Hagan, 21696.

38. Succession of Lucy Ann Hagan, 21696.

39. Succession of Lucy Ann Hagan, 21696.

40. Will of John Hagan #10362, vol. 10, Orleans Parish, NOPL; "One Hundred Dollars Reward," *Daily Picayune*, 10 Sept. 1848.

41. Will of John Hagan, 10362; Schafer, *Becoming Free*, 14.

42. Will of John Hagan, 10362, In a reflection of his varied business interests, some of the financial paper John Hagan owned belonged to slave traders, but some did not. The largest promissory note was from W. G. Hewes, president of the New Orleans & Opelousas Railroad, and endorsed by B. F. Flanders, secretary of said company, for $15,000. He invested in another railroad company, as well, among other corporations. In June 1856 he possessed ten shares capital stock of the New Orleans and Jackson Railroad Company and 182 shares in the Citizens Bank of Louisiana worth $28,210.00. The Great Northern Railroad Company had given Hagan twenty-five bonds as collateral for a $15,000 note. Hagan had also previously invested in the expansion of the cotton kingdom farther south: he owned "Certificate number 453 & 464 for fifteen hundred dollars Cuba funds signed by G. Betancourt," which was, by 1856, "considered of no value by the appraisers." Hagan additionally had accounts at three banks—the Citizen's Bank of Louisiana, the Union Bank of Louisiana, and the Bank of Louisiana—with varying balances in his favor.

43. Will of John Hagan, 10362. John Hagan may have left additional, private instructions to Alexander Hagan and Edward Barnett to look after Lucy and their children. John left to Alexander the "remainder" of his estate after all bequests had been made and debts paid. Alexander Hagan and Barnett must have carried out John's wishes in regard to Cheatham. At least part of the children's inheritance ended up being in the form of Louisiana State Bank stock, which Hagan had not specified in his will. Cheatham maintained contact with both Alexander Hagan and Barnett. Alexander continued to operate the slave jail on Esplanade for several years before his own death, meaning that Cheatham likely shared the household with him. When Alexander became ill, shortly after his brother, Cheatham nursed him, just as she had John. The remaining brother, Hugh, recorded a payment to her for her services after Alexander's death. Succession of Alexander Hagan 11945, Second District Court, Orleans Parish, NOPL.

44. *Louisa Hackman v. J & JF Garnier*, Docket 16805, Third District Court, Orleans Parish NOPL.

45. Gamber, *Boardinghouse*, 39.

46. Data from author's database of the 1860 U.S. Census; Gamber, *Boardinghouse*, 7.

47. Gamber, *Boardinghouse*, 7; Henry J. Lovejoy, *The Laws and Revised Ordinances of the City of New Orleans* (New Orleans: E. C. Wharton, 1857), 131, 240, 242, 246. Historic New Orleans Collection JS1201.A9.A3 1857-70-12-L; data from author's database.

48. Gamber, *Boardinghouse*, 62–64, 74.

49. Gamber, *Boardinghouse*, 74.

50. Gamber, *Boardinghouse*, 13; *Eliza Hammond v. TB Blackburn*, Docket 8730, Fourth District Court, Orleans Parish, NOPL.

51. *Eliza Hammond v. TB Blackburn*, 8730.

52. Gamber, *Boardinghouse*, 8.

53. "A Resident," *New Orleans As It Is . . .* , 44.

54. Picquet and Mattison, *The Octoroon*, 11.

55. Johnson, *Slavery's Metropolis*, 95.

56. *Mary Powell alias Elvire Malotte v. Joseph McQuiston*, Docket 14875, Third District Court, Orleans Parish, NOPL.

57. *Lucy Cheatham v. Her Creditors*, Docket 19579, Second District Court, Orleans Parish, NOPL. Cheatham also acquired additional real estate; the 1860 census valued her real estate holdings at $15,000, well beyond the $4,000 property Hagan left her. In 1859, for instance, she purchased seven lots in the Second District of New Orleans. New Orleans Notarial Archives, Deed Book 81, 265–67.

58. *Lucy Cheatham v. Her Creditors*, 19579.

59. New Orleans Notarial Archives, Deed Book 72, 651; Deed Book 77, 73; Deed Book 81, 265–67.

60. *Lucy Cheatham v. Her Creditors*, 19579.

61. *Lucy Cheatham v. Her Creditors*, 19579.

62. *Lucy Cheatham v. Her Creditors*, 19579; *Louisa Hackman v. J & JF Garnier*, 16805.

63. *Lucy Ann Cheatham, f.w.c. praying to be tutrix . . .* , Docket 19388, Second District Court, Orleans Parish, NOPL.

64. *Lucy Ann Cheatham, f.w.c. praying to be tutrix . . .* , 19388.

65. *Lucy Ann Cheatham f.w.c. v. Her Creditors*, 19579. After the sale Cheatham was still left in possession of her children's half interest in the lots on Esplanade. In 1864, however, she convened another family meeting, where it was decided that the land should be sold and the proceeds used for their benefit.

66. *Samuel Barrett v. Mrs. L. A. Hagan & John Ray*, Docket 35350, Supreme Court of Louisiana (unreported). With few assets of her own, Cheatham had to turn to someone with racial privilege to assist her in paying her daughter's tuition. John Ray, a lawyer who was likely one of Cheatham's boarders, cosigned Cheatham's promissory notes to the school and was thus cited to appear in court with her when the notes went unpaid.

67. Succession of Lucy Ann Hagan, 21696; U.S. Census Bureau, *Ninth Census, 1870*, Fifth Ward, New Orleans, Orleans Parish, Louisiana s.v. "Lucy Hagan"; U.S. Census Bureau, *Tenth Census, 1880*, New Orleans, Orleans Parish, Louisiana s.v. "Lucy Hagan."

68. Succession of Lucy Ann Hagan, 21696.

69. Succession of Lucy Ann Hagan, 21696.

70. Succession of Lucy Ann Hagan, 21696.

71. Succession of Lucy Ann Hagan, 21696.

72. Succession of Lucy Ann Hagan, 21696.

73. Succession of Lucy Ann Hagan, 21696.

74. "Personal," *New Orleans Republican*, 3 Apr. 1875. Lulu White's famous Storyville Brothel was also named Mahogany Hall. Brothels like White's in many ways played upon the transgressive sex across the color line of the antebellum era, advertising "octoroon" prostitutes in language familiar to the fancy trade and "tragic mulatto" literature. Landau, *Spectacular Wickedness*; Long, *Great Southern Babylon*.

75. Camp, *Closer to Freedom*, 3.

Conclusion

1. *Boyd's 1892 Directory of the District of Columbia*, 322; *Boyd's 1887 Directory of the District of Columbia*, 324.

2. Bianchi, Sayer, Milkie, and Robinson, "Housework"; Bittman et al. "When Does Gender Trump Money?"; Brines, "Economic Dependency, Gender, and the Division of Labor at Home"; Sayer, "Gender, Time, and Inequality."

3. Yeung, *In a Day's Work*, 79. See Anderson, *Doing the Dirty Work*; Bernam and Theodore, *Home Economics*; Ehrenreich and Hochschild, eds., *Global Woman*; Hochschild, *Commercialization of Intimate Life*; Nadasen, *Household Workers Unite*; Palmer, *Domesticity and Dirt*; Perea, "The Echoes of Slavery"; Rollins, *Between Women*; Romero, *Maid in the U.S.A.*; Romero, Preston, and Giles, eds., *When Care Work Goes Global*. For more on the National Domestic Workers' Alliance and how to take action, visit https://www.domesticworkers.org/.

4. Olivo quoted in Yeung, *In a Day's Work*, 79.

Epilogue

1. "Mrs. C Omohundro," *Union Provost Marshals' File of Papers Relating to Individual Citizens* NARA Microfilm publication M345 Roll 207.

2. "Mrs. C Omohundro."

Bibliography

Abbreviations

LVA   Library of Virginia
NARA   National Archives and Records Administration
NCSA   North Carolina State Archives
NOPL   New Orleans Public Library City Archives and Louisiana Division
SCA   South Carolina Department of Archives and History
VHS   Virginia Historical Society

Primary Sources

Manuscripts

Illinois
  Chicago History Museum
    Hector Davis Account Book
    R. H. Dickinson Letters
Kentucky
  Frankfort: Kentucky Department of Archives
    Fayette County Circuit Court Records
Louisiana
  Baton Rouge: Louisiana State Archives
    Louisiana Death Certificates
  New Orleans: City Archives/Louisiana Division, New Orleans Public Library
    Louisiana Register of Free Colored Persons Entitled to Remain in the State,
        Volume 1, 1840–1856
    New Orleans City Directories
    Orleans Parish Civil District Court Cases
    Orleans Parish First District Court Cases
    Orleans Parish Second District Court Cases
    Orleans Parish Third District Court Cases
    Orleans Parish Fourth District Court Cases
    Orleans Parish Fifth District Court Cases
    Orleans Parish Will Books
  New Orleans: Historic New Orleans Collection
    City of New Orleans Antebellum Collection MSS462
    New Orleans City Directories
    Henry J. Lovejoy, *The Laws and Revised Ordinances of the City of New Orleans*
    "A Resident," *New Orleans As It Is: Its Manners and Customs . . .* (1849)

New Orleans: Notarial Archives
    Orleans Parish Deed Books
University of New Orleans
    Louisiana Supreme Court Cases Database
Massachusetts
    Boston Public Library
        Ziba Oakes Papers
North Carolina
    Chapel Hill: University of North Carolina at Chapel Hill
        John Caldwell Papers
        Cameron Family Papers
        Charles Dewey Papers
        F. H. Elmore Papers
        William Ethelbert Ervin Journals
        Herndon Haralson Papers
        James Thomas Harrison Papers
        Isaac Jarratt Papers
        George W. Mordecai Papers
        A. Walker and A. T. Walker Account Book, 1851–1861
    Durham: Rubenstein Library, Duke University
        Obadiah Fields Papers
        William A. J. Finney Papers
        Tyre Glen Papers
        William Haynie Hatchett Papers
        Henry A. Ince Papers
        Jarratt-Puryear Papers
        Malvern Hill Omohundro Papers
        D. M. Pulliam Papers
        Slave Transporters' Notebook, 1845
        Samuel O. Woods Papers
        Southwest Railroad Bank Records
    Raleigh: North Carolina State Archives
        Badgett Family Papers
        Elias W. Ferguson Papers
Pennsylvania
    Haverford: Haverford College Special Collections
        Julia Wilbur Diary
    Lancaster: Lancaster County Courthouse
        Lancaster County Miscellaneous Books
    Lancaster: Lancaster County Historical Society
        Records of the Estate of Silas Omohundro in the Orphans' Court of Lancaster
            County, Pennsylvania
    Philadelphia: Philadelphia City Archives
        Philadelphia Death Records
        Philadelphia Deed Books

  Philadelphia Marriage Records
  Philadelphia Orphans' Court Records
 Philadelphia: National Archives Repository
  U.S. District Court Eastern District of Virginia Records
South Carolina
 Charleston: South Carolina Historical Society
  Bank of Charleston Records
  Southwest Railroad Bank Records
 Charleston: State Library of South Carolina
  Petitions to the Legislature of South Carolina
 Columbia: South Caroliniana Library
  John Christopher Faber Papers
  McGee and Charles Family Papers
  Planters and Mechanics Bank of Charleston Accounts
  John D. Warren Papers
Virginia
 Charlottesville: University of Virginia Alderman Library
  Cocke Family Papers, 1725–1939
  Silas and R. F. Omohundro Accounts of Slave Trade and Farm Accounts,
   1857–1864
 Richmond: John Marshall Court Building
  Richmond City Chancery Court Case Files
 Richmond: Library of Virginia
  Alonzo Brock Collection
  Beasley, Wood, & Jones Slave Trade Account Book, 1835–1851
  Dickinson, Hill & Co. (Richmond, Va.) Account Books, 1846–1849, 1855–1858
  Richmond City Records
   Richmond City Circuit Court Will Book 2, 1861–1865
   Richmond City Common Hall Records
   Richmond City Hustings Court Deed Books, 1831–1867
   Richmond City Hustings Court Minutes, 1853–1867
   Richmond City Hustings Court Order Books, 1846–1867
   Richmond City Hustings Court Will Books 2, 24
   Richmond City Hustings Wills, Inventories, and Accounts, 1824–1828
  Silas Omohundro Business and Estate Records, 1842–1882
 Richmond: Virginia Historical Society
  Bank of the Commonwealth Records, 1859–1865
  Bassett Family Papers Section 28
  Edmund Berkeley Accounts, 1824–1915
  Branch and Company Records
  Dabney Family Papers
  Early Family Papers Section 48
  Farmers Bank of Virginia Records, 1812–1853
  Fauquier Savings Institution Records, 1835–1839
  William Mayo Fulton Papers

George Family Papers
Gwathney Family Papers
Henry Lee Letter, July 17, 1827
Robert E. Lee Letter, May 11, 1861
Mason Papers Section 48
Matthew Bates Nowlin Papers, 1792–1856
Silas Omohundro Receipt of Sale, Mss2Om653 a 1
Thomas Randolph Price Papers
Signet Banking Corporation Records, 1795–1996
Charles Simeon Stringfellow Papers
P.M. Tabb & Son Letter
Wyllie Family Papers, 1798–1881, Section 1
   Williamsburg: College of William & Mary Special Collections
      Austin-Twyman Papers
Washington, DC
   National Archives
      Union Provost Marshals' File of Papers Relating to Individual Citizens

Books

Abdy, Edward S. *Journal of a Residence and Tour in the United States of North America, from April, 1833, to October, 1834*. 3 vols. London, 1835.
Adams, Nemiah. *A South-Side View of Slavery, or, Three Months at the South, in 1854.* Boston, 1855.
Andrews, Ethan Allen. *Slavery and the Domestic Slave Trade in the United States.* Boston: Light and Stearns, 1836.
Ball, Charles. *Fifty Years in Chains, or, the Life of an American Slave.* New York, 1859.
Beecher, Catherine E. *A Treatise on Domestic Economy, for the Use of Young Ladies at Home, and at School.* Boston: Thomas H. Webb and Co., 1843.
Blair, John S. ed. *The Washington Law Reporter*, vol. 15. Washington, D.C.: Law Reporter Print, 1887.
Bremer, Fredrika. *The Homes of the New World; Impressions of America.* Translated by Mary Howitt. 2 vols. New York: Harper and Bros., 1853. Reprint, New York: Johnson Reprint, 1968.
Brown, John. *Slave Life in Georgia: A Narrative of the Life, Sufferings, and Escape of John Brown, a Fugitive Slave.* Edited by F. N. Boney. Savannah, GA: Beehive Press, 1991.
Brown, William Wells. *Clotel; or, The President's Daughter: A Narrative of Slave Life in the United States.* London: Partridge and Oakey, 1853.
———. *From Fugitive Slave to Free Man: The Autobiographies of William Wells Brown.* Edited by William L. Andrews. New York: Mentor Books, 1993.
Browning, Orville. *The Diary of Orville Hickman Browning*, vol. 1. Edited by Theodore Calvin Pease. Springfield: Illinois State Historical Library, 1925.
Buckingham, James S. *The Slave States of America.* 2 vols. London, 1842.
Business Directory of the Cities of Richmond, Petersburg, Norfolk, and Portsmouth, Virginia, For 1859-'60. New York: William F. Bartlett, 1859.

Chambers, William. *Things as They Are in America*. London, 1854.

Chesnut, Mary Boykin. *A Diary from Dixie*. Edited by Isabella D. Martin and Myrta Lockett Avary. New York: D. Appleton and Co., 1905.

Clark, Washington Augustus. *The History of the Banking Institutions Organized in South Carolina Prior to 1860*. Columbia, SC, 1922.

Coffin, Levi. *Reminiscences of Levi Coffin, the Reputed President of the Underground Railroad; Being a Brief History of the Labors of a Lifetime in Behalf of the Slave, with the Stories of Numerous Fugitives, Who Gained Their Freedom through His Instrumentality, and Many Other Incidents*. Cincinnati: Robert Clarke and Co., 1880.

Collins, Winfield H. *The Domestic Slave Trade of the Southern States*. New York: Broadway, 1904.

Corey, Charles H. *A History of the Richmond Theological Seminary, with Reminiscences of Thirty Years' Work among the Colored People of the South*. Richmond, VA: J. W. Randolph Co., 1895.

de Tocqueville, Alexis. *Journey to America*. 1831. Reprint, New Haven, CT: Yale University Press, 1960.

Duke, Basil W. *History of the Bank of Kentucky, 1792–1895*. Louisville, KY: John P. Morton and Co., 1895.

Ellyson's Richmond City Directory, and Business Reference Book Carefully Arranged for 1845–46. Richmond, VA: H. K. Ellyson, 1846.

Engels, Friedrich. *The Origin of the Family, Private Property, and the State*. Zurich: 1884. Reprint, Moscow: Progress, 1968.

Fairbank, Calvin. *Rev. Calvin Fairbank during Slavery Times: How He "Fought the Good Fight" to Prepare "the Way."* Chicago: R. R. McCabe, 1890.

Featherstonhaugh, George William. *Excursion through the Slave States, from Washington on the Potomac, to the Frontier of Mexico; with Sketches of Popular Manners and Geological Notices*. New York, 1844.

Ferslew, W. Eugene, comp. *First Annual Directory for the City of Richmond, to Which Is Added a Business Directory for 1859*. Richmond: Geo. M. West, 1859.

———. *Second Annual Directory for the City of Richmond, to Which Is Added a Business Directory for 1860*. Richmond, VA, 1860.

Fitzhugh, George. *Cannibals All! Or, Slaves without Masters*. Richmond, VA: A. Morris, 1857.

———. *Sociology for the South, or the Failure of Free Society*. Richmond, VA: A. Morris, 1854.

Gibbon, James S. *The Banks of New-York, Their Dealers, the Clearing House, and the Panic of 1857*. New York, 1859.

Grose, Francis. *Classical Dictionary of the Vulgar Tongue, Revised and Corrected . . .* London, 1823.

Harper, William, James Henry Hammond, Thomas Roderick Dew, and William Gilmore Simms. *The Pro-Slavery Argument*. Philadelphia: Lippincott, Grambo and Co., 1853.

Hotten, James Camden. *The Slang Dictionary; Or, the Vulgar Words, Street Phrases, and 'Fast' Expressions of High and Low Society . . .* London, 1864.

Jacobs, Harriet. *Incidents in the Life of a Slave Girl.* Boston: 1861. Reprint, New York: Signet Classics, 2000.

Keckley, Elizabeth. *Behind the Scenes or, Thirty Years a Slave, and Four Years in the White House.* New York, 1868. Reprint, New York: Penguin Classics, 2005.

Loguen, Jermain Wesley. *The Rev. J. W. Loguen, as a Slave and as a Freeman: A Narrative of Real Life.* Syracuse, NY: 1859.

Martineau, Harriet. *Society in America.* 3 vols. 2nd ed. London: Saunders and Otley, 1837.

———. *Writings on Slavery and the American Civil War.* Edited by Deborah Ann Logan. DeKalb: Northern Illinois University Press, 2002.

Marx, Karl. *Capital: A Critique of Political Economy.* New York: Modern Library, 1906.

McElroy's 1865 Philadelphia Directory. Philadelphia: A. McElroy and Co., 1865.

Montague, William L. *Montague's Richmond Directory and Business Advertiser for 1850–1851* . . . Richmond, VA, 1851.

Newman, Rev. A. M. "Reminiscences." *Baptist Home Mission Monthly* 10, no. 11 (Nov. 1888).

Northup, Solomon, Joseph Logsdon, and Sue L. Eakin. *Twelve Years a Slave.* Baton Rouge: Louisiana State University Press, 1975.

Olmsted, Frederick Law. *The Cotton Kingdom: A Traveller's Observations on Cotton and Slavery in the American Slave States, 1853–1861.* 2 vols. New York: Mason Bros., 1861.

Picquet, Louisa, and Hiram Mattison. *The Octoroon: Or Inside Views of Southern Domestic Life.* New York, 1861.

Redpath, James. *The Roving Editor: Or, Talks with Slaves in the Southern States.* New York: A. B. Burdick, 1859.

Roper, Moses. *A Narrative of the Adventures and Escape of Moses Roper from American Slavery.* London, 1838.

Smith, P. Frazer, ed. *Pennsylvania State Reports*, vol. 66, *Comprising Cases Adjudged in the Supreme Court of Pennsylvania.* Philadelphia: Kay and Bro., 1871.

Stevens, Charles Emery. *Anthony Burns: A History.* Boston: John P. Jewett and Co., 1856. Reprint, New York: Arno Press, 1969.

Stowe, Harriet Beecher. *The Key to Uncle Tom's Cabin.* Boston, 1852. Reprint, New York: Arno Press, 1968.

Tasistro, L. F. *Random Shots and Southern Breezes: Containing Critical Remarks on the Southern States and Southern Institutions, with Semi-Serious Observations on Men and Manners.* New York: Harper and Bros., 1842.

Weld, Theodore Dwight. *American Slavery As It Is: Testimony of a Thousand Witnesses.* New York: American Anti-Slavery Society, 1839.

Newspapers

Anti-Slavery Bugle (New Lisbon, Ohio)

Charleston Mercury (Charleston, South Carolina)

The Daily Crescent (New Orleans, Louisiana)

The Daily Dispatch (Richmond, Virginia)

The Daily Picayune (New Orleans, Louisiana)

The Liberator

The Mercury (New York City, New York)

The Mississippi Free Trader
  (Natchez, Mississippi)
New Bern Sentinel (North Carolina)
Philadelphia Enquirer
Richmond Enquirer

Richmond Whig and
  Daily Advertiser
The Times Picayune
  (New Orleans, Louisiana)
The Washington Critic

Secondary Sources

Albelda, Randy, Christopher Gunn, and William Waller, eds. *Alternatives to Economic Orthodoxy: A Reader in Political Economy*. Armonk, NY: M. E. Sharpe, 1987.

Alexander, Adele Logan. *Ambiguous Lives: Free Women of Color in Rural Georgia, 1789–1879*. Fayetteville: University of Arkansas Press, 1991.

Anderson, Bridget. *Doing the Dirty Work: The Global Politics of Domestic Labour*. London: Zed Books, 2000.

Bancroft, Frederic. *Slave-Trading in the Old South*. Baltimore: J. H. Furst Co., 1931.

Baptist, Edward E. "'Cuffy,' 'Fancy Maids,' and 'One-Eyed Men': Rape, Commodification, and the Domestic Slave Trade in the United States." *American Historical Review* 106, no. 5 (Dec. 2001): 1619–650.

———. *The Half Has Never Been Told: Slavery and the Making of American Capitalism*. New York: Basic Books, 2014.

———. "Toxic Debt, Liar Loans, and Securitized Human Beings: The Panic of 1837 and the Fate of Slavery." *Common-Place: The Interactive Journal of American History* 10 (Apr. 2010).

Baptist, Edward E., and Stephanie M. H. Camp, eds. *New Studies in the History of American Slavery*. Athens: University of Georgia Press, 2006.

Bardaglio, Peter Winthrop. *Reconstructing the Household: Families, Sex, and the Law in the Nineteenth-Century South*. Chapel Hill: University of North Carolina Press, 1995.

Barnes, L. Diane, Brian Schoen, and Frank Towers, eds. *The Old South's Modern Worlds: Slavery, Region, and Nation in the Age of Progress*. New York: Oxford University Press, 2011.

Baucom, Ian. *Specters of the Atlantic: Finance Capital, Slavery, and the Philosophy of History*. Durham, NC: Duke University Press, 2005.

Baxter, William T. "Observations on Money, Barter, and Bookkeeping," *Accounting Historians Journal* 31, no. 1 (June 2004): 129–39.

Beckert, Sven. *Empire of Cotton: A Global History*. New York: Alfred A. Knopf, 2014.

Beckert, Sven, and Christine Desan, eds. *American Capitalism: New Histories*. New York: Columbia University Press, 2018.

Beckert, Sven, and Seth Rockman, eds. *Slavery's Capitalism: A New History of American Economic Development*. Philadelphia: University of Pennsylvania Press, 2016.

Bernam, Linda, and Nik Theodore. *Home Economics: The Invisible and Unregulated World of Domestic Work*. New York: National Domestic Workers Alliance, 2012.

Berry, Daina Ramey. *The Price for Their Pound of Flesh: The Value of the Enslaved, from Womb to Grave, in the Building of a Nation*. Boston: Beacon Press, 2017.

Bianchi, Suzanne M., Liana C. Sayer, Melissa A. Milkie, and John P. Robinson. "Housework: Who Did, Does or Will Do It, and How Much Does It Matter?" *Social Forces* 91, no. 1 (September 2012): 55–63.

Bittman, Michael, Paula England, Liana Sayer, Nancy Folbre, and George Matheson. "When Does Gender Trump Money? Bargaining and Time in House-hold Work." *American Journal of Sociology* 109, no. 1 (2003): 186–214.

Billings, Dwight B. *Planters and the Making of a New South*. Chapel Hill: University of North Carolina Press, 1979.

Bleser, Carol K., ed. *In Joy and in Sorrow: Women, Family, and Marriage in the Victorian South, 1830–1900*. New York: Oxford University Press, 1991.

Block, Sharon. *Rape and Sexual Power in Early America*. Chapel Hill: University of North Carolina Press, 2006.

Bodenhorn, Howard. *A History of Banking in Antebellum America: Financial Markets and Economic Development in an Era of Nation Building*. Cambridge: Cambridge University Press, 2000.

———. *State Banking in Early America: A New Economic History*. New York: Oxford University Press, 2003.

Bowers, Q. David. *Obsolete Paper Money Issued by Banks in the United States, 1782–1866*. Atlanta, GA: Whitman, 2006.

Boydston, Jeanne. *Home and Work: Housework, Wages, and the Ideology of Labor in the Early Republic*. New York: Oxford University Press, 1990.

Brier, Jennifer, Jim Downs, and Jennifer Morgan, eds., *Connexions: Histories of Race and Sex in North America*. Urbana: University of Illinois Press, 2016.

Brines, Julie. "Economic Dependency, Gender, and the Division of Labor at Home." *American Journal of Sociology* 100, no. 3 (Nov. 1994): 652–88.

Buckley, Thomas E. *The Great Catastrophe of My Life: Divorce in the Old Dominion*. Chapel Hill: University of North Carolina Press, 2001.

Buckridge, Steeve O. *The Language of Dress: Resistance and Accommodation in Jamaica, 1760–1890*. Jamaica: University of West Indies Press, 2004.

Burnard, Trevor. *Mastery, Tyranny, and Desire: Thomas Thistlewood and His Slaves in the Anglo-Jamaican World*. Chapel Hill: University of North Carolina Press, 2004.

Caldwell, Stephen A. *A Banking History of Louisiana*. Baton Rouge: Louisiana State University Press, 1935.

Camp, Stephanie M. H. *Closer to Freedom: Enslaved Women and Everyday Resistance in the Plantation South*. Chapel Hill: University of North Carolina Press, 2004.

Cheung, Floyd D. "'Les Cenelles' and Quadroon Balls: 'Hidden Transcripts' of Resistance and Domination in New Orleans, 1803–1845." *Southern Literary Journal* 29, no. 2 (Spring 1997): 5–16.

Clark, Emily. *The Strange History of the American Quadroon: Free Women of Color in the Revolutionary Atlantic World*. Chapel Hill: University of North Carolina Press, 2013.

Clark-Pujara, Christy. *Dark Work: The Business of Slavery in Rhode Island*. New York: NYU Press, 2016.

Clinton, Catharine. *The Plantation Mistress: Woman's World in the Old South*. New York: Pantheon Books, 1982.

Clinton, Catherine, and Michele Gillespie, eds. *The Devil's Lane: Sex and Race in the Early South*. New York: Oxford University Press, 1997.

Clinton, Catherine, and Nina Silber, eds. *Divided Houses: Gender and the Civil War*. New York: Oxford University Press, 1992.

Coleman, J. Winston. *Slavery Times in Kentucky*. Chapel Hill: University of North Carolina Press, 1940.

Collins, Patricia Hill. *Black Feminist Thought: Knowledge, Consciousness, and the Politics of Empowerment*. 2nd ed. New York: Routledge, 2000.

———. "It's All in the Family: Intersections of Gender, Race, and Nation." *Hypatia* 13, no. 3 (Summer 1998): 62–82.

Cordwell, Justine M., and Ronald A. Schwarz, eds. *The Fabrics of Culture: The Anthropology of Clothing and Adornment*. New York: Mouton, 1979.

Cott, Nancy F. *The Bonds of Womanhood: Woman's Sphere in New England, 1780–1835*. New Haven, CT: Yale University Press, 1977.

———. *Public Vows: A History of Marriage and the Nation*. Cambridge, MA: Harvard University Press, 2000.

Cowan, Ruth Schwartz. *More Work for Mother: The Ironies of Household Technology from the Open Hearth to the Microwave*. New York: Basic Books, 1983.

Dalla Costa, Mariarosa, and Selma James. *The Power of Women and the Subversion of the Community*. Bristol: Falling Wall Press, 1972.

Davis, Adrienne. "'Don't Let Nobody Bother Yo' Principle': The Sexual Economy of American Slavery." In *Sister Circle: Black Women and Work*, edited by Sharon Harley and The Black Women and Work Collective, 128–45. New Brunswick, NJ: Rutgers University Press, 2002.

———. "The Private Law of Race and Sex: An Antebellum Perspective." *Stanford Law Review* 51, no. 2 (Jan. 1999): 221–88.

Davis, Angela Y. *Women, Race and Class*. 1st Vintage Books ed. New York: Vintage Books, 1983.

Deetz, Kelly Fanto. *Bound to the Fire: How Virginia's Enslaved Cooks Helped Invent American Cuisine*. Lexington: University Press of Kentucky, 2017.

Delphy, Christine. *Close to Home: A Materialist Analysis of Women's Oppression*. Translated and edited by Diana Leonard. Amherst: University of Massachusetts Press, 1984.

Deyle, Steven. *Carry Me Back: The Domestic Slave Trade in American Life*. New York: Oxford University Press, 2005.

Dimand, Robert, and Chris Nyland, eds. *The Status of Women in Classical Economic Thought*. Cheltenham: Edward Elgar, 2003.

Dublin, Thomas. *Women at Work: The Transformation of Work and Community in Lowell, Massachusetts, 1826–1860*. New York: Columbia University Press, 1979.

Dudden, Faye E. *Serving Women: Household Service in Nineteenth-Century America*. Middletown, CT: Wesleyan University Press, 1983.

Duval, Kathleen. "Intermarriage and Métissage in Colonial Louisiana." *William and Mary Quarterly* 65, no. 2 (Apr. 2008): 267–304.

Edwards, Laura F. "Enslaved Women and the Law: Paradoxes of Subordination in the Post-Revolutionary Carolinas." *Slavery and Abolition* 26, no. 2 (Aug. 2005): 305–23.

Eggert, Gerald G. "A Pennsylvanian Visits the Richmond Slave Market." *Pennsylvania Magazine of History and Biography* 109, no. 4 (Oct. 1985): 571–76.

Ehrenreich, Barbara, and Arlie Russell Hochschild. *Global Woman: Nannies, Maids, and Sex Workers in the New Economy*. New York: Henry Holt, 2002.

Faflike, David. *Boarding Out: Inhabiting the American Urban Literary Imagination, 1840–1860*. Evanston, IL: Northwestern University Press, 2012.

Ferber, Marianne A., and Julie A. Nelson, eds. *Beyond Economic Man: Feminist Theory and Economics*. Chicago: University of Chicago Press, 1993.

Fett, Sharla. *Working Cures: Healing, Health, and Power on Southern Slave Plantations*. Chapel Hill: University of North Carolina Press, 2002.

Fiege, Mark, and Stephen Mihm. "On Bank Notes." *Environmental History* 13, no. 2 (Apr. 2008): 350–59.

Folbre, Nancy. "Exploitation Comes Home: A Critique of the Marxian Theory of Family Labor." *Cambridge Journal of Economics* 6, no. 4 (1982): 317–29.

———. "The Unproductive Housewife: Her Evolution in Nineteenth Century Economic Thought." *Signs* 16, no. 3 (Spring 1991): 463–84.

Forret, Jeff. *Williams' Gang: A Notorious Slave Trader and His Cargo of Black Convicts*. New York: Cambridge University Press, 2019.

Forret, Jeff, and Bruce Baker, eds. *The Scoundrels, Shysters, and Confidence Men of Nineteenth-Century Southern Capitalism*. Baton Rouge: Louisiana State University Press, 2020.

Fossett, Judith Jackson and Jeffrey A. Tucker, eds. *Race Consciousness: African American Studies for the New Century*. New York: New York University Press, 1997.

Foster, Helen Bradley. *New Raiments of Self: African American Clothing in the Antebellum South*. New York: Berg, 1997.

Foster, Thomas A. *Rethinking Rufus: Sexual Violations of Enslaved Men*. Athens: University of Georgia Press, 2019.

Fox, Bonnie, ed. *Hidden in the Household: Women's Domestic Labour under Capitalism*. Toronto: Women's Press, 1980.

Fox-Genovese, Elizabeth. *Within the Plantation Household: Black and White Women of the Old South*. Chapel Hill: University of North Carolina Press, 1988.

Frederickson, Mary E., and Delores M. Walters, eds. *Gendered Resistance: Women, Slavery, and the Legacy of Margaret Garner*. Urbana: University of Illinois Press, 2013.

Friend, Craig Thompson, and Anya Jabour, eds. *Family Values in the Old South*. Gainesville: University of Florida Press, 2010.

Fuentes, Marisa J. *Dispossessed Lives: Enslaved Women, Violence, and the Archive*. Philadelphia: University of Pennsylvania Press, 2016.

Gallagher, Catherine. *The Body Economic: Life, Death, and Sensation in Political Economy and the Victorian Novel*. Princeton: Princeton University Press, 2003.

Gamber, Wendy. *The Boardinghouse in Nineteenth-Century America*. Baltimore: John Hopkins University Press, 2007.

———. *The Female Economy: The Millinery and Dressmaking Trades, 1860–1930*. Urbana: University of Illinois Press, 1997.

————. "Tarnished Labor: The Home, the Market, and the Boardinghouse in Antebellum America." *Journal of the Early Republic* 22, no. 2 (Summer 2002): 177–204.

Garrigus, John D. *Before Haiti: Race and Citizenship in French Saint-Domingue*. New York: Palgrave Macmillan, 2006.

Gaspar, David Barry, and Darlene Clark Hine, eds. *Beyond Bondage: Free Women of Color in the Americas*. Urbana: University of Illinois Press, 2004.

Genovese, Eugene D. *Roll Jordan Roll: The World the Slaves Made*. New York: Vintage Books, 1976.

Ghosh, Durba. *Sex and the Family in Colonial India: The Making of Empire*. Cambridge: Cambridge University Press, 2006.

Glymph, Thavolia. *Out of the House of Bondage: The Transformation of the Plantation Household*. Cambridge: Cambridge University Press, 2008.

Gordon-Reed, Annette. *The Hemingses of Monticello: An American Family*. New York: W. W. Norton, 2008.

————. *Thomas Jefferson and Sally Hemings: An American Controversy*. Charlottesville: University of Virginia Press, 1997.

Gould, Virginia Meacham, "'If I Can't Have My Rights, I Can Have My Pleasures, and if They Won't Give Me Wages, I Can Take Them': Gender and Slave Labor in Antebellum New Orleans." In *Discovering the Women in Slavery: Emancipating Perspectives on the American Past*, edited by Patricia Morton, 179–201. Athens: University of Georgia Press, 1996.

Green, George D. *Finance and Economic Development in the Old South: Louisiana Banking, 1804–1861*. Stanford: Stanford University Press, 1972.

Green, Sharony. "'Mr. Ballard, I Am Compelled to Write Again': Beyond Bedrooms and Brothels, a Fancy Girl Speaks." *Black Women, Gender, & Families* 5, no. 1 (Spring 2011): 17–40.

————. *Remember Me to Miss Louisa: Hidden Black-White Intimacies in Antebellum America*. DeKalb: Northern Illinois University Press, 2015.

Gross, Ariela J. *Double Character: Slavery and Mastery in the Antebellum Courtroom*. Princeton, NJ: Princeton University Press, 2000.

Gudmestad, Robert H. *A Troublesome Commerce: The Transformation of the Interstate Slave Trade*. Baton Rouge: Louisiana State University Press, 2003.

Guillory, Monique. "Some Enchanted Evening on the Auction Block: The Cultural Legacy of the New Orleans Quadroon Balls." PhD diss., New York University, 1999.

Hartigan-O'Connor, Ellen. "Abigail's Accounts: Economy and Affection in the Early Republic." *Journal of Women's History* 17, no. 3 (Fall 2005): 35–58.

————. *The Ties That Buy: Women and Commerce in Revolutionary America*. Philadelphia: University of Pennsylvania Press, 2009.

Hartman, Saidiya V. *Lose Your Mother: A Journey along the Atlantic Slave Route*. New York: Farrar, Straus and Giroux, 2007.

————. *Scenes of Subjection: Terror, Slavery, and Self-Making in Nineteenth-Century America*. New York: Oxford University Press, 1997.

————. "Venus in Two Acts." *Small Axe: A Caribbean Journal of Criticism* 12, no. 2 (June 2008): 1–14.

Hartmann, Heidi. "The Family as the Locus of Gender, Class and Political Struggle: The Example of Housework." *Signs* 6, no. 3 (Sept. 1981): 366–94.

Heier, Jan Richard. "Accounting for the Business of Suffering: A Study of the Antebellum Richmond, Virginia, Slave Trade." *Abacus* 46, no. 1 (2010): 60–82.

Hendrick, George, and Willene Hendrick. *The Creole Mutiny: A Tale of Revolt Aboard a Slave Ship*. Chicago: Ivan R. Dee, 2003.

Hewitson, Gillian J. *Feminist Economics: Interrogating the Masculinity of Rational Economic Man*. Northampton, MA: Edward Elgar, 1999.

Higginbotham, Evelyn Brooks. "African-American Women's History and the Metalanguage of Race." *Signs* 17, no. 2 (Winter 1992): 251–74.

Hine, Darlene Clark. "Rape and the Inner Lives of Black Women in the Middle West." *Signs* 14, no. 4 (Summer 1989): 912–20.

Hine, Darlene Clark, and Kate Wittenstein. "Female Slave Resistance: The Economics of Sex." In *Black Woman Cross-Culturally*, edited by Filomina Chioma Steady, 289–300. Cambridge, MA: Schenkman, 1981.

Hobbs, Allyson. *A Chosen Exile: A History of Racial Passing in American Life*. Cambridge, MA: Harvard University Press, 2014.

Hochschild, Arlie Russell. *The Commercialization of Intimate Life: Notes from Home and Work*. Berkeley: University of California Press, 2003.

———. *The Managed Heart: The Commercialization of Human Feeling*. Berkeley: University of California Press, 1983.

Hodes, Martha Elizabeth, ed. *Sex, Love, Race: Crossing Boundaries in North American History*. New York: NYU Press, 1999.

———. *White Women, Black Men: Illicit Sex in the Nineteenth-Century South*. New Haven, CT: Yale University Press, 1997.

Hunter, Tera W. *To 'Joy My Freedom: Southern Black Women's Lives and Labors after the Civil War*. Cambridge, MA: Harvard University Press, 1997.

Inman, Mary. *In Woman's Defense*. Los Angeles: Mercury, 1940.

Ipsen, Pernille. *Daughters of the Trade: Atlantic Slavers and Interracial Marriage on the Gold Coast*. Philadelphia: University of Pennsylvania Press, 2015.

Johnson, Rashauna. *Slavery's Metropolis: Unfree Labor in New Orleans during the Age of Revolutions*. Cambridge: Cambridge University Press, 2016.

Johnson, Walter. "The Pedestal and the Veil: Rethinking the Capitalism/Slavery Question." *Journal of the Early Republic* 24, no. 2 (Summer 2004): 299–308.

———. *River of Dark Dreams: Slavery and Empire in the Cotton Kingdom*. Cambridge, MA: Harvard University Press, 2013.

———. "The Slave Trader, the White Slave, and the Politics of Racial Determination in the 1850s." *Journal of American History* 87, no. 1 (June 2000): 13–38.

———. *Soul by Soul: Life Inside the Antebellum Slave Market*. Cambridge, MA: Harvard University Press, 1999.

Jones, Bernie D. *Fathers of Conscience: Mixed-Race Inheritance in the Antebellum South*. Athens: University of Georgia Press, 2009.

Jones, Hillary. "From Mariage à la Mode to Weddings at Town Hall: Marriage, Colonialism, and Mixed-Race Society in Nineteenth-Century Senegal." *International Journal of African Historical Studies* 38, no. 1 (2005): 27–48.

———. *The Métis of Senegal: Urban Life and Politics in French West Africa.* Bloomington: Indiana University Press, 2012.

Jones, Jacqueline. *Labor of Love, Labor of Sorrow: Black Women, Work, and the Family from Slavery to Present.* New York: Vintage Books, 1986.

Jones-Rogers, Stephanie. *They Were Her Property: White Women as Slaveholders in the American South.* New Haven, CT: Yale University Press, 2019.

Jordan, Winthrop D. *White Over Black: American Attitudes towards the Negro, 1550–1812.* Chapel Hill: University of North Carolina Press, 1968.

Kaplan, Amy. "Manifest Domesticity." *American Literature* 70, no. 3 (Sept. 1998): 581–606.

Katzman, David M. *Seven Days a Week: Women and Service in Industrializing America.* New York: Oxford University Press, 1978.

Kennedy, Lynn. "A Slave to Fashion: White Women, Black Women, Sewing, and Power in the Antebellum South." Presented at the Southern Association of Women Historians Annual Meeting, June 7–9, 2018 (University of Alabama).

Kessler-Harris, Alice. *Out to Work: A History of Wage-Earning Women in the United States.* Oxford: Oxford University Press, 1982.

Kierner, Cynthia A. *Beyond the Household: Women's Place in the Early South, 1700–1835.* Ithaca, NY: Cornell University Press, 1998.

Kilbourne, Richard Holcombe, Jr. *Debt, Investment, Slaves: Credit Relations in East Feliciana Parish, Louisiana 1825–1885.* Tuscaloosa: University of Alabama Press, 1995.

———. *Slave Agriculture and Financial Markets in Antebellum America: The Bank of the United States in Mississippi, 1831–1852.* London: Pickering and Chatto, 2006.

Kimball, Gregg D. *American City, Southern Place: A Cultural History of Antebellum Richmond.* Athens: University of Georgia Press, 2000.

King, Stewart R. *Blue Coat or Powdered Wig: Free People of Color in Pre-Revolutionary Saint Domingue.* Athens: University of Georgia Press, 2001.

Kraus, Lisa. "Archaeology of the Bruin Slave Jail." PhD diss., University of Texas–Austin, 2009.

Kreisel, Deanna. *Economic Woman: Demand, Gender, and Narrative Closure in Eliot and Hardy.* Toronto: University of Toronto Press, 2012.

Kuhn, Annette, and AnnMarie Wolpe. *Feminism and Materialism: Women and Modes of Production.* London: Routledge and Kegan Paul, 1978.

Laird, Matthew R. *Preliminary Archeological Investigation of the Lumpkin Jail Site.* Williamsburg, VA: James River Institute for Archeology, 2006.

Landau, Emily Epstein. *Spectacular Wickedness: Sex, Race, and Memory in Storyville, New Orleans.* Baton Rouge: Louisiana State University Press, 2013.

Laslett, Barbara, and Johanna Brenner. "Gender and Social Reproduction: Historical Perspectives." *Annual Review of Sociology* 15 (1989): 381–404.

Lebsock, Suzanne. *The Free Women of Petersburg: Status and Culture in a South Town, 1784–1860.* New York: W. W. Norton, 1984.

Leghorn, Lisa, and Katherine Parker. *Woman's Work: Sexual Economics and the World of Women.* Boston: Routledge and Kegan Paul, 1981.

Lerner, Gerda. *The Creation of Patriarchy.* New York: Oxford University Press, 1986.

————. "The Lady and the Mill Girl: Changes in the Status of Women in the Age of Jackson." *American Studies* 10, no. 1 (Spring 1969): 5–15.

Lesesne, J. Mauldin. *The Bank of the State of South Carolina: A General and Political History*. Columbia: University of South Carolina Press, 1970.

Leslie, Kent Anderson. *Woman of Color, Daughter of Privilege: Amanda America Dickson, 1849–1893*. Athens: University of Georgia Press, 1995.

Lewis, Jan Ellen, and Peter S. Onuf, eds. *Sally Hemings and Thomas Jefferson: History, Memory, and Civil Culture*. Charlottesville: University Press of Virginia, 1999.

Lightner, David L. *Slavery and the Commerce Power: How the Struggle against the Interstate Slave Trade Led to the Civil War*. New Haven, CT: Yale University Press, 2006.

Livesay, Daniel Alan. "Children of Uncertain Fortune: Mixed-Race Migration from the West Indies to Britain, 1750–1820." PhD diss., University of Michigan, 2010.

Long, Alecia P. *The Great Southern Babylon: Sex, Race, and Respectability in New Orleans, 1865–1920*. Baton Rouge: Louisiana State University Press, 2004.

Luskey, Brian P., and Wendy A. Woloson, eds. *Capitalism by Gaslight: Illuminating the Economy of Nineteenth-Century America*. Philadelphia: University of Pennsylvania Press, 2015.

MacKinnon, Catherine, and Reva B. Siegel, eds. *Directions in Sexual Harassment*. New Haven, CT: Yale University Press, 2003.

Malos, Ellen, ed. *The Politics of Housework*. London: Allison and Busby, 1980.

Manganelli, Kimberly Snyder. *Transatlantic Spectacles of Race: The Tragic Mulatta and the Tragic Muse*. New Brunswick, NJ: Rutgers University Press, 2012.

Manion, Jen. *Liberty's Prisoners: Carceral Culture in Early America*. Philadelphia: University of Pennsylvania Press, 2015.

Marler, Scott P. *The Merchants' Capital: New Orleans and the Political Economy of the Nineteenth-Century South*. Cambridge: Cambridge University Press, 2013.

Martin, Bonnie M. "Slavery's Invisible Engine: Mortgaging Human Property." *Journal of Southern History* 76, no. 4 (Nov. 2010): 817–66.

Matthews, Glenna. *Just a Housewife: The Rise and Fall of Domesticity in America*. New York: Oxford University Press, 1987.

May, Ann Mari. "The Feminist Challenge to Economics." *Challenge* 45, no. 6 (Nov.–Dec. 2002): 45–69.

McBride, Kari Boyd. "A (Boarding) House Is Not a Home: Women's Work and Woman's Worth on the Margins of Domesticity." *Frontiers: A Journal of Women Studies* 17, no. 1 (1996): 90–112.

McCurry, Stephanie. *Masters of Small Worlds: Yeoman Households, Gender Relations, and the Political Culture of the Antebellum South Carolina Low Country*. New York: Oxford University Press, 1995.

McGinnis, Callie, ed. "Hatcher and McGehee Negro Book," *Muscogiana* 4 (Summer 1993): 8–16.

McInnis, Maurie D. *Slaves Waiting for Sale: Abolitionist Art and the American Slave Trade*. Chicago: University of Chicago Press, 2011.

McMichael, Phillip. "Slavery in Capitalism: The Rise and Demise of the U.S. Antebellum Cotton Culture." *Theory and Society* 20, no. 3 (June 1991): 321–49.

Meillasoux, Claude. *The Anthropology of Slavery: The Womb of Iron and Gold*. Chicago: University of Chicago Press, 1991.

Michel, Bernard E. "Christian Schussele: Portrayer of America." *Transactions of the Moravian Historical Society* 22, no. 2 (1965): 249–67.

Mies, Maria. *Patriarchy and Accumulation on a World Scale*. London: Zed Books, 1986.

Miles, Tiya. *The Ties That Bind: The Story of an Afro-Cherokee Family in Slavery and Freedom*. Berkeley: University of California Press, 2006.

Miller, Marla R. *The Needle's Eye: Women and Work in the Age of Revolution*. Amherst: University of Massachusetts Press, 2006.

Mills, Gary B. "Miscegenation and the Free Negro in Antebellum 'Anglo' Alabama: A Reexamination of Southern Race Relations." *Journal of American History* 68, no. 1 (June 1981): 16–34.

Montalvo, Maria R. "The Slavers' Archive: Enslaved People, Power, and the Production of the Past in the Antebellum Courtroom." PhD diss., Rice University, 2018.

Morgan, Jennifer L. *Laboring Women: Reproduction and Gender in New World Slavery*. Philadelphia: University of Pennsylvania Press, 2004.

Morrison, Karen Y. "Slave Mothers and White Fathers: Defining Family and Status in Late Colonial Cuba." *Slavery and Abolition* 31, no. 1 (Mar. 2010): 29–55.

Nadasen, Premilla. *Household Workers Unite: The Untold Story of African American Women Who Built a Movement*. Boston: Beacon Press, 2015.

Nelson, Julie A. "Feminism and Economics." *Journal of Economic Perspectives* 9, no. 2 (Spring 1995): 131–48.

Nelson, Scott Reynolds. *A Nation of Deadbeats: An Uncommon History of America's Financial Disasters*. New York: Alfred A. Knopf, 2012.

———. "Who Put Their Capitalism in My Slavery?" *Journal of the Civil War Era* 5, no. 2 (June 2015): 289–310.

Omohundro, Malvern Hill. *The Omohundro Genealogical Record*. Staunton, VA: McClure, 1951.

Owens, Deirdre Cooper. *Medical Bondage: Race, Gender, and the Origins of American Gynecology*. Athens: University of Georgia Press, 2017.

Owens, Emily Alyssa. "Fantasies of Consent: Black Women's Sexual Labor in 19th Century New Orleans." PhD diss., Harvard University, 2015.

Palmer, Phyllis. *Domesticity and Dirt: Housewives and Domestic Servants in the United States, 1920–1945*. Philadelphia: Temple University Press, 2010.

Pascoe, Peggy. *What Comes Naturally: Miscegenation Law and the Making of Race in America*. Oxford: Oxford University Press, 2009.

Pateman, Carol. *The Sexual Contract*. Stanford: Stanford University Press, 1988.

Perdue, Charles L., Jr., Thomas E. Barden, and Robert K. Phillips, eds. *Weevils in the Wheat: Interviews with Virginia Ex-Slaves*. Charlottesville: University Press of Virginia, 1976.

Perea, Juan F. "The Echoes of Slavery: Recognizing the Racist Origins of the Agricultural and Domestic Workers Exclusion from the National Labor Relations Act." *Ohio State Law Journal* 72, no. 1 (Jan. 2011): 95–138.

Powell, Williams S., ed. *Dictionary of North Carolina Biography*, vol. 1. Chapel Hill: University of North Carolina Press, 1979.

Reiter, Rayna R., ed. *Toward an Anthropology of Women*. New York: Monthly Review Press, 1975.

Roach, Joseph. "Slave Spectacles and Tragic Octoroons: a Cultural Genealogy of Antebellum Performance." *Theater Survey* 33, no. 2 (Nov. 1992): 167–87.

Robinson, Charles F. "'Most Shamefully Common': Arkansas and Miscegenation." *Arkansas Historical Quarterly* 60, No. 3 (Autumn 2001): 265–83.

Rockman, Seth. *Scraping By: Wage Labor, Slavery, and Survival in Early Baltimore*. Baltimore: John Hopkins University Press, 2009.

———. "Slavery and Capitalism." In "Forum on the Future of Civil War Era Studies," online supplement, *Journal of the Civil War Era* 2 (Mar. 2012).

Rogers, Dominique. "Les libres de couleur dans les capitals de Saint-Domingue: Fortune, mentalités et intégration à la fin de l'Ancien Régime (1776-1789)." PhD diss., L'université Michel de Montaigne, 1999.

Rollins, Judith. *Between Women: Domestics and Their Employers*. Philadelphia: Temple University Press, 1985.

Romero, Lora. *Home Fronts: Domesticity and Its Critics in the Antebellum United States*. Durham, NC: Duke University Press, 1997.

Romero, Mary. *Maid in the U.S.A.* New York: Routledge, 2002.

Romero, Mary, Valeria Preston, and Wenona Giles, eds. *When Care Work Goes Global: Gender in a Global/Local World*. New York: Routledge, 2016.

Rosenthal, Caitlin. *Accounting for Slavery: Masters and Management*. Cambridge, MA: Harvard University Press, 2018.

Rothman, Joshua D. *Flush Times and Fever Dreams: A Story of Capitalism and Slavery in the Age of Jackson*. Athens: University of Georgia Press, 2014.

———. *The Ledger and the Chain: The Masterminds of America's Domestic Slave Trade* (forthcoming).

———. *Notorious in the Neighborhood: Sex and Families across the Color Line in Virginia, 1787-1861*. Chapel Hill: University of North Carolina Press, 2003.

Sayer, Liana C. "Gender, Time, and Inequality: Trends in Women's and Men's Paid Work, Unpaid Work, and Free Time." *Social Forces* 84, no. 1 (Sep. 2005): 285–303.

Schafer, Judith Kelleher. *Becoming Free, Remaining Free: Manumission and Enslavement in New Orleans, 1846-1862*. Baton Rouge: Louisiana State University Press, 2003.

———. *Brothels, Depravity, and Abandoned Women: Illegal Sex in Antebellum New Orleans*. Baton Rouge: Louisiana State University Press, 2009.

———. "Open and Notorious Concubinage: The Emancipation of Slaves Mistresses by Will and the Supreme Court in Antebellum Louisiana." *Louisiana History* 28, no. 2 (Spring 1987): 165–82.

Schermerhorn, Calvin. *The Business of Slavery and the Rise of American Capitalism, 1815-1860*. New Haven, CT: Yale University Press, 2015.

———. *Money Over Mastery, Family Over Freedom: Slavery in the Antebellum Upper South*. Baltimore: John Hopkins University Press, 2011.

Schwartz, Marie Jenkins. *Birthing a Slave: Motherhood and Medicine in the Antebellum South*. Cambridge, MA: Harvard University Press, 2010.

Schweninger, Loren. "Property Owning Free African-American Women in the South, 1800- 1870." *Journal of Women's History* 1, no. 3 (Winter 1990): 13–44.

Scott, Joan Wallach. *Gender and the Politics of History*. Rev. ed. New York: Columbia University Press, 1999.

Searing, James F. *West African Slavery and Atlantic Commerce: The Senegal River Valley, 1700-1860*. Cambridge, MA: Harvard University Press, 1993.

Sharpless, Rebecca. *Cooking in Other Women's Kitchens: Domestic Workers in the South, 1865-1900*. Chapel Hill: University of North Carolina Press, 2010.

Shaw, Madelyn. "Slave Cloth and Clothing Slaves: Craftsmanship, Commerce, and Industry." *MESDA Journal* (2012), http://www.mesdajournal.org/2012/slave-cloth -clothing-slaves-craftsmanship-commerce-industry/.

Shire, Laurel Clark. *The Threshold of Manifest Destiny*. Philadelphia: University of Pennsylvania Press, 2016.

Smithers, Gregory D. *Slave Breeding: Sex, Violence, and Memory in African American History*. Gainesville: University Press of Florida, 2012.

Sollors, Werner. *An Anthology of Interracial Literature: Black-White Contacts in the Old World and the New*. New York: NYU Press, 2004.

———. *Interracialism: Black-White Marriage in American History, Literature, and Law*. New York: Oxford University Press, 2000.

Sommerville, Diane Miller. *Rape and Race in the Nineteenth-Century South*. Chapel Hill: University of North Carolina Press, 2004.

Spear, Jennifer M. *Race, Sex, and Social Order in Early New Orleans*. Baltimore: Johns Hopkins University Press, 2009.

Stanley, Amy Dru. *From Bondage to Contract: Wage Labor, Marriage, and the Market in the Age of Slave Emancipation*. Cambridge: Cambridge University Press, 1998.

Stansell, Christine. *City of Women: Sex and Class in New York, 1789-1860*. Urbana: University of Illinois Press, 1987.

Stephenson, Wendell Holmes. *Isaac Franklin: Slave Trader and Planter of the Old South*. Baton Rouge: Louisiana State University Press, 1938.

Sterling, Dorothy, ed. *We Are Your Sisters: Black Women in the Nineteenth Century South*. New York: W. W. Norton, 1984.

Stevenson, Brenda E. *Life in Black and White: Family and Community in the Slave South*. New York: Oxford University Press, 1996.

———. "What's Love Got to Do with It? Concubinage and Enslaved Women and Girls in the Antebellum South." *Journal of African American History* 98, no. 1 (Winter 2013): 99–125.

Stoler, Ann L. "Making Empire Respectable: The Politics of Race and Sexual Morality in 20th-Century Colonial Cultures." *American Ethnologist* 16, no. 4 (Nov. 1989): 634–60.

Tadman, Michael. "The Hidden History of Slave Trading in Antebellum South Carolina: John Springs III and Other 'Gentlemen Dealing in Slaves.'" *South Carolina Historical Magazine* 97, no. 1 (Jan. 1996): 6–29.

———. *Speculators and Slaves: Masters, Traders, and Slaves in the Old South*. Madison: University of Wisconsin Press, 1989.

Takagi, Midori. *"Rearing Wolves to Our Own Destruction": Slavery in Richmond, Virginia, 1787-1865*. Charlottesville: University Press of Virginia, 1999.

Tansey, Richard. "Bernard Kendig and the New Orleans Slave Trade." *Louisiana History* 23, no. 2 (Spring 1982): 159–78.

Taylor, Nikki M. *Frontiers of Freedom: Cincinnati's Black Community, 1802–1868.* Athens: Ohio University Press, 2005.

Thorne, Barrie, and Marilyn Yalom, eds. *Rethinking the Family: Some Feminist Questions.* 2nd ed. Boston: Northeastern University Press, 1992.

Trent, Hank. *The Secret Life of Bacon Tait, a White Slave Trader Married to a Free Woman of Color.* Baton Rouge: Louisiana State University Press, 2017.

Turner, Sasha. *Contested Bodies: Pregnancy, Childrearing, and Slavery in Jamaica.* Philadelphia: University of Pennsylvania Press, 2017.

Tyler-McGraw, Marie, and Gregg D. Kimball. *In Bondage and Freedom: Antebellum Black Life in Richmond, Virginia.* Richmond, VA: Valentine Museum, 1988.

Waring, Marilyn. *If Women Counted: A New Feminist Economics.* New York: Harper and Row, 1998.

Washington, Margaret. "'From Motives of Delicacy': Sexuality and Morality in the Narratives of Sojourner Truth and Harriet Jacobs." *Journal of African American History* 92, no. 1 (Winter 2007): 57–73.

Weaver, Karol K. "Fashioning Freedom: Slave Seamstresses in the Atlantic World." *Journal of Women's History* 24, no. 1 (Spring 2012): 44–59.

Welter, Barbara. "The Cult of True Womanhood, 1800–1860." *American Quarterly* 18 (1966): 151–74.

West, Emily. *Chains of Love: Slave Couples in Antebellum South Carolina.* Urbana: University of Illinois Press, 2004.

White, Deborah Gray. *Ar'n't I a Woman?: Female Slaves in the Plantation South.* New York: W. W. Norton, 1999.

Williamson, Joel. *New People: Miscegenation and Mulattoes in the United States.* New York: Free Press, 1980.

Winter, Kari J. *The American Dreams of John B. Prentis, Slave Trader.* Athens: University of Georgia Press, 2011.

Women's Work Study. "Loom, Broom, and Womb: Producers, Maintainers, and Reproducers." *Frontiers: A Journal of Women Studies* 1, no. 1 (Autumn 1975): 1–41.

Wood, Kirsten E. "Making a Home in Public: Domesticity, Authority, and Family in the Old South's Public Houses," in *Southern Families*, edited by Craig Friend and Anya Jabour. Gainesville: University Press of Florida, 2009.

———.*Masterful Women: Slaveholding Widows from the American Revolution through the Civil War.* Chapel Hill: University of North Carolina Press, 2004.

Woodman, Harold D. *King Cotton and His Retainers: Financing and Marketing the Cotton Crop of the South, 1800–1925.* Lexington: University of Kentucky Press, 1968.

Wright, Gavin. *The Political Economy of the Cotton South: Households, Markets, and Wealth in the Nineteenth Century.* New York: W. W. Norton, 1978.

———. *Slavery and American Economic Development.* Baton Rouge: Louisiana State University Press, 2006.

Yeung, Bernice. *In a Day's Work: The Fight to End Sexual Violence against America's Most Vulnerable Workers.* New York: New Press, 2018.

Zaborney, John J. *Slaves for Hire: Renting Enslaved Laborers in Antebellum Virginia.* Baton Rouge: Louisiana State University Press, 2012.

Zakim, Michael. *Ready Made Democracy: A History of Men's Dress in the American Republic, 1760–1860.* Chicago: University of Chicago Press, 2003.

Ze Winters, Lisa. *The Mulatta Concubine: Terror, Intimacy, Freedom, and Desire in the Black Transatlantic.* Athens: University of Georgia Press, 2016.

Index

abolitionists, 25–26, 42–44, 91, 144n45

abuse, 31–32. *See also* emotional abuse; physical abuse; sexual abuse; violence

accessories, 19–21, 26–27, 38–41, 50–53, 56, 63, 94, 117, 135n1, 150n70

accounts, 8–15, 19, 27, 34, 39–40, 46–47, 51–53, 56–63, 133n1, 153n42

activism, 126

advertising, 52–57, 59–60, 64–66, 98, 112–14, 142n19, 143n32, 154n74

African American women. *See* black women

American Bank Note Company, 66, 144n55

Amis, Junius, 77, 85, 148n47

Andrews, E. A., 49–50

Anti-Slavery Bugle, 91

archiving, 14, 47, 69, 104, 130

auctions, 4, 16, 26–27, 33, 51, 77–80, 89, 119, 125, 140n1

Ballard, Rice, 28, 37, 145n3

bank notes. *See* cash

Bank of Kentucky, 85–90, 149n51–149n52

bankruptcy, 57, 78, 85, 88, 117–19

Banks, Ann, 36, 46

Banks, Matilda, 36

bank stock, 116–18, 140n1, 153n42–153n43

Barbour, Betsy, 37

Barclay, Ann Maria, 108

Barnett, Edward, 110–11, 118, 153n43

Beckert, Sven, 13

Beecher, Catherine, 5, 32

Betts, William, 101, 137n26

Binford, Mayo, & Blair, 19

Bissel, Austin, & Co., 54

Blackburn, T. B., 113–14

black women: commodification of, 24, 63, 71; as concubines, 68–95; domestic labor and, 6, 98; as fancy girls, 19–45; free, 4, 75, 114–15; as housekeepers, 96–122; as seamstresses, 46–67; sexuality and, 12, 20–22, 71, 123, 152n21. *See also* race; sexuality; slavery; slave trade

Blakeley, James G., 23–25, 52, 70, 145n3

Block, Sharon, 105, 137n28

board (as complement to room), 3–5, 8, 32–33, 48–49, 83–84, 113–15, 119, 125–26

boardinghouses: domestic labor and, 98–99, 112–15; the Omohundros and, 16, 31–36; slave trade and, 4, 27, 37–38, 68, 72, 76

Boazman, J. W, 52

Boggs, Susan, 48

Botts, George Ann, 108

Boyd's City Directory of the District of Columbia, 124

Boydston, Jeanne, 6

Boylan, Thomas N., 93

Bremer, Frederika, 10, 107, 152n30

Brooks, Mary Ellen, 23–27, 52, 65

Brown, John, 25, 27–28

Brown, William Wells, 49, 100

Bruin, Joseph, 63

Buchanan, A. M., 80, 88

Cammeyer, Charles, 90–92

Camp, Stephanie, 38, 108, 123

Cannon, Elisha, 52

capitalism, 4–16, 44, 67, 71, 125, 133n3, 145n6

Carey, Mathew, 58

domesticity, 7–8, 32, 61, 65, 98, 104. *See also* domestic labor

domestic labor: capitalism and, 14–16; by enslaved concubines, 28, 74, 78, 81; the fancy trade and, 31–35; by housekeepers, 98–102, 113–14; sexual abuse and, 114, 125–26; sexual economy and, 3–9, 13, 17, 45, 50. *See also* women's labor

Downing, Salem, 37

dressmakers, 8, 51, 58, 64

Dumas Hotel, 76

Dunbar, A. F., 85–89

Eacho, E. D., 64–65

earrings. *See* accessories

economy. *See* sexual economy

Edmondson, Emily, 63

Edmondson, Mary, 63

education, 28, 36, 41, 119, 121

Edwards, Ann, 24

Edwards, John M., 29

emancipation, 17, 73–74, 78–83, 86–90, 108, 115, 149n51, 152n33. *See also* self purchase

emotional abuse, 126. *See also* abuse

emotional labor, 5, 20, 99–100, 104–6, 113, 126

employment, 8, 35, 48–52, 58–60, 68–69, 82–83, 126

Engels, Friedrich, 8–9, 43–44

enslaved women: children and, 62, 117–18; clothing and, 27, 32, 52, 55–57, 61; as commodities, 49–50; domestic labor of, 64–67, 98–101; hiring out of, 69, 71; reproductive labor and, 7, 45, 68, 72; resistance by, 108–9; sexual economy of slavery and, 9–17, 70–71, 104–5, 114, 130; sexuality and, 13, 23; violence against, 21, 25–26, 102, 115

estates. *See* inheritance

Etter, Alderman, 90–92

Eustler, G.W., 38

Faber, Ellen, 99

Fairbank, Calvin, 25–26

family: as an ideal, 26, 98; domestic labor and the, 32, 113, 126; as property, 30, 40; reproductive labor and, 8–9; slave trade and, 38–39, 43–45, 101. *See also* children

fancy girls, 10–16, 19–45, 51, 65, 70–71, 101

fantasies, 20–26. *See also* consent

Farmer's Bank of Virginia, 2, 133n1

fashion, 20, 27, 39–41, 58. *See also* clothing; negro cloth; ready-made clothing

Faurie, Charles, 118

feminine labor, 67. *See also* women's labor

feminism, 7–9, 44, 76

Feminist Economics (journal), 9

Ferguson, Elias, 38, 63

fiction, 98, 100. *See also* literature

Fitzhugh, George, 44–45

Folger, N. C., 57, 60. *See also* N. C. Folger & Co.

food. *See* board

Foster, Helen Bradley, 53

Foster, L. M., 57

Fountain, Courtney, 37

Franklin, Isaac, 25, 28

Franklin & Armfield, 15, 28–29, 49–50, 70, 137n23, 145n3

freedom. *See* emancipation

Freeman, Laurette, 120

Freeman, Theophilus, 17, 49, 68, 73–88, 91–95, 100, 104

free market economy, 44–45, 130. *See also* capitalism; sexual economy

free men of color, 74

friendship, 17, 108–9, 119, 123. *See also* resistance

Fuentes, Marisa, 31, 139n49, 148n43

furnished rooms, 72, 93, 96, 112, 117. *See also* rented rooms

furniture, 40, 94–96, 111, 116–17, 147n40, 150n70

www.ingramcontent.com/pod-product-compliance
Lightning Source LLC
Chambersburg PA
CBHW030837270326
41928CB00007B/1091